Astro-Dinos

Astro-Dinos

Matthew Petchinsky

Astro-Dinos: The Cosmic Guide to Prehistoric Wisdom
By: Matthew Petchinsky

Introduction: Welcome to Astro-Dinos

Welcome to *Astro-Dinos: The Cosmic Guide to Prehistoric Wisdom*, where the timeless mysteries of the cosmos meet the awe-inspiring world of dinosaurs. This book is a unique exploration of how celestial energies—the planets, stars, and moon phases—intertwine with the prehistoric wonder of Earth's most magnificent creatures. As we dive into the fusion of astrology and paleontology, prepare to uncover a new way of understanding the universe and our place within it.

Why Combine Dinosaurs and Astrology?

Dinosaurs ruled the Earth for millions of years, embodying strength, resilience, and adaptability. They left behind a legacy written in the fossils and rocks of our planet. Similarly, astrology reflects the story of human existence through the movements and alignments of celestial bodies, offering insight into our personality, destiny, and universal connections.

Though dinosaurs and astrology come from vastly different realms, they share a profound commonality: the essence of cycles, change, and balance. By combining the two, this guide seeks to honor the wisdom of the past while uncovering cosmic lessons that are as relevant today as they were millions of years ago.

Imagine the planets, moons, and stars as energetic forces that shaped the environment in which dinosaurs thrived. The meteor showers that lit up prehistoric skies, the solstices that marked the turning of seasons, and the eclipses that cast shadows on ancient landscapes—all were cosmic events that influenced life on Earth in ways we are only beginning to understand.

The Astrological Dinosaur Zodiac

What if each zodiac sign could be represented by a dinosaur whose traits align with its astrological qualities? This book introduces the **Dinosaur Zodiac**, where mighty creatures like the fierce Tyrannosaurus Rex symbolize Leo's courage, and the steadfast Triceratops embodies Taurus's reliability. Each dinosaur serves as a totem, channeling cosmic energy and prehistoric wisdom to inspire and guide you.

By exploring the Dinosaur Zodiac, you will gain deeper insight into your own astrological chart and how its themes reflect the enduring truths of nature. Whether you are a bold Aries Allosaurus or a sensitive Pisces Plesiosaurus, this book will help you uncover the unique strengths and challenges that define your path.

The Role of Celestial Events in Prehistoric Times

The cosmos has always played a pivotal role in life on Earth, influencing everything from weather patterns to evolutionary changes. For dinosaurs, celestial events such as meteor impacts and solar eclipses could have been awe-inspiring phenomena—or catastrophic forces of change. These events remind us of the delicate interplay between cosmic energy and terrestrial existence.

This guide will explore the significance of celestial events, including lunar phases, planetary alignments, and even the mysterious nodes that shape destiny. You'll discover how these cycles, just like the rise and fall of the dinosaurs, hold lessons about growth, transformation, and renewal.

The Modern Relevance of Prehistoric Astrology

Astrology offers a timeless lens through which we can interpret the cycles of life. By incorporating the themes of prehistoric resilience and adaptation, this book provides a fresh perspective on astrological wisdom. You'll learn practical ways to integrate the lessons of the Dinosaur Zodiac into your daily life, from understanding your personality traits to navigating challenges with the strength of a Stegosaurus or the cleverness of a Velociraptor.

In a world that is constantly evolving, the stories of dinosaurs remind us of the importance of adapting to change while staying grounded in our true nature. The celestial map of astrology serves as a guide, helping us navigate these changes with grace and understanding.

What to Expect in This Book

Astro-Dinos is divided into several sections to make your journey through prehistoric and cosmic wisdom both engaging and enlightening.

- **Dinosaur Zodiac**: Each chapter explores how a specific dinosaur aligns with a zodiac sign, uncovering its symbolic traits and astrological influence.
- **Planetary Energies**: Learn how the sun, moon, and planets shaped the lives of dinosaurs and how they continue to impact us today.
- **Celestial Events**: Discover the power of eclipses, solstices, equinoxes, and meteor showers, and how they connect prehistoric history to astrological cycles.
- **Moon Phases**: Understand the rhythm of lunar cycles and their connection to life's ebb and flow, from the time of the dinosaurs to our modern era.
- **Practical Applications**: Dive into rituals, journaling prompts, and practices to align yourself with the cosmic energies explored in this book.

Additionally, the appendices provide quick-reference guides to Dinosaur Zodiac dates, a calendar of upcoming celestial events, and a glossary of key terms to deepen your understanding.

Embark on Your Astro-Dino Journey

Whether you are an astrology enthusiast, a dinosaur lover, or simply curious about the intersection of ancient wisdom and prehistoric lore, this book invites you to step into a world where the stars and Earth's oldest creatures unite. Together, we will uncover the secrets of the cosmos and learn to channel the power of dinosaurs as cosmic allies.

Get ready to roar with the wisdom of the stars and the strength of the Earth's most legendary creatures. Let *Astro-Dinos* guide you on an unforgettable journey through time, space, and the infinite connections that shape our universe.

Part 1: Dinosaur Zodiac

Chapter 1: Aries the Allosaurus
The Fierce Pioneer of the Prehistoric Zodiac
Characteristics of Aries the Allosaurus

Aries, the first sign of the zodiac, represents boldness, passion, and an unyielding drive to forge new paths. Similarly, the Allosaurus, one of the most formidable predators of the Jurassic period, embodies these same traits. Known as the "different lizard," the Allosaurus was a top-tier carnivore, fearless in its pursuits and adaptable in its environment.

Aries the Allosaurus is defined by the following key characteristics:

1. **Courageous Leader**:
   Much like Aries individuals who thrive on being at the forefront, the Allosaurus was an apex predator, unafraid to take on challenges that required strategy and power. It symbolizes the unrelenting bravery that pushes through obstacles.
2. **Restless Energy**:
   Allosaurus was an active and dynamic creature, constantly moving and adapting to its surroundings. This reflects the Aries trait of boundless energy and a need for action.
3. **Impulsivity**:
   The Allosaurus, while powerful, was sometimes impulsive, acting quickly rather than planning extensively—just like Aries natives, who are known for leaping headfirst into situations without hesitation.
4. **Fiercely Independent**:
   Aries individuals cherish their independence, much like the Allosaurus, which relied on its own skills and instincts to survive. This dinosaur is a symbol of self-reliance and individuality.

Strengths of Aries the Allosaurus

Aries the Allosaurus is a powerful blend of fiery energy and instinctual cunning, making it a natural leader in both prehistoric and astrological realms. Here are its strengths:

1. **Fearlessness**:
   Aries the Allosaurus embodies raw courage. This dinosaur didn't back down from a challenge, no matter the size of its opponent. This reflects Aries's ability to tackle challenges head-on, no matter the risks involved.
2. **Resourcefulness**:
   Known for its adaptability, the Allosaurus could thrive in various environments and situations. Similarly, Aries individuals possess the ability to navigate through life's twists and turns with creativity and resilience.
3. **Charismatic Presence**:
   Aries-born people have an undeniable charisma that draws others to them, much like the awe-inspiring Allosaurus, whose very presence commanded attention in its prehistoric world.
4. **Determined Spirit**:
   The Allosaurus's hunting strategy was one of persistence, using its powerful jaws and sharp claws to overpower prey. Aries natives share this determination, rarely giving up until they achieve their goals.
5. **Trailblazer Energy**:
   As a symbol of leadership and innovation, Aries the Allosaurus reminds us of the importance of forging new paths and embracing change.

Celestial Influences on Aries the Allosaurus

Astrologically, Aries is ruled by **Mars**, the planet of action, energy, and aggression. Mars's fiery influence perfectly aligns with the bold and combative nature of the Allosaurus, highlighting the following celestial connections:

1. **Mars and the Allosaurus's Warrior Spirit**:
   Mars infuses Aries with a warrior-like energy, which is mirrored in the Allosaurus's role as a dominant predator. This celestial influence enhances the Allosaurus's ferocity, making it a force to be reckoned with in the prehistoric landscape.
2. **The Element of Fire**:
   Aries is a fire sign, associated with passion, ambition, and intensity. The Allosaurus's fiery determination to hunt and survive reflects the untamed flames of Aries energy.
3. **Seasonal Beginnings**:
   Aries marks the start of the astrological year and the season of spring—a time of renewal and fresh beginnings. Similarly, the Allosaurus symbolizes evolution and the constant rebirth of nature's cycle, representing life's ever-forward march.
4. **Celestial Impulsiveness**:
   Aries is known for its impulsive and headstrong nature, traits enhanced by Mars's influence. The Allosaurus's quick, decisive actions in the hunt embody this celestial impulsivity, showing how Mars fuels both instinct and courage.

How Aries the Allosaurus Inspires Us

Aries the Allosaurus teaches us the importance of embracing life with courage, passion, and an adventurous spirit. Here are ways this prehistoric zodiac sign can guide us:

1. **Channel Your Inner Leader**:
   Just as the Allosaurus ruled its domain, Aries reminds us to take charge of our lives and lead with confidence.
2. **Embrace Challenges**:
   Life's difficulties can feel overwhelming, but the spirit of Aries the Allosaurus encourages us to face them head-on with determination and resolve.
3. **Find Strength in Independence**:
   While collaboration has its place, Aries the Allosaurus shows the power of trusting your own instincts and forging your path.
4. **Act with Passion**:
   Whether it's pursuing a goal or protecting those you care about, let the fire of Aries energy fuel your actions, much like the Allosaurus's relentless drive for survival.

Modern Aries Lessons from the Allosaurus

1. **Balance Impulsiveness with Strategy**:
   While the Allosaurus thrived on quick action, it also knew when to be patient and strategic. Aries individuals can learn from this balance, tempering their natural impulsivity with thoughtful planning.
2. **Harness the Power of Mars**:
   Mars energy is a double-edged sword—it can ignite passion but also burn out quickly. Aries the Allosaurus reminds us to channel this energy wisely, using it to fuel persistence rather than recklessness.
3. **Be Fearless but Wise**:
   Boldness is an Aries strength, but combining it with wisdom can lead to greater success. The Allosaurus's adaptive hunting methods are a reminder to use your resources intelligently.

Astrological Reflection for Aries the Allosaurus

- **Birth Chart Placement**:
  If Aries or Mars plays a significant role in your astrological chart, you may resonate strongly with the Allosaurus's traits. Use this connection to tap into your inner courage and determination.
- **Celestial Rituals**:
  Align your energy with Mars by incorporating fiery symbols, red candles, or assertive affirmations into your daily routine. Honor the Allosaurus as a totem for strength and leadership in your astrological practice.

In the Dinosaur Zodiac, Aries the Allosaurus is a fiery, determined, and fearless symbol of cosmic strength. By embracing its energy, you can lead with confidence, conquer challenges, and channel the unstoppable power of the prehistoric warrior within. Let Aries the Allosaurus be your guide to unlocking your primal instincts and cosmic potential.

Chapter 2: Taurus the Triceratops
The Steadfast Guardian of the Prehistoric Zodiac
Symbolism of Taurus the Triceratops

Taurus, the second sign of the zodiac, represents grounded stability, unwavering determination, and a deep connection to the Earth. These qualities align seamlessly with the majestic Triceratops, one of the most iconic herbivorous dinosaurs of the Cretaceous period. With its three prominent horns and a large protective frill, the Triceratops embodies strength, resilience, and a calm but unshakable demeanor.

Taurus the Triceratops is a symbol of steadfast reliability, a protector of its domain, and a being in tune with its surroundings. Its traits reflect the Taurus archetype of loyalty, practicality, and a love for life's simple pleasures.

Key Characteristics of Taurus the Triceratops

1. **Grounded Stability**:
   The Triceratops was a creature deeply rooted in its environment, much like Taurus natives who find strength in stability and routine. With its powerful build and defensive nature, this dinosaur thrived by staying grounded and practical in its approach to survival.

2. **Protective Nature**:
   Taurus individuals are known for their fierce loyalty and protective instincts. Similarly, the Triceratops used its horns and frill to defend itself and its herd, symbolizing Taurus's commitment to safeguarding loved ones.

3. **Strength and Patience**:
   Despite its intimidating appearance, the Triceratops was a peaceful herbivore unless provoked. This mirrors the Taurus trait of patience, where individuals are calm and composed until their boundaries are crossed.

4. **Connection to Earth**:
   Taurus, an Earth sign, has a natural affinity for nature and the physical world. The Triceratops, as a grazing herbivore, relied on the land for sustenance, embodying this deep connection to Earth's resources.

5. **Appreciation for Simplicity**:
   Taurus enjoys life's simple pleasures, whether it's good food, comfort, or tranquility. The Triceratops, content in its grazing habits, reflects this love for stability and enjoyment of the essentials.

Stability of Taurus the Triceratops

At the core of Taurus is a profound sense of stability, which is mirrored in the Triceratops's physical and behavioral attributes. This stability is expressed in the following ways:

1. **Emotional Stability**:
   Taurus individuals are known for their even-tempered nature and ability to remain calm under pressure. The Triceratops, with its patient and steady demeanor, mirrors this emotional resilience. It only reacted defensively when truly threatened, preferring peace over conflict.
2. **Physical Strength**:
   The Triceratops's sturdy body and massive frill represent the unshakable strength of Taurus. This physical resilience is symbolic of Taurus's ability to endure hardships and remain grounded, no matter the challenges.
3. **Dependability**:
   Much like Taurus natives, the Triceratops was a reliable protector of its herd. This dependability reflects the Taurus trait of being someone others can count on, whether for emotional support or practical solutions.
4. **Persistence**:
   Taurus is ruled by the fixed modality, meaning it is persistent and determined. The Triceratops's ability to survive in its environment despite threats from predators like the Tyrannosaurus Rex is a testament to its enduring spirit.

Planetary Alignments of Taurus the Triceratops

Taurus is ruled by **Venus**, the planet of love, beauty, and abundance. Venus's influence imbues Taurus the Triceratops with a harmonious connection to nature, a love for the finer things in life, and a sense of loyalty and protection. The following celestial alignments define Taurus the Triceratops:

1. **Venus and Earthly Pleasures**:
   Venus governs Taurus's appreciation for comfort, beauty, and the physical world. This aligns with the Triceratops's role as a peaceful grazer, living harmoniously in lush prehistoric landscapes. Taurus individuals, like the Triceratops, find joy in life's simple yet fulfilling pleasures.

2. **The Element of Earth**:
   As an Earth sign, Taurus is deeply rooted in the physical and material world. The Triceratops, dependent on the land for survival, symbolizes this Earthy connection, teaching us the importance of grounding ourselves in our environment and appreciating the resources around us.

3. **Planetary Stability**:
   Taurus is a fixed sign, associated with consistency and reliability. The Triceratops's sturdy build and enduring presence in its ecosystem reflect this celestial stability. Under Venus's influence, Taurus teaches us to build strong foundations and find peace in life's routines.

4. **Celestial Balance**:
   Venus also brings a sense of harmony and balance to Taurus. The Triceratops, while powerful and capable of defense, maintained a peaceful existence unless threatened. This duality of strength and calm mirrors the Venusian gift of finding balance in all things.

Lessons from Taurus the Triceratops

Taurus the Triceratops serves as a guide for embracing life with patience, resilience, and a deep appreciation for the present moment. Here are key lessons from this prehistoric zodiac sign:

1. **Build a Strong Foundation**:
   Like the Triceratops's sturdy body and grounded nature, Taurus reminds us to create a stable base in our lives—whether in relationships, careers, or personal goals.
2. **Value Simplicity**:
   Life's greatest joys often come from simple pleasures. Taurus the Triceratops encourages us to slow down, appreciate the beauty of the natural world, and savor the small things that bring comfort and happiness.
3. **Protect What Matters**:
   Taurus is fiercely loyal, and the Triceratops's role as a protector teaches us the importance of standing firm for the people and values we hold dear.
4. **Practice Patience**:
   In a fast-paced world, patience is a virtue. Taurus the Triceratops demonstrates the power of remaining calm and composed, showing us that persistence and steady effort yield long-lasting results.
5. **Connect with the Earth**:
   Taurus's Earthy nature is a reminder to stay connected to the physical world. Spend time in nature, nurture your body, and cultivate gratitude for the resources that sustain you.

Astrological Reflection for Taurus the Triceratops

- **Birth Chart Placement**:
  If Taurus or Venus is prominent in your astrological chart, you may resonate with the traits of the Triceratops. Use this connection to enhance your groundedness, patience, and ability to build lasting relationships.
- **Celestial Rituals**:
  Work with Venus's energy by incorporating green or earthy tones into your surroundings, practicing self-care, and engaging in grounding exercises such as walking in nature or gardening. Honor the Triceratops as a symbol of protection and stability in your astrological practice.

In the Dinosaur Zodiac, Taurus the Triceratops stands as a beacon of strength, patience, and harmony. By channeling its energy, you can navigate life with grace, protect what you hold dear, and find joy in the beauty of the present moment. Let Taurus the Triceratops remind you to stand firm in your values and embrace the peaceful yet powerful side of your nature.

Chapter 3: Gemini the Gallimimus
The Swift Messenger of the Prehistoric Zodiac
Duality of Gemini the Gallimimus

Gemini, the third sign of the zodiac, is the epitome of duality, adaptability, and quick-witted communication. Represented by the twins, Gemini thrives in the ability to see both sides of any situation, embracing complexity and change. In the Dinosaur Zodiac, this energy is embodied by the Gallimimus, a swift and intelligent dinosaur whose agility and social behavior make it a perfect match for Gemini's dual nature.

The Gallimimus, often referred to as the "chicken mimic," was a lightweight, bird-like dinosaur known for its incredible speed and adaptability. Its dual nature is reflected in its ability to thrive in diverse environments and work cohesively in groups, while still retaining individuality.

Key Characteristics of Gemini the Gallimimus

1. **Quick Thinking:**
   Like Gemini individuals who possess sharp intellect and mental agility, the Gallimimus was quick to adapt, whether evading predators or foraging for food.
2. **Duality and Versatility:**
   Geminis are known for their duality—the ability to balance contrasting traits such as logic and creativity or seriousness and playfulness. Similarly, the Gallimimus could shift between roles: a swift individual runner when needed and a cooperative herd member when advantageous.
3. **Natural Communicators:**
   Geminis thrive on interaction and connection, and the Gallimimus, a highly social dinosaur, is a prehistoric mirror of this quality. Its likely communication through body language and movement symbolizes Gemini's talent for conveying ideas in dynamic ways.
4. **Curiosity and Exploration:**
   With its agile build and keen senses, the Gallimimus explored its environment with curiosity. Geminis share this thirst for knowledge and a love of learning through diverse experiences.
5. **Energy and Movement:**
   Gallimimus's unmatched speed is symbolic of Gemini's restless energy, always in motion and seeking new adventures.

Communication Skills of Gemini the Gallimimus

Communication is a cornerstone of Gemini energy, and the Gallimimus reflects this through its cooperative and interactive nature. The following traits highlight Gemini the Gallimimus's role as a prehistoric messenger:

1. **Nonverbal Communication:**
   While modern interpretations suggest the Gallimimus didn't "speak" in the traditional sense, its movements and social behaviors were likely crucial for coordinating with others in its herd. This mirrors Gemini's skill at expressing thoughts through actions, gestures, and creative forms of communication.

2. **Adaptability in Expression:**
   Geminis excel at adjusting their communication style to fit the audience, whether through wit, charm, or logic. The Gallimimus's ability to quickly react and adapt to environmental changes shows a similar mastery of versatile communication.

3. **Connecting the Herd:**
   Geminis are natural networkers, linking people and ideas. The Gallimimus's role in its herd was likely one of cohesion, where its movements and signals helped keep the group synchronized and safe.

4. **Storytelling Through Motion:**
   Gemini the Gallimimus teaches us that communication isn't always verbal. Its swift, deliberate movements can inspire us to think about how we "speak" through our actions and how our body language conveys messages.

Cosmic Impacts on Gemini the Gallimimus

Astrologically, Gemini is ruled by Mercury, the planet of communication, intellect, and swift movement. Mercury's influence imbues Gemini the Gallimimus with an energetic and cerebral presence, as well as the ability to thrive in complex situations. Here's how Mercury's energy enhances this prehistoric sign:

1. Mercury's Speed:
   Just as Mercury is the fastest-moving planet, Gallimimus's incredible speed makes it a perfect representation of Gemini's quick and dynamic energy. This swiftness symbolizes the mental agility and adaptability that Geminis are known for.
2. Duality of Mercury:
   Mercury governs both reason and imagination, creating the duality that defines Gemini. Gallimimus embodies this by balancing its instincts for survival with its social and exploratory tendencies.
3. Cosmic Curiosity:
   Mercury's influence fuels curiosity and the desire to learn, a trait shared by both Geminis and the Gallimimus. This connection inspires exploration and the constant pursuit of knowledge.
4. The Air Element:
   Gemini is an Air sign, associated with intellect, communication, and movement. The Gallimimus's light, bird-like frame and swift movements resonate with the Air element's ethereal and ever-changing qualities.

Lessons from Gemini the Gallimimus

Gemini the Gallimimus offers valuable lessons on embracing life's complexities and thriving through adaptability. Here are some key takeaways:

1. **Embrace Duality:**
   Just as Gemini balances opposing forces, the Gallimimus teaches us to navigate the dualities of life—logic and emotion, independence and connection—finding harmony in complexity.
2. **Stay Curious:**
   The Gallimimus's exploratory nature is a reminder to remain curious and open to new ideas. Gemini energy thrives when learning and growing, so take time to seek knowledge and explore uncharted territories.
3. **Communicate Effectively:**
   Like the Gallimimus that likely communicated through movement and group dynamics, Gemini energy encourages us to express ourselves clearly and adapt our communication style to connect with others.
4. **Move with Purpose:**
   Gallimimus's speed wasn't just random—it served a purpose, whether evading predators or finding food. Similarly, Gemini the Gallimimus inspires us to use our energy and intellect intentionally, channeling our restless spirit into meaningful pursuits.

Astrological Reflection for Gemini the Gallimimus

1. **Harness Mercury's Energy:**
   If Gemini or Mercury is prominent in your chart, you may resonate with the quick-witted and adaptable nature of the Gallimimus. Use this energy to excel in communication, networking, and intellectual growth.
2. **Celebrate Your Versatility:**
   Gemini the Gallimimus teaches us that versatility is a strength. By embracing your ability to adapt and multitask, you can navigate life's challenges with grace and creativity.
3. **Explore Your World:**
   Geminis thrive on variety and exploration. Take inspiration from the Gallimimus's curious nature by seeking out new experiences and expanding your horizons.

Practical Applications of Gemini the Gallimimus

1. **Communication Practices:**
   Focus on improving your communication skills, whether through journaling, public speaking, or learning new languages. Let the Gallimimus inspire you to stay dynamic and expressive.
2. **Mind-Body Connection:**
   Channel the swift energy of Gemini the Gallimimus by engaging in activities that combine mental and physical agility, such as yoga, dance, or running.
3. **Build a Network:**
   Like the social Gallimimus, use your Gemini energy to connect with others and build meaningful relationships. Networking and collaboration can open doors to new opportunities.

In the Dinosaur Zodiac, Gemini the Gallimimus is a symbol of duality, communication, and adaptability. By channeling its energy, you can embrace life's complexities, connect with others, and move through the world with the grace and curiosity of this swift prehistoric messenger. Let Gemini the Gallimimus inspire you to explore, communicate, and thrive in your own dynamic journey.

Chapter 4: Cancer the Camarasaurus
The Gentle Nurturer of the Prehistoric Zodiac
Nurturing Nature of Cancer the Camarasaurus

Cancer, the fourth sign of the zodiac, is deeply tied to nurturing, emotional sensitivity, and the rhythms of life. Represented by the crab, Cancer brings an intuitive connection to home, family, and security. In the Dinosaur Zodiac, these qualities align beautifully with the Camarasaurus, a large, herbivorous dinosaur known for its protective and community-oriented behaviors. Its name, meaning "chambered lizard," references the spacious air chambers in its vertebrae, symbolizing a heart and spirit spacious enough to hold love, compassion, and care.

The Camarasaurus was a gentle giant of the Jurassic period, thriving in herds and relying on cooperation for survival. Like Cancer individuals, this dinosaur balanced its massive physical presence with a peaceful and nurturing demeanor.

Key Characteristics of Cancer the Camarasaurus

1. **Protective Instincts**:
   Cancer individuals are natural protectors, fiercely guarding their loved ones. The Camarasaurus displayed similar behaviors, moving in herds where adults likely shielded the young from predators, demonstrating a strong sense of communal care.

2. **Emotional Sensitivity**:
   Cancer is ruled by the moon, which governs emotions and intuition. The Camarasaurus's peaceful, herbivorous lifestyle reflects a calm and gentle nature, akin to Cancer's emotional depth and desire for harmony.

3. **Connection to Home and Family**:
   Just as Cancers prioritize their home and loved ones, the Camarasaurus relied on its herd for safety and companionship. This bond mirrors Cancer's commitment to creating a secure and loving environment.

4. **Adaptability to Rhythms**:
   Cancer is a cardinal sign, initiating change and adapting to the rhythms of life. Similarly, the Camarasaurus thrived by adjusting to seasonal vegetation and the challenges of its environment.

5. **Intuitive Wisdom**:
   Cancers are known for their strong intuition, often sensing the needs of others without being told. The Camarasaurus's instincts for survival, especially in protecting its herd, symbolize this deep inner knowing.

The Role of Lunar Phases in Cancer's Energy

The moon plays a central role in Cancer's astrological identity, governing its emotional tides and intuitive powers. For Cancer the Camarasaurus, lunar phases offer a symbolic rhythm for its nurturing and protective qualities:

1. **New Moon (Beginnings and Inner Reflection):**
   The New Moon symbolizes new beginnings and introspection. Cancer the Camarasaurus teaches us to pause and reflect during this phase, focusing on setting intentions for emotional growth and family well-being.

2. **Waxing Crescent (Building and Nurturing):**
   As the moon begins to grow, Cancer energy focuses on nurturing and development. For the Camarasaurus, this reflects the time spent caring for the young and fostering growth within the herd.

3. **First Quarter (Action and Protection):**
   The First Quarter Moon symbolizes action and overcoming challenges. Cancer the Camarasaurus demonstrates the strength needed to protect loved ones and navigate life's obstacles with courage and determination.

4. **Full Moon (Connection and Fulfillment):**
   The Full Moon is a time of heightened emotion and connection. Cancer the Camarasaurus reflects this by strengthening bonds within its herd, teaching us the importance of celebrating relationships and collective unity.

5. **Waning Phases (Release and Renewal):**
   As the moon wanes, Cancer energy turns inward, focusing on emotional release and renewal. For the Camarasaurus, this phase represents the quiet, restorative moments that sustain its gentle nature.

Intuition of Cancer the Camarasaurus

Cancer is one of the most intuitive zodiac signs, often guided by feelings and a profound connection to the unseen. The Camarasaurus embodies this through its instinctual behaviors and harmonious existence within its ecosystem.

1. **Emotional Awareness**:
   Cancer the Camarasaurus teaches us to tune into our emotions, recognizing them as valuable tools for navigating life. Like the Camarasaurus, which relied on instinct for survival, Cancers benefit from trusting their gut feelings.
2. **Empathy and Compassion**:
   Cancers are deeply empathetic, often sensing the needs of others before they are expressed. The communal life of the Camarasaurus, where cooperation ensured survival, mirrors this quality.
3. **Inner Strength Through Intuition**:
   Just as the Camarasaurus remained steadfast in its protective role, Cancer individuals can draw on their intuition to find strength in challenging times.

Cosmic Impacts on Cancer the Camarasaurus

Astrologically, Cancer is ruled by the **Moon**, which governs the emotional and intuitive aspects of life. This celestial influence enhances Cancer the Camarasaurus's nurturing qualities and deep connection to life's rhythms. Here's how lunar energy shapes this prehistoric zodiac sign:

1. **The Moon's Emotional Pull**:
   The moon's gravitational influence mirrors Cancer's emotional depth, pulling on the tides of the heart just as it does the ocean. Cancer the Camarasaurus symbolizes the ebb and flow of feelings, teaching us to embrace emotional cycles as part of life's natural rhythm.
2. **Connection to Water**:
   Cancer is a Water sign, representing intuition, emotion, and adaptability. While the Camarasaurus was a land creature, its reliance on vegetation and ecosystems tied to water sources reflects Cancer's affinity for the life-giving and restorative properties of water.
3. **Lunar Cycles and Herd Dynamics**:
   The phases of the moon influence Cancer's energy, encouraging moments of reflection, action, and connection. For Cancer the Camarasaurus, these cycles are symbolic of the rhythms of herd life, where nurturing and protection are balanced with the need for individual rest and renewal.

Lessons from Cancer the Camarasaurus

Cancer the Camarasaurus offers timeless lessons about care, intuition, and emotional strength. Here are key takeaways:

1. **Nurture Your Loved Ones**:
   Like the Camarasaurus that protected its young and stayed close to its herd, Cancer reminds us to prioritize the people and relationships that matter most.
2. **Trust Your Intuition**:
   The instincts of the Camarasaurus were vital for survival, just as Cancer's intuition is a guiding force. Learn to trust your inner voice and let it lead you toward safety and fulfillment.
3. **Embrace Emotional Cycles**:
   Life is full of emotional highs and lows, much like the phases of the moon. Cancer the Camarasaurus teaches us to honor these cycles and find strength in both growth and renewal.
4. **Build a Safe Haven**:
   Cancer values home as a place of comfort and security. Take inspiration from the Camarasaurus by creating an environment that nurtures and protects, whether it's a physical space or an emotional support system.
5. **Balance Giving and Receiving**:
   While Cancers are natural caregivers, it's important to allow yourself to receive care and rest. The Camarasaurus, though a protector, also relied on its herd for mutual support.

Astrological Reflection for Cancer the Camarasaurus

1. **Honor Lunar Energy**:
   Use the moon's phases to guide your emotional journey. Set intentions during the New Moon, connect with others during the Full Moon, and release burdens during the Waning phases.
2. **Practice Intuitive Living**:
   Cancer the Camarasaurus encourages you to live intuitively, tuning into the subtle cues of your environment and emotions.
3. **Foster Community**:
   Like the Camarasaurus's herd, surround yourself with a support network that values care and connection. Strengthen these bonds through acts of kindness and mutual respect.

Practical Applications of Cancer the Camarasaurus

1. **Moon Rituals**:
   Align your activities with the moon's phases. Use the New Moon for setting goals, the Full Moon for gratitude and connection, and the Waning Moon for rest and reflection.
2. **Create a Safe Space**:
   Design a home environment that feels nurturing and secure. Incorporate elements that bring comfort, such as soft lighting, soothing scents, or cherished mementos.
3. **Embrace Emotional Expression**:
   Allow yourself to feel and express your emotions fully. Journaling, meditation, or creative activities can help you connect with and honor your feelings.

In the Dinosaur Zodiac, Cancer the Camarasaurus is a gentle and intuitive guide, teaching us the value of nurturing, emotional connection, and living in harmony with life's natural rhythms. By embracing its energy, you can deepen your relationships, trust your instincts, and find comfort in the cycles of change. Let Cancer the Camarasaurus inspire you to protect, nurture, and grow with the strength of your heart and spirit.

Chapter 5: Leo the Tyrannosaurus Rex
The Regal Ruler of the Prehistoric Zodiac
The Majestic Nature of Leo the Tyrannosaurus Rex

Leo, the fifth sign of the zodiac, is synonymous with leadership, confidence, and the radiant energy of the Sun. Represented by the lion, Leo embodies courage, dominance, and an undeniable charisma that commands attention. In the Dinosaur Zodiac, this energy is perfectly captured by the Tyrannosaurus Rex (T-Rex), the undisputed king of its domain during the Late Cretaceous period. Known for its massive size, powerful bite, and commanding presence, the T-Rex exudes all the qualities of a true Leo.

The T-Rex was not just a predator—it was a symbol of strength, resilience, and dominance. Much like Leo individuals, it thrived at the top of its ecosystem, embodying the qualities of leadership, courage, and an unshakable confidence that made it both feared and revered.

Key Characteristics of Leo the Tyrannosaurus Rex

1. **Leadership**:
   Leo individuals are natural-born leaders, exuding confidence and charisma that inspire others to follow. The T-Rex, as an apex predator, ruled its environment with unmatched authority, embodying this leadership quality.
2. **Courage and Strength**:
   Just as Leos face challenges with boldness, the T-Rex's sheer power and fearlessness made it a dominant force in its world. This dinosaur's ability to hunt and defend its territory symbolizes Leo's bravery in the face of adversity.
3. **Commanding Presence**:
   Leos are known for their magnetic personalities that draw others toward them. Similarly, the T-Rex's size and reputation made it the center of attention in its ecosystem, reflecting Leo's innate ability to captivate and inspire.
4. **Loyalty and Protection**:
   While the T-Rex is often depicted as a fierce predator, recent studies suggest it may have cared for its young and protected its territory with unwavering dedication. This mirrors Leo's protective nature toward their loved ones and community.
5. **Passion for Life**:
   Leo is ruled by the Sun, the life-giving star that fuels creativity, vitality, and joy. The T-Rex, thriving in its role as a dominant creature, represents the Leo zest for life and its desire to shine brightly in all endeavors.

Leadership Qualities of Leo the Tyrannosaurus Rex

The T-Rex's leadership qualities were not just about its physical prowess but also its ability to dominate and adapt within its ecosystem. These traits align seamlessly with Leo's leadership archetype:

1. **Confidence in Action**:
   The T-Rex hunted with precision and skill, relying on its strength and instincts. Similarly, Leos approach challenges with confidence, trusting in their abilities to lead and succeed.
2. **Inspiring Dominance**:
   Just as the T-Rex inspired awe and fear among other creatures, Leos naturally command respect through their presence and determination. They lead by example, showing others the power of courage and conviction.
3. **Protective Leadership**:
   Leadership for Leo is not just about dominance but also about care and protection. The T-Rex's potential role as a guardian of its young mirrors Leo's dedication to safeguarding their family, friends, and community.
4. **Creative Solutions**:
   Leos are creative problem-solvers who thrive under pressure. The T-Rex, despite its size, was a highly adaptable predator that used its intelligence and instincts to overcome challenges, reflecting Leo's ability to find innovative solutions.

Courage of Leo the Tyrannosaurus Rex

Courage is a defining trait of both Leo and the T-Rex, manifesting in their ability to face challenges with unyielding determination. Here's how this quality is reflected:

1. **Fearless Predator**:
   The T-Rex's role as an apex predator required immense bravery, as it often faced formidable opponents. This mirrors Leo's boldness in tackling life's obstacles head-on, no matter the odds.
2. **Inner Strength**:
   Leos possess an inner strength that allows them to persevere through difficulties. The T-Rex, surviving and thriving in a competitive and dangerous world, symbolizes this resilience.
3. **Facing Adversity**:
   Whether defending their territory or hunting for survival, the T-Rex displayed a relentless courage that parallels Leo's ability to rise to any occasion with confidence and determination.
4. **Leading by Example**:
   Leos inspire others through their courage, much like the T-Rex's dominance inspired respect and awe among its contemporaries. This quality makes them natural leaders who encourage others to be brave and bold.

Solar Energies and Leo the Tyrannosaurus Rex

Leo is ruled by the **Sun**, the celestial body that represents vitality, creativity, and self-expression. The T-Rex's powerful presence and thriving existence align perfectly with the radiant energy of the Sun:

1. **The Sun as a Life Force**:
   Just as the Sun sustains life on Earth, Leo the T-Rex symbolizes the driving force that keeps ecosystems in balance. Its role as a predator ensured the survival of other species through natural selection, reflecting the Sun's vital role in maintaining order.
2. **Radiance and Confidence**:
   The Sun's brilliance mirrors Leo's natural confidence and charisma. The T-Rex's commanding presence and unparalleled strength are expressions of this solar energy, reminding us to embrace our inner light and let it shine.
3. **Creativity and Expression**:
   Solar energy fuels Leo's creativity and self-expression, qualities that are reflected in the T-Rex's ability to adapt its hunting techniques and assert its dominance in creative ways.
4. **Warmth and Generosity**:
   While the T-Rex may seem like an unlikely symbol of warmth, its potential role in caring for its offspring reflects the Sun's nurturing qualities. Similarly, Leos radiate warmth and generosity, often going out of their way to support and uplift others.

Lessons from Leo the Tyrannosaurus Rex

Leo the Tyrannosaurus Rex offers powerful lessons about leadership, courage, and self-expression. Here's what we can learn from this regal creature:

1. **Lead with Confidence**:
   The T-Rex thrived as a leader of its ecosystem, demonstrating the importance of confidence in achieving success. Leos can channel this energy to lead others with courage and conviction.
2. **Face Challenges Head-On**:
   The T-Rex didn't back down from challenges, and neither should you. Leo energy reminds us that bravery and persistence are key to overcoming obstacles.
3. **Shine Brightly**:
   Leos are ruled by the Sun, and like the T-Rex, they are meant to stand out. Embrace your unique talents and let your light shine in all that you do.
4. **Protect What Matters**:
   Just as the T-Rex likely protected its young, Leos are called to safeguard their loved ones and stand up for their values with unwavering loyalty.
5. **Embrace Your Inner Power**:
   The T-Rex's physical strength and dominance are symbols of the inner power we all possess. Leos teach us to harness this power to achieve our goals and inspire others.

Astrological Reflection for Leo the Tyrannosaurus Rex

1. **Honor the Sun's Energy:**
   Leos thrive when they connect with the Sun's energy. Spend time outdoors, meditate on solar imagery, or use affirmations to boost your confidence and vitality.
2. **Celebrate Your Leadership:**
   Embrace opportunities to lead, whether in your personal or professional life. Like the T-Rex, you have the strength and charisma to inspire others and make a difference.
3. **Radiate Positivity:**
   Leo the T-Rex encourages us to share our warmth and generosity with the world. Practice acts of kindness and let your enthusiasm uplift those around you.

Practical Applications of Leo the Tyrannosaurus Rex

1. **Confidence Building:**
   Develop rituals that boost your self-confidence, such as positive affirmations, power poses, or setting and achieving small goals.
2. **Creative Expression:**
   Use the T-Rex's adaptability as inspiration to explore your creative side. Whether through art, writing, or problem-solving, let your creativity shine.
3. **Leadership Development:**
   Take steps to hone your leadership skills, such as taking on new responsibilities, mentoring others, or practicing effective communication.

In the Dinosaur Zodiac, Leo the Tyrannosaurus Rex reigns as the fearless and charismatic ruler of the prehistoric world. By channeling its energy, you can embrace your inner leader, face challenges with courage, and shine brightly as a source of inspiration and strength. Let Leo the T-Rex remind you of your power, confidence, and the limitless potential of your unique light.

Chapter 6: Virgo the Velociraptor
The Analytical Strategist of the Prehistoric Zodiac
The Methodical Nature of Virgo the Velociraptor

Virgo, the sixth sign of the zodiac, represents precision, intellect, and an unparalleled attention to detail. Ruled by Mercury, Virgo is known for its analytical prowess, practicality, and dedication to improvement. In the Dinosaur Zodiac, this energy is perfectly embodied by the Velociraptor, a small yet highly intelligent predator of the Late Cretaceous period. Famous for its cunning tactics, sharp instincts, and strategic approach to hunting, the Velociraptor encapsulates Virgo's meticulous and resourceful nature.

Despite its relatively small size compared to other dinosaurs, the Velociraptor was a master strategist, relying on precision and intellect to survive and thrive. Similarly, Virgo individuals excel at using their mental acuity and problem-solving skills to navigate challenges and achieve their goals.

Key Characteristics of Virgo the Velociraptor

1. **Strategic Thinker**:
   Much like Virgo's penchant for planning and organization, the Velociraptor used calculated strategies when hunting, often working in coordinated groups to outsmart prey.

2. **Precision and Detail-Oriented**:
   Virgo thrives on accuracy and meticulous attention to detail, traits mirrored in the Velociraptor's precise movements, sharp claws, and efficient hunting techniques.

3. **Resourcefulness**:
   Virgos are highly resourceful, finding practical solutions to complex problems. The Velociraptor's ability to adapt to various environments and maximize its strengths exemplifies this quality.

4. **Intellectual Curiosity**:
   The Velociraptor's keen intelligence mirrors Virgo's natural curiosity and thirst for knowledge, symbolizing a deep drive to understand and master its surroundings.

5. **Dependability and Discipline**:
   Virgos are known for their reliability and dedication to their tasks. Similarly, the Velociraptor's disciplined approach to survival showcases its focus and determination.

Precision of Virgo the Velociraptor

Precision is a defining trait of both Virgo and the Velociraptor, reflected in their ability to execute tasks with accuracy and efficiency. Here's how this characteristic manifests:

1. **Calculated Movements**:
   The Velociraptor was known for its swift, precise attacks, targeting specific vulnerabilities in its prey. This mirrors Virgo's calculated approach to problem-solving, ensuring every action is intentional and effective.
2. **Attention to the Smallest Details**:
   Virgos excel at noticing nuances others might overlook. The Velociraptor's sharp vision and acute senses allowed it to identify opportunities and threats with remarkable accuracy.
3. **Methodical Hunting Style**:
   Unlike larger, brute-force predators, the Velociraptor relied on strategy and precision, much like Virgo's methodical approach to achieving success in their endeavors.
4. **Efficiency in Action**:
   Virgos value efficiency and dislike wasted effort. The Velociraptor's ability to conserve energy while pursuing its goals reflects this focus on maximizing results with minimal resources.

Intellect of Virgo the Velociraptor

Virgo is one of the most intellectually driven signs of the zodiac, known for its analytical mind and ability to synthesize information. The Velociraptor's intelligence is legendary, making it a perfect representation of Virgo's mental agility:

1. **Problem-Solving Skills**:
   The Velociraptor's ability to plan and execute complex hunting strategies showcases its problem-solving abilities, a hallmark of Virgo's intellect.
2. **Adaptability and Learning**:
   Virgos are quick learners, constantly seeking ways to improve. The Velociraptor's adaptability in various environments and its ability to learn from experience reflect this trait.
3. **Collaborative Intelligence**:
   While Virgos are independent thinkers, they also excel in teamwork when the situation demands. The Velociraptor's cooperative hunting tactics mirror Virgo's ability to work with others to achieve a common goal.
4. **Mental Sharpness**:
   Virgo's sharp intellect allows them to analyze situations quickly and accurately. The Velociraptor's quick reflexes and keen decision-making skills exemplify this mental clarity.

Astrological Influences on Virgo the Velociraptor

Virgo is ruled by **Mercury**, the planet of communication, intellect, and analysis. Mercury's influence enhances Virgo's natural precision, intellect, and adaptability, making it a perfect match for the Velociraptor's cunning nature. Here's how Mercury's energy shapes this prehistoric zodiac sign:

1. **Mercury's Analytical Power**:
   Mercury infuses Virgo with a sharp, detail-oriented mind, enabling them to analyze complex situations with ease. The Velociraptor's strategic hunting style reflects this analytical prowess.
2. **Earth Element Grounding**:
   Virgo is an Earth sign, symbolizing practicality, stability, and connection to the material world. The Velociraptor's ability to navigate its physical environment with precision and resourcefulness highlights this Earthy grounding.
3. **Duality of Mercury**:
   As Mercury governs both intellect and adaptability, Virgo the Velociraptor excels in balancing mental acuity with practical action, ensuring success in both planning and execution.
4. **Precision of Communication**:
   Mercury's influence also enhances Virgo's communication skills. The Velociraptor's ability to coordinate with its pack demonstrates a form of prehistoric "communication," mirroring Virgo's clarity and effectiveness in interactions.

Lessons from Virgo the Velociraptor

Virgo the Velociraptor offers valuable lessons about precision, intellect, and adaptability. Here are the key takeaways:

1. **Master the Details**:
   Success often lies in the small details. Like the Velociraptor, take the time to analyze and plan, ensuring every step is purposeful and effective.
2. **Think Strategically**:
   Virgo the Velociraptor teaches us to approach challenges with a strategic mindset, breaking problems into manageable steps and focusing on solutions.
3. **Adapt to Your Environment**:
   The Velociraptor's adaptability reminds us to remain flexible and resourceful, using our surroundings and skills to our advantage.
4. **Embrace Collaboration**:
   While independence is valuable, teamwork can amplify success. Virgo the Velociraptor demonstrates the power of working with others to achieve shared goals.
5. **Focus on Continuous Improvement**:
   Virgo's drive for self-improvement aligns with the Velociraptor's instinct to learn and adapt. Use this energy to refine your skills and strive for excellence.

Astrological Reflection for Virgo the Velociraptor

1. **Harness Mercury's Energy**:
   If Virgo or Mercury is prominent in your chart, channel its analytical power to excel in planning, problem-solving, and communication.
2. **Stay Grounded**:
   Virgo's Earth element encourages you to remain practical and connected to reality. Use the Velociraptor's precision and focus as inspiration to stay grounded in your goals.
3. **Celebrate Your Intellect**:
   Virgo the Velociraptor reminds us that intellect is a powerful tool. Embrace your analytical abilities and use them to navigate challenges with confidence.

Practical Applications of Virgo the Velociraptor

1. **Develop a Strategic Plan**:
   Whether for personal or professional goals, create a detailed plan that outlines specific steps to achieve your objectives. Think like the Velociraptor, considering all angles before acting.
2. **Refine Your Skills**:
   Dedicate time to honing a particular skill or talent. Virgo's energy thrives on mastery and improvement, much like the Velociraptor's evolutionary adaptations.
3. **Organize Your Environment**:
   Use Virgo's love of order to declutter and organize your space. A well-organized environment fosters clarity and productivity.
4. **Practice Mindfulness**:
   Precision and focus come naturally when you're fully present. Practice mindfulness techniques to enhance your concentration and decision-making abilities.

In the Dinosaur Zodiac, Virgo the Velociraptor is a symbol of precision, intellect, and strategic mastery. By channeling its energy, you can approach life's challenges with confidence, focus, and an analytical mindset. Let Virgo the Velociraptor inspire you to embrace your mental agility, refine your skills, and navigate the world with precision and purpose.

Chapter 7: Libra the Lambeosaurus
The Harmonious Diplomat of the Prehistoric Zodiac
The Balanced Nature of Libra the Lambeosaurus

Libra, the seventh sign of the zodiac, is the embodiment of balance, relationships, and harmony. Represented by the scales, Libra seeks equilibrium in all aspects of life, thriving in partnerships and fostering peaceful connections. In the Dinosaur Zodiac, these qualities are reflected in the Lambeosaurus, a graceful herbivorous dinosaur from the Late Cretaceous period. Known for its distinctive crest and likely social nature, the Lambeosaurus is a symbol of cooperative relationships and the beauty of living in harmony with one's surroundings.

The Lambeosaurus, with its elongated, hollow cranial crest, stands out not only for its appearance but also for its possible role in communication and social bonding. Like Libras, who are natural diplomats, the Lambeosaurus likely relied on connections and relationships within its herd to thrive.

Key Characteristics of Libra the Lambeosaurus

1. **Balance and Grace**:
   Libras strive for harmony and balance in all they do, a quality mirrored in the Lambeosaurus's elegant movements and peaceful existence as a herbivore.
2. **Social Connectivity**:
   Libra thrives in relationships and partnerships. The Lambeosaurus, thought to live in herds, symbolizes the importance of social bonds and mutual support.
3. **Beauty and Aesthetic Appeal**:
   Ruled by Venus, Libra has an eye for beauty and elegance. The Lambeosaurus's unique and striking crest embodies this aesthetic quality, making it one of the more visually distinct dinosaurs.
4. **Diplomatic Nature**:
   Libras are peacemakers, often resolving conflicts and bringing people together. The Lambeosaurus's cooperative behavior within its herd reflects this ability to maintain harmony in social settings.
5. **Equilibrium in Life**:
   Just as Libra seeks balance between work and leisure, action and rest, the Lambeosaurus exemplifies a balanced existence, thriving through its peaceful and community-oriented lifestyle.

Balance of Libra the Lambeosaurus

Balance is the cornerstone of Libra energy, and the Lambeosaurus's lifestyle offers a prehistoric model for achieving equilibrium:

1. **Dietary Harmony**:
   As a herbivore, the Lambeosaurus lived in balance with its environment, grazing on vegetation without disrupting the ecosystem. This mirrors Libra's desire to live in harmony with nature and others.
2. **Social Stability**:
   Herd living requires balance between individual needs and group dynamics. The Lambeosaurus likely found this equilibrium, teaching us the importance of maintaining harmony in our relationships.
3. **Adaptation and Flexibility**:
   Libras are skilled at adapting to maintain balance, and the Lambeosaurus's ability to thrive in varying habitats shows a similar adaptability in response to environmental changes.
4. **Inner Peace and Outer Calm**:
   Libras prioritize both inner serenity and external harmony. The Lambeosaurus's calm demeanor and role as a non-aggressive herbivore reflect this peaceful balance.

Relationships of Libra the Lambeosaurus

Libra's strength lies in its ability to forge and nurture relationships, a trait shared by the Lambeosaurus. Here's how this dinosaur symbolizes Libra's relational qualities:

1. **Cooperative Herd Behavior**:
   The Lambeosaurus likely lived in herds, depending on mutual cooperation for safety and survival. This mirrors Libra's talent for fostering partnerships and working collaboratively with others.
2. **Effective Communication**:
   The hollow crest of the Lambeosaurus is thought to have been used for producing sounds, possibly for communication. This highlights Libra's gift for clear and harmonious communication in building connections.
3. **Diplomatic Problem-Solving**:
   Libras excel at resolving conflicts with tact and fairness. While the Lambeosaurus was not a predator or aggressor, its social dynamics likely involved resolving group tensions peacefully, reflecting Libra's diplomatic nature.
4. **Emphasis on Togetherness**:
   Just as Libras value companionship, the Lambeosaurus thrived as part of a herd, teaching us the importance of relationships and mutual care.

Celestial Harmony and Libra the Lambeosaurus

Libra is ruled by **Venus**, the planet of love, beauty, and harmony, which enhances Libra's desire for balance and relational focus. Here's how celestial influences shape Libra the Lambeosaurus:

1. **Venusian Beauty**:

    Venus imbues Libra with an appreciation for aesthetics, which is reflected in the Lambeosaurus's striking crest. This physical feature symbolizes the beauty and uniqueness Libras seek in the world around them.

2. **Harmony Through Relationships**:

    Venus fosters love and connection, emphasizing Libra's relational strengths. The Lambeosaurus's herd behavior demonstrates how mutual support and communication create a harmonious existence.

3. **Air Element Connection**:

    As an Air sign, Libra is intellectual and communicative, thriving on interaction. The Lambeosaurus's crest-based communication aligns with this Air element energy, emphasizing the importance of exchanging ideas and maintaining social bonds.

4. **Celestial Balance**:

    Libra seeks to align personal needs with those of others, much like the Lambeosaurus balanced its role within the herd. Venus's influence enhances this ability to find and maintain equilibrium.

Lessons from Libra the Lambeosaurus

Libra the Lambeosaurus offers profound insights into the value of balance, relationships, and harmony. Here are the key lessons:

1. **Strive for Balance**:
   Just as the Lambeosaurus lived in harmony with its environment, Libras teach us to seek balance in our own lives—whether between work and rest, giving and receiving, or independence and togetherness.
2. **Value Your Relationships**:
   The Lambeosaurus's herd behavior reminds us of the importance of community and connection. Nurture your relationships and create a supportive network.
3. **Communicate with Clarity**:
   Libra the Lambeosaurus emphasizes the power of communication. Whether resolving conflicts or building connections, use your words and actions to promote understanding and harmony.
4. **Celebrate Beauty and Harmony**:
   Venus encourages us to appreciate life's beauty, just as the Lambeosaurus's crest inspires awe. Surround yourself with things and people that bring joy and balance into your life.
5. **Be a Diplomat**:
   The Lambeosaurus's peaceful nature reminds us to approach conflicts with fairness and tact. Strive to be a mediator, bringing people together rather than driving them apart.

Astrological Reflection for Libra the Lambeosaurus

1. **Embrace Venus's Energy**:
   Use Venus's influence to enhance your relationships, appreciate beauty, and create harmony in your surroundings. Activities like decorating your space, practicing self-care, or fostering connections with loved ones can amplify this energy.
2. **Seek Social Balance**:
   Libra the Lambeosaurus teaches us to balance our personal needs with those of the group. Reflect on how you can maintain equilibrium in your relationships.
3. **Practice Fairness and Diplomacy**:
   Strive to resolve conflicts with empathy and fairness, channeling Libra's diplomatic nature in your interactions.

Practical Applications of Libra the Lambeosaurus

1. **Build Strong Relationships**:
   Dedicate time to nurturing your friendships and partnerships. Show appreciation for those who support you and create opportunities to connect.
2. **Enhance Communication Skills**:
   Practice active listening and thoughtful expression. Like the Lambeosaurus, use your unique voice to strengthen bonds and foster understanding.
3. **Create a Harmonious Environment**:
   Surround yourself with beauty and balance. Arrange your space to reflect Libra's love for harmony, incorporating elements that bring you peace and joy.
4. **Foster Group Dynamics**:
   Whether at work, home, or in your community, focus on building cohesive, supportive groups. Be a leader in promoting collaboration and mutual respect.

In the Dinosaur Zodiac, Libra the Lambeosaurus stands as a beacon of balance, relationships, and celestial harmony. By channeling its energy, you can cultivate meaningful connections, foster peace, and create a life filled with beauty and equilibrium. Let Libra the Lambeosaurus inspire you to embrace your diplomatic nature, strengthen your bonds, and find harmony in every aspect of life.

Chapter 8: Scorpio the Spinosaurus
The Intense Transformer of the Prehistoric Zodiac
The Powerful Presence of Scorpio the Spinosaurus

Scorpio, the eighth sign of the zodiac, represents intensity, transformation, and an unparalleled depth of emotion. Ruled by Pluto, the planet of rebirth and regeneration, Scorpio thrives in the realms of power, mystery, and profound change. In the Dinosaur Zodiac, this energy finds its perfect match in the Spinosaurus, a unique and fearsome predator that dominated both land and water during the Cretaceous period. With its massive size, iconic sail-like spine, and adaptability, the Spinosaurus is a living symbol of Scorpio's transformative and mysterious nature.

The Spinosaurus, one of the largest carnivorous dinosaurs, was an enigmatic creature that thrived in diverse environments. Its dual existence between aquatic and terrestrial habitats reflects Scorpio's ability to navigate emotional and physical depths, embracing transformation and renewal at every turn.

Key Characteristics of Scorpio the Spinosaurus

1. **Intensity and Power**:
   Scorpio individuals are known for their immense emotional and physical intensity. The Spinosaurus, with its commanding presence and apex predator status, embodies this raw power.

2. **Mystery and Enigma**:
   Just as Scorpio exudes a sense of mystery, the Spinosaurus's unique physiology and behavior continue to intrigue scientists, symbolizing the allure of the unknown.

3. **Adaptability and Transformation**:
   Scorpios are masters of transformation, thriving in situations that require change and reinvention. The Spinosaurus's ability to transition seamlessly between aquatic and terrestrial environments reflects this adaptability.

4. **Resilience and Survival**:
   Scorpio is associated with the ability to endure and rise from the ashes. Similarly, the Spinosaurus's evolutionary adaptations for survival in challenging conditions mirror Scorpio's resilience.

5. **Dominance in Hidden Realms**:
   Scorpios excel in exploring the unseen and unknown. The Spinosaurus, as one of the few dinosaurs adept at both swimming and hunting in water, thrived in environments that others could not dominate.

Intensity of Scorpio the Spinosaurus

Intensity is at the core of Scorpio's identity, driving their passion and focus in all endeavors. The Spinosaurus, with its powerful presence and hunting prowess, reflects this intense nature in the following ways:

1. **Predatory Power**:
   The Spinosaurus was a formidable predator, capable of taking down large prey in both water and on land. This reflects Scorpio's relentless drive and determination to achieve their goals.
2. **Focused Energy**:
   Scorpios channel their intensity into precise and purposeful actions. The Spinosaurus's calculated hunting techniques demonstrate this focused and deliberate energy.
3. **Emotional Depth**:
   While the Spinosaurus's intensity was physical, Scorpio's depth is emotional and psychological. Together, they teach us to embrace and harness our inner strength for personal and external transformations.
4. **Unyielding Determination**:
   Scorpio's persistence is unmatched, much like the Spinosaurus's tenacity in surviving and thriving in diverse habitats. This shared intensity highlights the power of staying committed to one's goals.

Transformation of Scorpio the Spinosaurus

Transformation is the defining theme of Scorpio, ruled by Pluto, the planet of rebirth and regeneration. The Spinosaurus exemplifies this energy through its evolutionary and adaptive abilities:

1. **Evolutionary Adaptation**:
   The Spinosaurus's semi-aquatic lifestyle required significant adaptations, including its elongated skull, webbed feet, and iconic sail. These changes reflect Scorpio's ability to evolve and transform when faced with challenges.
2. **Symbol of Rebirth**:
   Pluto's influence ties Scorpio to cycles of death and rebirth, both literal and metaphorical. The Spinosaurus's ability to thrive in the unforgiving environments of rivers and swamps mirrors this regenerative energy.
3. **Power Through Change**:
   Scorpios find their strength in transformation, much like the Spinosaurus, which used its unique adaptations to dominate its ecosystem. This dinosaur reminds us that embracing change is essential for growth and survival.
4. **Navigating Depths**:
   Just as Scorpio dives into the depths of the psyche, the Spinosaurus thrived in watery habitats, symbolizing the exploration of hidden realms and the courage to face the unknown.

Pluto's Power and Scorpio the Spinosaurus

Scorpio is ruled by **Pluto**, the planet of transformation, power, and the underworld. Pluto's influence imbues Scorpio the Spinosaurus with an aura of mystery and a capacity for profound change:

1. **Pluto and Regeneration**:
   Pluto governs the cycles of life, death, and rebirth. The Spinosaurus's dominance in harsh and changing environments symbolizes the ability to adapt and regenerate under Pluto's transformative energy.

2. **Mastery of Hidden Realms**:
   Pluto rules the unseen, and Scorpio thrives in exploring the depths of the psyche and the mysteries of life. The Spinosaurus's ability to dominate both land and water reflects mastery over dual and hidden realms.

3. **Raw and Elemental Power**:
   Pluto enhances Scorpio's raw energy, fueling their ambition and resilience. The Spinosaurus, as one of the most powerful predators of its time, exemplifies this primal force.

4. **Magnetism and Mystery**:
   Pluto gives Scorpio a magnetic and enigmatic presence. The Spinosaurus, with its distinctive sail and unique adaptations, continues to captivate and intrigue, embodying this Plutonian allure.

Lessons from Scorpio the Spinosaurus

Scorpio the Spinosaurus offers profound lessons about intensity, transformation, and embracing one's power. Here are key takeaways:

1. **Harness Your Intensity**:
   Like the Spinosaurus, channel your energy into purposeful and deliberate actions. Scorpio reminds us that intensity, when focused, can lead to incredible achievements.

2. **Embrace Transformation**:
   Life is full of changes, and Scorpio teaches us to embrace them as opportunities for growth. The Spinosaurus's adaptations remind us that transformation is essential for survival and success.

3. **Explore Hidden Depths**:
   Just as the Spinosaurus thrived in watery habitats, Scorpio encourages us to explore the depths of our emotions, thoughts, and desires. This self-discovery leads to greater understanding and empowerment.

4. **Be Resilient**:
   Challenges are a natural part of life. Scorpio the Spinosaurus reminds us to remain resilient and use adversity as a catalyst for strength and renewal.

5. **Own Your Power**:
   Scorpio's connection to Pluto emphasizes the importance of stepping into your personal

power. The Spinosaurus's commanding presence inspires us to embrace our strength and lead with confidence.

Astrological Reflection for Scorpio the Spinosaurus

1. **Tap into Pluto's Energy**:
   Use Pluto's transformative power to embrace change and growth. Reflect on how challenges in your life have shaped you and explore ways to harness this energy for future success.
2. **Strengthen Emotional Depth**:
   Scorpio the Spinosaurus encourages you to dive into your emotions and address hidden fears or desires. Journaling, meditation, or therapy can help unlock and process these depths.
3. **Balance Power and Intensity**:
   Use Scorpio's intense energy wisely, ensuring it empowers rather than overwhelms. The Spinosaurus's calculated actions remind us to channel power in a focused and balanced way.

Practical Applications of Scorpio the Spinosaurus

1. **Embrace Transformation**:
   Identify an area of your life that requires change and take intentional steps to evolve. Whether it's a career shift, a relationship adjustment, or personal growth, let Scorpio the Spinosaurus guide you through the process.
2. **Harness Resilience**:
   Practice resilience by facing challenges head-on and learning from setbacks. Build a mindset that embraces obstacles as opportunities for growth.
3. **Explore Your Inner World**:
   Dedicate time to self-reflection and emotional exploration. Use tools like meditation, shadow work, or astrology to uncover and understand your inner depths.
4. **Channel Intensity into Creativity**:
   Scorpio energy thrives when focused on creative or transformative projects. Use your passion to fuel artistic endeavors, problem-solving, or personal achievements.

In the Dinosaur Zodiac, Scorpio the Spinosaurus is a powerful symbol of intensity, transformation, and the ability to navigate life's depths with strength and purpose. By channeling its energy, you can embrace change, harness your power, and explore the hidden realms of your emotions and mind. Let Scorpio the Spinosaurus inspire you to transform, thrive, and rise stronger with every challenge.

Chapter 9: Sagittarius the Stegosaurus
The Adventurous Visionary of the Prehistoric Zodiac
The Free-Spirited Nature of Sagittarius the Stegosaurus

Sagittarius, the ninth sign of the zodiac, is the embodiment of exploration, freedom, and the pursuit of wisdom. Ruled by Jupiter, the planet of expansion, philosophy, and higher learning, Sagittarius thrives on adventure, curiosity, and the quest for meaning. In the Dinosaur Zodiac, these qualities align seamlessly with the Stegosaurus, a gentle yet determined herbivore of the Late Jurassic period. With its distinctive plates and spiked tail, the Stegosaurus symbolizes resilience, discovery, and a harmonious connection to its environment.

The Stegosaurus, known for its iconic armored plates and nomadic tendencies, mirrors Sagittarius's desire for freedom and exploration. Despite its imposing size and strength, this dinosaur was peaceful, embodying Sagittarius's philosophical and visionary traits.

Key Characteristics of Sagittarius the Stegosaurus

1. **Adventurous Spirit**:
   Sagittarius thrives on adventure and exploration, a quality reflected in the Stegosaurus's roaming lifestyle. This dinosaur likely traveled vast distances in search of food, showcasing a Sagittarian desire for movement and discovery.

2. **Freedom-Loving Nature**:
   Sagittarians cherish freedom and independence, much like the Stegosaurus, which lived a nomadic existence, unbound by territorial constraints.

3. **Optimism and Resilience**:
   Sagittarius is known for its optimistic outlook and ability to overcome challenges. The Stegosaurus, with its protective plates and spiked tail, symbolizes the strength and resilience needed to thrive in a complex ecosystem.

4. **Curiosity and Learning**:
   Jupiter fuels Sagittarius's thirst for knowledge and understanding. The Stegosaurus, with its unique physiology, represents the Sagittarian quest to learn and grow through experience.

5. **Philosophical Connection to Nature**:
   Sagittarius seeks to understand the world on a deeper level, much like the Stegosaurus's peaceful existence reflects a harmonious relationship with its environment.

Exploration of Sagittarius the Stegosaurus

Exploration is central to Sagittarius's essence, and the Stegosaurus's lifestyle exemplifies this wandering spirit:

1. **Nomadic Habits**:
   The Stegosaurus likely migrated in search of food and water, demonstrating the Sagittarian love for travel and exploration. Its journeys reflect a desire to expand horizons and embrace new experiences.
2. **Navigating Challenges**:
   Sagittarius is unafraid to venture into the unknown, much like the Stegosaurus, which roamed diverse landscapes and adapted to changing environments.
3. **Seeking Abundance**:
   Sagittarius, ruled by Jupiter, is associated with expansion and abundance. The Stegosaurus's grazing habits align with this energy, symbolizing the pursuit of sustenance and growth.
4. **Freedom to Roam**:
   The Stegosaurus's lack of territorial aggression reflects Sagittarius's need for freedom and openness, emphasizing the importance of unencumbered exploration.

Freedom of Sagittarius the Stegosaurus

Freedom is a cornerstone of Sagittarius's identity, and the Stegosaurus embodies this through its independent and peaceful existence:

1. **Unrestricted Movement**:
   Like Sagittarius, which thrives on independence, the Stegosaurus's roaming lifestyle allowed it to explore vast territories without being tied to a specific region.
2. **Self-Reliance**:
   Despite its social tendencies, the Stegosaurus was a self-sufficient herbivore, mirroring Sagittarius's ability to balance freedom with personal responsibility.
3. **Harmonious Coexistence**:
   Sagittarians value relationships that honor their independence. Similarly, the Stegosaurus coexisted peacefully with other species, emphasizing mutual respect and freedom.
4. **Expansive Perspective**:
   Sagittarius views the world as a place of infinite possibilities, and the Stegosaurus's ability to adapt and thrive in varied environments reflects this expansive mindsct.

Jupiter's Wisdom and Sagittarius the Stegosaurus
Sagittarius is ruled by **Jupiter**, the planet of expansion, philosophy, and higher learning. Jupiter's influence enhances Sagittarius the Stegosaurus's visionary qualities and adventurous spirit:

1. **Jupiter's Expansive Energy**:
   Jupiter encourages growth and exploration, which is evident in the Stegosaurus's migratory habits and its ability to adapt to diverse environments.
2. **Philosophical Depth**:
   Jupiter fuels Sagittarius's quest for meaning and understanding. The Stegosaurus, with its peaceful and purposeful existence, symbolizes a connection to the natural world and the philosophical insights it offers.
3. **Optimism and Abundance**:
   Jupiter brings an optimistic and abundant energy to Sagittarius. The Stegosaurus's ability to find sustenance and thrive in challenging ecosystems reflects this belief in life's potential for growth and prosperity.
4. **Learning Through Experience**:
   Jupiter inspires learning through exploration and firsthand experience. The Stegosaurus's nomadic lifestyle represents this Sagittarian pursuit of knowledge and understanding through active engagement with the world.

Lessons from Sagittarius the Stegosaurus
Sagittarius the Stegosaurus offers timeless lessons about exploration, freedom, and the pursuit of wisdom. Here are the key takeaways:

1. **Embrace the Journey**:
   Life is an adventure, and Sagittarius the Stegosaurus reminds us to approach it with curiosity and enthusiasm. Explore new ideas, places, and experiences to expand your perspective.
2. **Honor Your Freedom**:
   Like the Stegosaurus, prioritize independence and freedom in your life. Seek relationships and environments that support your desire for growth and movement.
3. **Cultivate Resilience**:
   Challenges are opportunities for growth. The Stegosaurus's protective adaptations remind us to stay strong and optimistic in the face of adversity.
4. **Seek Abundance and Growth**:
   Sagittarius, ruled by Jupiter, teaches us to pursue abundance in all forms—knowledge, relationships, and personal growth. The Stegosaurus's constant search for sustenance reflects this expansive energy.
5. **Connect with Nature's Wisdom**:
   Sagittarius the Stegosaurus encourages us to find meaning and harmony in the natural world. Spend time outdoors, reflect on life's interconnectedness, and draw inspiration from the cycles of nature

Astrological Reflection for Sagittarius the Stegosaurus

1. **Expand Your Horizons**:
   Use Jupiter's energy to explore new opportunities, whether through travel, education, or personal development. Let Sagittarius the Stegosaurus inspire your quest for growth.
2. **Foster Optimism**:
   Embrace a positive outlook and trust in life's abundance. Sagittarius the Stegosaurus teaches us to focus on possibilities rather than limitations.
3. **Balance Freedom with Responsibility**:
   While freedom is vital, Sagittarius reminds us to balance it with accountability. The Stegosaurus's self-sufficient nature encourages us to take ownership of our choices.

Practical Applications of Sagittarius the Stegosaurus

1. **Pursue Knowledge and Adventure**:
   Dedicate time to learning and exploring. Read books, take classes, or plan trips that broaden your understanding of the world.
2. **Connect with Nature**:
   Spend time in natural settings to ground yourself and gain perspective. Reflect on the Stegosaurus's peaceful coexistence with its environment.
3. **Set Expansive Goals**:
   Use Sagittarius's optimistic energy to set ambitious goals. Focus on growth and abundance, and take steps toward achieving your dreams.
4. **Celebrate Freedom**:
   Create space in your life for independence and exploration. Prioritize activities and relationships that honor your need for freedom and growth.

In the Dinosaur Zodiac, Sagittarius the Stegosaurus is a beacon of exploration, freedom, and wisdom. By channeling its energy, you can embrace life's adventures, seek knowledge, and approach the world with optimism and curiosity. Let Sagittarius the Stegosaurus inspire you to roam boldly, grow endlessly, and find meaning in the journey of life.

Chapter 10: Capricorn the Ceratosaurus
The Ambitious Achiever of the Prehistoric Zodiac
The Disciplined Nature of Capricorn the Ceratosaurus

Capricorn, the tenth sign of the zodiac, symbolizes discipline, ambition, and a steadfast determination to achieve greatness. Ruled by Saturn, the planet of structure, responsibility, and life lessons, Capricorn is a master of hard work, perseverance, and climbing to the top against all odds. In the Dinosaur Zodiac, these traits are embodied by the Ceratosaurus, a medium-sized carnivore of the Late Jurassic period known for its adaptability, unique physical characteristics, and ability to thrive in challenging environments.

With its distinctive horned snout and balance of strength and strategy, the Ceratosaurus mirrors Capricorn's resilience, ambition, and ability to succeed through disciplined effort and calculated actions.

Key Characteristics of Capricorn the Ceratosaurus

1. **Ambition and Drive**:
   Capricorns are natural goal-setters who steadily work toward their ambitions. Similarly, the Ceratosaurus's prowess as a predator demonstrates its determination and resourcefulness in achieving its goals.

2. **Practicality and Strategy**:
   Capricorns excel at creating structured plans and executing them with precision. The Ceratosaurus, with its adaptable hunting techniques, exemplifies this practical and strategic approach to survival.

3. **Resilience and Endurance**:
   Capricorn thrives on perseverance, often enduring hardships to achieve success. The Ceratosaurus's ability to adapt to diverse environments and challenges reflects this resilience.

4. **Leadership and Authority**:
   Capricorns are natural leaders who earn respect through their work ethic and accomplishments. The Ceratosaurus's dominant presence in its ecosystem mirrors this authoritative and commanding energy.

5. **Structure and Discipline**:
   Ruled by Saturn, Capricorns value structure and discipline. The Ceratosaurus, with its balanced hunting and survival methods, embodies this grounded and methodical energy.

Discipline of Capricorn the Ceratosaurus

Discipline is a defining trait of Capricorn, driving their ability to achieve long-term success through consistent effort. The Ceratosaurus reflects this discipline in the following ways:

1. **Steady Approach**:
   Capricorns thrive on careful planning and methodical execution, much like the Ceratosaurus, which used a calculated approach to hunting and survival.
2. **Focused Energy**:
   Rather than wasting energy on unnecessary risks, Capricorns prioritize actions that align with their goals. The Ceratosaurus's efficient hunting techniques symbolize this focus and intentionality.
3. **Patience and Perseverance**:
   Capricorn's discipline enables them to endure challenges and delays. The Ceratosaurus's ability to persist in a competitive ecosystem highlights the value of patience and resilience.
4. **Structured Success**:
   Saturn's influence inspires Capricorns to build solid foundations for their achievements. The Ceratosaurus's balanced adaptation to its environment demonstrates this ability to create sustainable success.

Ambition of Capricorn the Ceratosaurus

Ambition is at the core of Capricorn's identity, fueling their drive to climb life's metaphorical mountains. The Ceratosaurus's ambitious traits include:

1. **Climbing to the Top**:
   Capricorns are known for their ability to rise above obstacles, much like the Ceratosaurus, which thrived in its ecosystem despite competition from larger predators like the Allosaurus.
2. **Self-Sufficiency**:
   Capricorns take pride in their independence and ability to achieve success on their own terms. The Ceratosaurus's solitary hunting habits reflect this self-reliant nature.
3. **Goal-Oriented Mindset**:
   Capricorns approach life with a clear sense of purpose, setting and achieving long-term goals. The Ceratosaurus's efficient strategies in securing prey symbolize this focused ambition.
4. **Legacy and Impact**:
   Ruled by Saturn, Capricorns often think about the long-term impact of their actions. The Ceratosaurus, with its distinctive horn and enduring presence in the fossil record, represents the lasting impression of Capricorn's accomplishments.

Saturn's Lessons and Capricorn the Ceratosaurus

Capricorn is ruled by **Saturn**, the planet of structure, discipline, and life's toughest lessons. Saturn's influence shapes Capricorn the Ceratosaurus into a symbol of responsibility and wisdom gained through experience:

1. **Saturn's Influence on Growth**:
   Saturn's energy teaches Capricorns that growth comes through effort and perseverance. The Ceratosaurus's ability to thrive in diverse and competitive environments reflects this hard-earned wisdom.
2. **Karmic Responsibility**:
   Saturn governs karma, encouraging Capricorns to take responsibility for their actions. The Ceratosaurus's balance of strength and strategy demonstrates the importance of thoughtful, intentional decisions.
3. **Structure and Boundaries**:
   Saturn inspires Capricorns to create order and structure in their lives. The Ceratosaurus's disciplined approach to survival mirrors this focus on building a stable foundation.
4. **Endurance Through Challenges**:
   Saturn's lessons often involve overcoming obstacles to achieve success. The Ceratosaurus's adaptability and resilience in the face of competition highlight Capricorn's ability to endure and emerge stronger.

Lessons from Capricorn the Ceratosaurus

Capricorn the Ceratosaurus teaches valuable lessons about discipline, ambition, and achieving greatness through hard work. Here are the key takeaways:

1. **Work Steadily Toward Your Goals**:
   Success rarely happens overnight. Capricorn the Ceratosaurus reminds us to stay focused, disciplined, and consistent in pursuing our ambitions.
2. **Build a Solid Foundation**:
   Saturn emphasizes the importance of structure and stability. Use Capricorn's energy to create a strong base for your personal and professional goals.
3. **Learn from Challenges**:
   Obstacles are opportunities for growth. The Ceratosaurus's adaptability reminds us to face challenges with resilience and learn from every experience.
4. **Balance Strength with Strategy**:
   Capricorn the Ceratosaurus demonstrates the power of combining strength with strategy. Use both physical and mental resources wisely to navigate life's complexities.

5. **Leave a Lasting Legacy**:
Capricorns are driven to create something meaningful and enduring. The Ceratosaurus's distinctive traits remind us to embrace our uniqueness and strive for impact.

Astrological Reflection for Capricorn the Ceratosaurus

1. **Harness Saturn's Energy**:
Use Saturn's influence to embrace discipline, responsibility, and long-term planning. Reflect on areas of your life where you can create more structure and focus.
2. **Pursue Ambitious Goals**:
Channel Capricorn's ambition to set high but achievable goals. Let the Ceratosaurus inspire you to work diligently and steadily toward success.
3. **Practice Patience and Resilience**:
Capricorn the Ceratosaurus encourages us to stay patient and persistent, even when progress feels slow. Trust that your efforts will yield results in time.

Practical Applications of Capricorn the Ceratosaurus

1. **Set Long-Term Goals**:
Define clear, achievable objectives for your personal and professional life. Break them into smaller steps to maintain focus and track your progress.
2. **Develop a Routine**:
Create a structured daily routine that supports your goals and builds discipline. Use Capricorn's energy to stay consistent and productive.
3. **Embrace Challenges**:
View obstacles as opportunities to learn and grow. Practice resilience by staying committed to your goals, even when faced with setbacks.
4. **Focus on Self-Improvement**:
Dedicate time to developing your skills and building your strengths. Like the Ceratosaurus, adapt to changing circumstances to maintain your edge.

In the Dinosaur Zodiac, Capricorn the Ceratosaurus stands as a powerful symbol of discipline, ambition, and the ability to achieve greatness through effort and resilience. By channeling its energy, you can embrace Saturn's lessons, overcome challenges, and build a life defined by meaningful accomplishments. Let Capricorn the Ceratosaurus inspire you to climb higher, work harder, and leave a legacy of strength and determination.

Chapter 11: Aquarius the Ankylosaurus
The Visionary Defender of the Prehistoric Zodiac
The Revolutionary Nature of Aquarius the Ankylosaurus

Aquarius, the eleventh sign of the zodiac, is a visionary force of innovation, independence, and progressive thinking. Ruled by Uranus, the planet of sudden change, rebellion, and ingenuity, Aquarius thrives on individuality, originality, and the drive to make the world a better place. In the Dinosaur Zodiac, these traits find their perfect counterpart in the Ankylosaurus, the armored herbivore of the Late Cretaceous period. Known for its heavily armored body and iconic club-like tail, the Ankylosaurus symbolizes ingenuity, self-reliance, and the ability to innovate for survival.

The Ankylosaurus's ability to adapt and protect itself through its unique physical defenses reflects Aquarius's independent and forward-thinking approach to life. As a peaceful yet formidable creature, the Ankylosaurus embodies the balance of individuality and communal harmony that defines Aquarius.

Key Characteristics of Aquarius the Ankylosaurus

1. **Innovation and Ingenuity**:
   Aquarius is synonymous with invention and originality, a quality mirrored in the Ankylosaurus's unique armor and defensive tail, which exemplify evolution's innovative brilliance.

2. **Independence and Self-Reliance**:
   Aquarians are fiercely independent and value self-sufficiency. The Ankylosaurus's ability to defend itself without relying on others reflects this autonomous nature.

3. **Unconventional Thinking**:
   Aquarius thrives on breaking boundaries and challenging norms. Similarly, the Ankylosaurus stands out with its unusual body structure and unconventional methods of survival.

4. **Defender of Peace**:
   While Aquarians are peaceful at heart, they are unafraid to stand up for their values and protect what matters. The Ankylosaurus, though a herbivore, could use its tail club with formidable force, defending itself against predators when necessary.

5. **Community Awareness**:
   Aquarius values collective well-being while maintaining individuality. The Ankylosaurus's likely social habits align with this balance, emphasizing cooperation without compromising autonomy.

Innovation of Aquarius the Ankylosaurus

Innovation is the driving force behind Aquarius, inspiring them to think outside the box and find creative solutions. The Ankylosaurus reflects this trait through its evolutionary adaptations:

1. **Armored Defenses**:
   The Ankylosaurus's heavy, bony plates and spiked armor are a marvel of nature's ingenuity, symbolizing Aquarius's ability to innovate in the face of challenges.
2. **Weaponized Tail**:
   Its club-like tail, used to ward off predators, showcases how innovation can turn defense into an art form. This is akin to Aquarius's ability to turn unconventional ideas into effective solutions.
3. **Adaptation to Survival**:
   Just as Aquarians adapt to new situations with creative thinking, the Ankylosaurus's unique defenses allowed it to thrive in dangerous environments where other herbivores might fail.
4. **Breaking the Mold**:
   Aquarius is unafraid to challenge traditional methods. The Ankylosaurus, with its unconventional body design, embodies the ability to stand out and succeed through originality.

Independence of Aquarius the Ankylosaurus

Aquarians are known for their independence and self-reliance, traits that align with the Ankylosaurus's solitary strength:

1. **Self-Sufficient Protection**:
   The Ankylosaurus didn't rely on speed or hiding to survive. Instead, it used its armor and tail club to independently protect itself, reflecting Aquarius's value of self-reliance.
2. **Autonomy in Action**:
   Aquarians thrive when they have the freedom to chart their own path. Similarly, the Ankylosaurus's ability to defend itself without depending on a herd symbolizes autonomy and confidence.
3. **Balancing Individuality and Community**:
   While Aquarians cherish their independence, they also value collective well-being. The Ankylosaurus likely lived in small groups or loosely connected herds, maintaining a balance between individuality and community.
4. **Rebel with a Cause**:
   Aquarians often challenge norms to create positive change. The Ankylosaurus's unique adaptations reflect the power of innovation and independence to overcome adversity.

Uranus's Influence and Aquarius the Ankylosaurus

Aquarius is ruled by **Uranus**, the planet of sudden change, rebellion, and forward-thinking ideas. Uranus's energy enhances Aquarius the Ankylosaurus's ability to adapt and thrive in unconventional ways:

1. **Uranian Innovation**:
   Uranus inspires radical breakthroughs and unconventional solutions. The Ankylosaurus's armored body and weaponized tail symbolize the kind of ingenuity that Uranus represents.
2. **Sudden Change and Adaptability**:
   Uranus governs upheaval and transformation. The Ankylosaurus's ability to survive in predator-dominated ecosystems reflects Aquarius's talent for adapting to sudden changes.
3. **Breaking Tradition**:
   Uranus pushes Aquarius to reject outdated norms and forge new paths. The Ankylosaurus, with its unique physical traits, represents the power of breaking the mold and embracing originality.
4. **Visionary Energy**:
   Uranus fuels Aquarius's vision for a better future. The Ankylosaurus, as a symbol of survival through innovation, teaches us to use creativity and foresight to overcome obstacles.

Lessons from Aquarius the Ankylosaurus

Aquarius the Ankylosaurus offers profound lessons about innovation, independence, and embracing change. Here are the key takeaways:

1. **Innovate to Overcome Challenges**:
   Like the Ankylosaurus, use your creativity and ingenuity to find solutions to life's problems. Aquarius teaches us to think outside the box and embrace unconventional ideas.
2. **Value Your Independence**:
   While collaboration is important, Aquarius the Ankylosaurus reminds us to trust our abilities and rely on ourselves when needed.
3. **Adapt to Change**:
   Life is full of unexpected shifts, but Aquarius's Uranian energy shows us how to adapt and thrive in the face of transformation.
4. **Stand Out Proudly**:
   The Ankylosaurus's unique design is a reminder to embrace your individuality. Aquarius teaches us that standing out is a strength, not a weakness.
5. **Balance Individuality with Community**:
   While independence is vital, Aquarius the Ankylosaurus also values collective well-being. Strive to find harmony between your personal goals and your contributions to society.

Astrological Reflection for Aquarius the Ankylosaurus

1. **Embrace Uranian Change**:
   Use Uranus's energy to embrace change and innovation. Reflect on areas of your life where you can break free from tradition and create something new.
2. **Foster Independence**:
   Trust in your abilities and embrace self-reliance. Let the Ankylosaurus inspire you to stand strong and protect yourself with confidence.
3. **Think Visionarily**:
   Channel Aquarius's visionary energy to explore new ideas and pursue goals that improve your life and the world around you.

Practical Applications of Aquarius the Ankylosaurus

1. **Innovate in Daily Life**:
   Look for ways to introduce creativity and originality into your routines. Solve problems with fresh ideas and unconventional approaches.
2. **Celebrate Your Individuality**:
   Embrace what makes you unique. Like the Ankylosaurus, use your distinctive qualities to your advantage.
3. **Adapt and Thrive**:
   Practice resilience and adaptability. Whether facing personal or professional challenges, channel Aquarius the Ankylosaurus's ability to adjust and overcome.
4. **Balance Independence and Community**:
   Find ways to contribute to your community while maintaining your personal freedom. Seek out relationships and projects that align with your values and individuality.

In the Dinosaur Zodiac, Aquarius the Ankylosaurus is a powerful symbol of innovation, independence, and the transformative energy of Uranus. By channeling its unique traits, you can embrace originality, adapt to change, and forge a path that reflects your vision for the future. Let Aquarius the Ankylosaurus inspire you to innovate, stand strong, and thrive in your individuality while contributing to the greater good.

Chapter 12: Pisces the Plesiosaurus
The Dreamy Visionary of the Prehistoric Zodiac
The Sensitive Nature of Pisces the Plesiosaurus

Pisces, the twelfth sign of the zodiac, symbolizes sensitivity, creativity, and a profound connection to the mystical and unseen. Ruled by Neptune, the planet of dreams, intuition, and the subconscious, Pisces thrives in the realms of imagination, emotion, and spiritual depth. In the Dinosaur Zodiac, these qualities align beautifully with the Plesiosaurus, a graceful marine reptile of the Mesozoic era. Known for its long neck, streamlined body, and ability to navigate vast oceans, the Plesiosaurus symbolizes the Piscean qualities of fluidity, intuition, and creative expression.

The Plesiosaurus's aquatic nature and elegant movements mirror Pisces's ability to flow through life's emotional and spiritual currents, exploring the mysteries of existence with an open heart and a curious mind.

Key Characteristics of Pisces the Plesiosaurus

1. **Emotional Sensitivity**:
   Pisces is deeply attuned to the emotional and energetic undercurrents of life. The Plesiosaurus, as a creature of the ocean, represents this connection to the fluid and ever-changing nature of emotions.

2. **Creativity and Imagination**:
   Pisces thrives on creative expression and visionary thinking. The Plesiosaurus's graceful form and movement symbolize the artistic and imaginative qualities that define Pisces.

3. **Intuition and Spirituality**:
   Ruled by Neptune, Pisces is naturally intuitive and connected to the mystical. The Plesiosaurus, navigating the depths of the ocean, embodies the exploration of life's hidden realms and spiritual mysteries.

4. **Compassion and Empathy**:
   Pisceans are known for their compassionate and empathetic nature. The Plesiosaurus's peaceful existence as a marine herbivore reflects this gentle and nurturing quality.

5. **Adaptability and Fluidity**:
   Like the ever-changing tides, Pisces and the Plesiosaurus share the ability to adapt to shifting circumstances with grace and resilience.

Sensitivity of Pisces the Plesiosaurus

Sensitivity is the cornerstone of Pisces's identity, allowing them to deeply connect with others and the world around them. The Plesiosaurus reflects this quality in the following ways:

1. **Attunement to Surroundings**:
   The Plesiosaurus's life in the ocean required a heightened awareness of its environment, mirroring Pisces's ability to sense and respond to subtle emotional and energetic shifts.
2. **Emotional Depth**:
   Pisces feels emotions on a profound level, often absorbing the feelings of others. The Plesiosaurus, swimming through the vast and mysterious ocean, symbolizes the depth of Pisces's emotional world.
3. **Peaceful Nature**:
   Pisceans often avoid conflict, seeking harmony instead. Similarly, the Plesiosaurus, as a peaceful creature, thrived by coexisting with its environment rather than dominating it.
4. **Vulnerability as Strength**:
   Pisces teaches that sensitivity is not a weakness but a source of strength and connection. The Plesiosaurus's reliance on its environment and fluid movements reflect this lesson.

Creativity of Pisces the Plesiosaurus

Creativity is a defining trait of Pisces, inspiring them to explore and express their inner world through art, imagination, and innovation. The Plesiosaurus represents this creative spirit through its form and behavior:

1. **Artistic Movement**:
   The Plesiosaurus's graceful, flowing movements through the water evoke a sense of artistry, symbolizing Pisces's ability to bring beauty and creativity into everything they do.
2. **Visionary Thinking**:
   Pisces is often ahead of their time, dreaming of possibilities that others cannot see. The Plesiosaurus, with its unique body structure and aquatic abilities, reflects this innovative and forward-thinking energy.
3. **Imagination and Exploration**:
   Just as Pisces loves to dream and explore the unknown, the Plesiosaurus's life in the vast and mysterious ocean mirrors this quest for discovery and creative inspiration.
4. **Connection to Nature's Beauty**:
   Pisceans are deeply inspired by the natural world. The Plesiosaurus, thriving in the ocean's beauty, symbolizes the importance of finding creativity and inspiration in one's surroundings.

Neptune's Mysteries and Pisces the Plesiosaurus

Pisces is ruled by **Neptune**, the planet of dreams, intuition, and the subconscious. Neptune's influence enhances Pisces the Plesiosaurus's mystical and spiritual qualities:

1. **Neptune's Intuition**:

   Neptune governs intuition and the ability to sense what lies beneath the surface. The Plesiosaurus, navigating the ocean's depths, symbolizes Pisces's intuitive understanding of life's mysteries.

2. **Connection to the Subconscious**:

   Neptune draws Pisces into the realms of dreams and the subconscious. The ocean, home to the Plesiosaurus, serves as a metaphor for these hidden and unexplored inner worlds.

3. **Dreamy and Visionary Energy**:

   Neptune fuels Pisces's imagination and creativity, inspiring them to dream big and think outside the box. The Plesiosaurus's graceful presence in the water reflects this ethereal and otherworldly quality.

4. **Spiritual Exploration**:

   Neptune encourages Pisces to seek spiritual understanding and connection. The Plesiosaurus, moving through the vast and interconnected ocean, represents the unity and oneness that Pisces seeks to experience.

Lessons from Pisces the Plesiosaurus

Pisces the Plesiosaurus offers profound lessons about sensitivity, creativity, and the mysteries of life. Here are the key takeaways:

1. **Embrace Your Sensitivity**:

   Like the Plesiosaurus, allow your sensitivity to guide you. Pisces teaches that being emotionally attuned is a strength that deepens your connection to yourself and others.

2. **Tap into Your Creativity**:

   Express your imagination and inner vision through creative outlets. Pisces the Plesiosaurus reminds us to explore and share the beauty of our dreams.

3. **Navigate Life's Depths**:

   Dive into the unknown with courage and curiosity. Just as the Plesiosaurus explored the ocean's depths, Pisces encourages us to trust our intuition and embrace life's mysteries.

4. **Practice Compassion and Empathy**:

   Pisces the Plesiosaurus teaches us to approach others with kindness and understanding. Use your empathy to create meaningful connections and support those around you.

5. **Find Fluidity in Change**:

   Life is ever-changing, like the tides. Pisces and the Plesiosaurus remind us to adapt with grace and remain open to new possibilities.

Astrological Reflection for Pisces the Plesiosaurus

1. **Connect with Neptune's Energy**:
   Use Neptune's influence to explore your dreams, intuition, and spiritual practices. Reflect on how you can integrate these insights into your daily life.
2. **Cultivate Creative Expression**:
   Dedicate time to creative activities that inspire you, whether it's art, music, writing, or daydreaming. Let the Plesiosaurus's graceful movements inspire your own creative flow.
3. **Embrace Emotional Depth**:
   Dive deep into your emotions and explore their meaning. Journaling, meditation, or therapy can help you connect with your inner world and grow from the experience.

Practical Applications of Pisces the Plesiosaurus

1. **Engage in Creative Practices**:
   Set aside time for creative exploration. Use art, writing, or other outlets to channel your imagination and bring your visions to life.
2. **Strengthen Your Intuition**:
   Practice listening to your inner voice through meditation, mindfulness, or intuitive exercises. Trust your instincts and let them guide you.
3. **Explore Spirituality**:
   Dive into spiritual practices that resonate with you, such as meditation, astrology, or dream journaling. Reflect on the interconnectedness of life and your place within it.
4. **Adapt to Emotional Currents**:
   Just as the Plesiosaurus navigated ocean tides, learn to adapt to life's emotional ups and downs. Practice self-care and compassion to stay balanced.

In the Dinosaur Zodiac, Pisces the Plesiosaurus represents sensitivity, creativity, and the ability to explore life's mysteries with grace and depth. By channeling its energy, you can embrace your intuition, express your imagination, and connect with the spiritual and emotional realms. Let Pisces the Plesiosaurus inspire you to dream deeply, feel profoundly, and flow gracefully through the tides of life.

Part 2: **Planets and Dinosaurs**

Chapter 13: The Sun and Dinosaurs
The Solar Influence on Prehistoric Life and Its Astrological Ties
The Central Role of the Sun in Prehistoric Times

The Sun, the center of our solar system, has always been a source of life, energy, and power. During the age of dinosaurs, the Sun played a critical role in shaping ecosystems, influencing behavior, and sustaining life. Its warming rays powered photosynthesis, which was essential for plant growth and the survival of herbivorous dinosaurs, creating the foundation of the prehistoric food chain. The Sun's cycles dictated the rhythms of life, from migration patterns to breeding seasons, weaving its influence into every aspect of existence.

Astrologically, the Sun represents vitality, identity, and the core essence of life. In the Dinosaur Zodiac, the Sun embodies the life force that fueled the prehistoric world, symbolizing the strength and power of these ancient creatures. Its energy is reflected in the traits and behaviors of dinosaurs, inspiring lessons about leadership, vitality, and the centrality of purpose in life.

The Sun's Influence on Prehistoric Ecosystems

1. **Energy for Plant Growth:**
   - The Sun's energy drove photosynthesis, enabling plants to flourish during the Mesozoic Era. From towering cycads to ferns and conifers, plant life formed the basis of the food web, sustaining herbivorous dinosaurs like the Stegosaurus and Triceratops.
   - These plants, in turn, supported carnivorous dinosaurs by sustaining the herbivores they preyed upon, creating a solar-powered ecosystem.
2. **Climate and Habitats:**
   - The Sun shaped the climates of prehistoric Earth, influencing the distribution of habitats. Tropical regions, bathed in abundant sunlight, supported lush vegetation and diverse dinosaur species.
   - Seasonal changes in sunlight affected the migration patterns and survival strategies of dinosaurs, prompting adaptations such as herding and nesting behaviors.
3. **Temperature Regulation:**
   - For many dinosaurs, sunlight was vital for thermoregulation. Cold-blooded species relied on basking in the Sun to raise their body temperatures, while warm-blooded dinosaurs needed the Sun to maintain energy efficiency in colder climates.
   - Dinosaurs with physical features like frills, plates, or sails—such as the Stegosaurus and Spinosaurus—may have used these adaptations to absorb or reflect sunlight, regulating their body heat.

The Sun and Dinosaur Behavior

The Sun's predictable cycles influenced various aspects of dinosaur behavior, mirroring the rhythms of life we associate with its astrological symbolism:

1. **Daily Rhythms:**
   - Dinosaurs likely followed diurnal patterns, with many species active during the day to maximize the benefits of sunlight. The Sun's energy powered their activities, from foraging to hunting.
   - Carnivores like the Tyrannosaurus Rex may have hunted at dawn or dusk to optimize their predatory efficiency, reflecting the Sun's transitional power.
2. **Seasonal Changes:**
   - The Sun's movement across the sky marked seasonal shifts that influenced breeding, nesting, and migration. Dinosaurs adapted to these changes, synchronizing their life cycles with solar rhythms.
   - Longer days in warmer months allowed for extended feeding and growth, critical for herbivores and their young.
3. **Communication and Mating:**
   - Some dinosaurs, like the Lambeosaurus with its crest, may have used visual displays enhanced by sunlight to communicate or attract mates. The Sun amplified their physical traits, showcasing their vitality and fitness.

Astrological Symbolism of the Sun and Dinosaurs
Astrologically, the Sun represents vitality, identity, and the central self. It governs how we express ourselves and shine our unique light in the world. In the Dinosaur Zodiac, the Sun's energy is reflected in the strength, leadership, and survival instincts of dinosaurs:

1. **Vitality and Life Force:**
   ◦ **The Sun was the life-giver of the Mesozoic Era, sustaining the ecosystems that supported dinosaur life. Astrologically, it represents the core essence of existence, the spark that animates all living beings.**
2. **Leadership and Power:**
   ◦ **The Sun governs leadership and authority, qualities mirrored in dominant dinosaurs like the Tyrannosaurus Rex, whose presence commanded respect and fear.**
3. **Identity and Individuality:**
   ◦ **Just as the Sun shapes individual traits in astrology, dinosaurs displayed unique characteristics and adaptations, from the Allosaurus's hunting skills to the Ankylosaurus's armored defenses. These distinctions highlight the Sun's influence on individuality and expression.**
4. **Cycles and Rhythms:**
   ◦ **The Sun's daily and yearly cycles symbolize continuity and renewal. Dinosaurs adapted to these rhythms, reflecting the astrological lesson of embracing life's natural ebbs and flows.**

Lessons from the Sun and Dinosaurs

The Sun's influence on the prehistoric world offers timeless lessons about vitality, purpose, and the interconnectedness of life:

1. **Embrace Your Inner Light:**
   - The Sun teaches us to shine brightly and embrace our unique identity. Like dinosaurs that thrived under the Sun's energy, we are called to express our true selves and live with purpose.
2. **Honor Life's Cycles:**
   - The Sun's rhythms remind us to align with life's natural flow, balancing activity with rest and growth with renewal. Dinosaurs synchronized their lives with the Sun, teaching us to live in harmony with nature.
3. **Find Strength in Adaptation:**
   - Just as dinosaurs adapted to the Sun's influence, we can draw strength from our ability to adjust and thrive in changing circumstances.
4. **Radiate Leadership and Positivity:**
   - The Sun inspires us to lead with confidence and warmth. Dinosaurs like the Triceratops protected their herds, reflecting the power of leadership rooted in care and responsibility.

Astrological Reflection for the Sun and Dinosaurs

1. **Connect with Your Solar Energy:**
   - Meditate on the Sun's role in your astrological chart, which represents your core identity and source of vitality. Reflect on how you can embody the Sun's energy in your life.
2. **Embrace Solar Rituals:**
   - Align with the Sun's power through rituals like sun salutations, outdoor meditation, or gratitude practices during sunrise or sunset.
3. **Shine Your Light:**
   - Let the Sun inspire you to live authentically and share your unique gifts with the world. Like the dinosaurs, thrive in the energy that fuels your essence.

Practical Applications of Solar Energy

1. **Harness Sunlight for Vitality:**
   - Spend time outdoors to soak in the Sun's energy, which supports physical and mental health. Like dinosaurs, we depend on sunlight for well-being.
2. **Create Sun-Focused Habits:**
   - Structure your day around the Sun's cycles. Engage in high-energy activities during daylight hours and embrace rest as the Sun sets.
3. **Celebrate Seasonal Shifts:**
   - Mark solstices and equinoxes as reminders of the Sun's influence on life. Use these transitions to set intentions and reflect on personal growth.

In the Dinosaur Zodiac, the Sun is the radiant force that shaped the prehistoric world, providing energy, structure, and rhythm to life. By connecting with the Sun's astrological and natural influence, we can draw inspiration from its role in sustaining the majestic dinosaurs and its enduring lessons about vitality, leadership, and purpose. Let the Sun and the legacy of dinosaurs remind you to shine brightly, live fully, and embrace the rhythms of life.

Chapter 14: The Moon and Dinosaur Habits
Lunar Phases and Their Symbolic Impact on Prehistoric Life
The Moon's Timeless Influence

For billions of years, the Moon has shaped life on Earth, influencing natural rhythms, behaviors, and ecosystems. During the age of dinosaurs, its gravitational pull regulated tides, impacted migration and reproductive cycles, and possibly shaped feeding and predator-prey interactions. The Moon's phases acted as a cosmic clock, governing subtle but profound changes in the environment.

In astrology, the Moon symbolizes intuition, emotions, and cycles of growth, reflection, and renewal. For dinosaurs, the Moon's influence connected them to the rhythm of Earth's natural processes, creating a dynamic interplay between the celestial and the terrestrial. This chapter explores how lunar phases may have impacted the habits of dinosaurs and draws symbolic lessons from these ancient connections.

The Moon's Role in Prehistoric Life

1. **Regulating Tides**:
    ◦ During the Mesozoic Era, the Moon's gravitational pull created tidal forces that influenced coastal and marine ecosystems. Dinosaurs like the Plesiosaurus, which thrived in aquatic environments, depended on these tidal rhythms for feeding and movement.
    ◦ Tides also created fertile coastal zones that supported plant growth, providing food for herbivorous dinosaurs.
2. **Light in the Darkness**:
    ◦ The Moon provided varying levels of light at night, influencing nocturnal behaviors. During a Full Moon, predators may have used the additional light for hunting, while prey species sought greater cover for protection.
    ◦ New Moons, with their lack of light, offered darker nights that could have reduced predator activity, providing safer opportunities for herbivores to forage.
3. **Triggering Reproductive Cycles**:
    ◦ Just as modern animals synchronize reproduction with lunar cycles, dinosaurs may have been influenced by the Moon when choosing mating or nesting times. Full Moons may have signaled the optimal time for courtship displays or egg-laying.
4. **Navigation and Migration**:
    ◦ Dinosaurs that migrated across vast distances, such as those in herds, may have used the Moon as a navigational aid. Its consistent phases and position in the sky provided a natural guide for orientation.

Lunar Phases and Dinosaur Behavior

The phases of the Moon likely played a key role in shaping dinosaur habits, mirroring the cycles of activity and rest, growth and renewal. Each phase offers symbolic insights into prehistoric life and behaviors:

1. **New Moon (Beginnings and Reflection):**
    - A New Moon signifies a time of darkness and introspection, offering protection to nocturnal herbivores as they foraged under the cover of night. Dinosaurs like the Ankylosaurus may have taken advantage of these darker nights to avoid predators.
2. **Waxing Crescent (Growth and Exploration):**
    - As the Moon grows in light, it symbolizes new opportunities and incremental progress. Dinosaurs may have explored new feeding grounds or prepared for seasonal changes during this phase.
3. **First Quarter (Action and Challenges):**
    - The First Quarter Moon represents decisive action and overcoming obstacles. Predatory dinosaurs, such as the Allosaurus, may have used the moderate moonlight during this phase for hunting, striking a balance between visibility and stealth.
4. **Waxing Gibbous (Preparation and Focus):**
    - As the Moon approaches fullness, it symbolizes refinement and preparation. Dinosaurs preparing for mating, nesting, or migration may have coordinated their efforts during this phase, using the increasing light to their advantage.
5. **Full Moon (Energy and Peak Activity):**
    - The Full Moon is a time of heightened energy and activity. Predators like the Tyrannosaurus Rex may have thrived under the bright moonlight, while herbivores gathered in groups for mutual protection.
    - The Full Moon also represents abundance and connection, aligning with the communal behaviors of herd-dwelling dinosaurs like the Triceratops.
6. **Waning Gibbous (Reflection and Gratitude):**
    - As the Moon begins to wane, it symbolizes a time for reflection and harvesting the fruits of labor. Dinosaurs may have focused on securing resources for the future or tending to nests during this phase.
7. **Last Quarter (Release and Adaptation):**
    - The Last Quarter Moon encourages letting go of what no longer serves and adapting to change. Dinosaurs might have shifted behaviors in response to dwindling resources or environmental changes.
8. **Waning Crescent (Rest and Renewal):**
    - The final phase of the lunar cycle represents rest and preparation for a new beginning. Dinosaurs may have taken this time to conserve energy, especially in challenging environments, mirroring the Moon's retreat before its rebirth.

Astrological Symbolism of the Moon and Dinosaurs

Astrologically, the Moon governs emotions, intuition, and cycles of change. Its influence on dinosaur habits highlights the connection between celestial rhythms and the natural world:

1. **Cycles of Life**:
   - The Moon's phases reflect the cycles of life, from birth to growth, culmination, and renewal. Dinosaurs lived in harmony with these natural rhythms, adapting their behaviors to the waxing and waning light.
2. **Emotional Intuition**:
   - The Moon symbolizes intuition and emotional depth. Dinosaurs, though not emotional in the human sense, relied on instinct to navigate their world, guided by the Moon's subtle cues.
3. **Harmony with Nature**:
   - The Moon teaches us to live in sync with nature's cycles. Dinosaurs exemplified this harmony, adjusting their behaviors to align with the Moon's influence on their environment.
4. **Adaptation and Resilience**:
   - The changing phases of the Moon remind us of the importance of adaptability. Dinosaurs, like the tides they relied upon, were resilient and fluid in their responses to environmental challenges.

Lessons from the Moon and Dinosaurs

The Moon's impact on dinosaurs offers profound lessons about living in harmony with natural cycles and embracing change:

1. **Honor Life's Rhythms**:
   - Just as dinosaurs adapted their habits to the Moon's cycles, we can align our lives with its phases to find balance and flow.
2. **Trust Your Instincts**:
   - The Moon symbolizes intuition, reminding us to trust our inner guidance. Like dinosaurs navigating their world, we can use our instincts to make wise decisions.
3. **Embrace Cycles of Renewal**:
   - The Moon's phases teach us that every ending brings a new beginning. Dinosaurs lived within these cycles, demonstrating the power of resilience and renewal.
4. **Balance Activity and Rest**:
   - The Moon's waxing and waning light encourages a balance between action and reflection. Dinosaurs, like all creatures, thrived by aligning their energy with these natural rhythms.

Astrological Reflection for the Moon and Dinosaurs

1. **Align with Lunar Phases**:
   - Observe the Moon's phases and reflect on how they influence your energy and emotions. Use the waxing Moon for growth and the waning Moon for rest and release.
2. **Explore Lunar Intuition**:
   - Practice tuning into your intuition, especially during the New and Full Moons. Reflect on how instinct guides your decisions, just as it guided prehistoric creatures.
3. **Celebrate Lunar Rituals**:
   - Honor the Moon's cycles with rituals that connect you to its energy, such as journaling, meditation, or spending time outdoors under its light.

Practical Applications of Lunar Wisdom

1. **Plan Activities with Lunar Phases**:
   - Schedule important tasks during the waxing Moon for momentum and use the waning Moon for reflection and completion.
2. **Observe Nature's Rhythms**:
   - Spend time in nature to observe how animals and plants respond to the Moon's influence. Reflect on the interconnectedness of all life.
3. **Cultivate Intuition**:
   - Strengthen your intuition through mindfulness practices, inspired by the Moon's role as a guide for prehistoric creatures.

In the Dinosaur Zodiac, the Moon represents the rhythmic, cyclical forces that shaped the habits and behaviors of dinosaurs. By connecting with its astrological and natural influence, we can learn to live in harmony with life's cycles, embrace intuition, and navigate change with resilience. Let the Moon and its impact on dinosaurs inspire you to align with the cosmic rhythms that govern your world.

Chapter 15: Mercury and Communication Among Dinosaurs
Travel, Migration, and Mental Agility in Prehistoric Times
The Role of Mercury in Prehistoric Life

Mercury, the planet of communication, intellect, and movement, governs how beings interact, navigate their surroundings, and adapt to changing circumstances. In the world of dinosaurs, Mercury's energy can be seen in their ability to travel vast distances, migrate in search of resources, and communicate within their ecosystems. Whether through vocalizations, physical displays, or environmental navigation, dinosaurs demonstrated remarkable adaptability and mental agility.

Astrologically, Mercury symbolizes quick thinking, exchange of ideas, and the ability to adapt. In the Dinosaur Zodiac, Mercury's influence highlights the mental and physical dexterity required for survival in a prehistoric world marked by constant change and challenges.

Mercury's Influence on Dinosaur Communication

Communication was vital for the survival and social structures of dinosaurs. While we cannot fully decode their communication methods, scientists believe they used a variety of signals, sounds, and body language, reflecting Mercury's domain over interaction and information exchange.

1. **Vocalizations and Sounds**:
   - Dinosaurs like the Parasaurolophus, with its distinctive crested skull, likely used low-frequency sounds to communicate over long distances. These sounds could warn of predators, establish territory, or coordinate herds.
   - The Lambeosaurus's hollow crest might have functioned as a resonating chamber, amplifying calls to communicate in complex ways.

2. **Physical Displays**:
   - Dinosaurs often used body language and physical attributes to communicate. Frills, horns, and colorful scales may have conveyed dominance, mating readiness, or warnings to rivals.
   - For example, Triceratops could have used its frilled head and horns in visual displays to assert dominance or attract mates.

3. **Environmental Cues**:
   - Dinosaurs also responded to environmental signals, such as the position of the Sun or Moon, weather changes, or resource availability. These cues helped them adapt to shifting conditions and informed their movements and behaviors.

Travel and Migration in the Dinosaur World

Mercury, as the planet of movement and travel, resonates strongly with the migratory behaviors of dinosaurs. Many species traveled vast distances in search of food, water, or suitable nesting grounds, relying on instincts and environmental cues to navigate.

1. **Seasonal Migrations**:
    ◦ Herbivorous dinosaurs like the Hadrosaurus likely migrated to follow seasonal vegetation patterns, ensuring access to fresh food and water. These migrations mirrored Mercury's influence over adaptability and resourcefulness.
    ◦ Carnivores, such as the Allosaurus, may have followed prey herds, demonstrating their ability to adapt their hunting strategies to migration patterns.
2. **Navigational Skills**:
    ◦ Dinosaurs likely relied on natural markers, such as rivers, mountain ranges, or celestial bodies, to navigate their environment. This reflects Mercury's role in guiding travel and facilitating exploration.
3. **Group Dynamics**:
    ◦ Herds of dinosaurs, such as the Diplodocus, coordinated their movements to migrate efficiently. Communication and collaboration were key to their survival, showcasing Mercury's influence over collective travel and interaction.

Mental Agility in Dinosaurs

Mercury's energy fosters quick thinking and adaptability, traits that were essential for dinosaurs to survive in dynamic and often hostile environments. From problem-solving to social interactions, dinosaurs demonstrated impressive mental agility:

1. **Problem-Solving Skills**:
   - Carnivorous dinosaurs like the Velociraptor are believed to have used intelligence and strategy when hunting, working in packs to outwit prey. This behavior reflects Mercury's influence over cleverness and collaboration.
2. **Adaptability to Change**:
   - Dinosaurs faced shifting climates, evolving ecosystems, and competition from other species. Their ability to adapt to these changes highlights Mercury's energy of resilience and mental flexibility.
3. **Social Intelligence**:
   - Social dinosaurs, such as the Iguanodon, likely relied on cooperation and shared knowledge within their groups. This collaborative spirit aligns with Mercury's focus on communication and collective problem-solving.
4. **Response to Threats**:
   - Dinosaurs needed to react quickly to predators or environmental changes. The swiftness of their responses, whether fleeing or defending, reflects Mercury's influence over speed and mental agility.

Astrological Symbolism of Mercury and Dinosaurs

Astrologically, Mercury governs communication, intellect, and mobility, traits that resonate with the behaviors and survival strategies of dinosaurs:

1. **Exchange of Information**:
   - Mercury's role as the messenger is mirrored in the ways dinosaurs shared information, from warning calls to visual signals, ensuring their survival in a world filled with threats and opportunities.
2. **Adaptability and Versatility**:
   - Mercury's energy encourages adaptability, seen in dinosaurs' ability to navigate diverse landscapes, shift behaviors, and adjust to changing conditions.
3. **Connection and Interaction**:
   - Just as Mercury fosters social interaction, dinosaurs demonstrated the importance of connection, whether through herd dynamics, parenting, or coordinated hunting strategies.
4. **Movement and Exploration**:
   - Mercury inspires exploration and curiosity, reflected in dinosaurs' migratory patterns and their constant search for resources and safety.

Lessons from Mercury and Dinosaurs

The influence of Mercury on dinosaurs offers timeless lessons about communication, adaptability, and the importance of mental agility. Here are the key takeaways:

1. **Communicate Effectively**:
   - Just as dinosaurs used sounds, signals, and behaviors to convey information, we can strengthen our communication skills to build connections and navigate challenges.
2. **Adapt to Change**:
   - Mercury reminds us to be flexible and resourceful. Dinosaurs thrived by adapting to their environment, teaching us to embrace change as an opportunity for growth.
3. **Collaborate and Cooperate**:
   - Whether migrating in herds or hunting in packs, dinosaurs showed the power of teamwork. Mercury's influence encourages us to work together for mutual benefit.
4. **Explore and Move Forward**:
   - Like migratory dinosaurs, we are called to explore new horizons and pursue opportunities. Mercury inspires us to stay curious and embrace the journey of discovery.

Astrological Reflection for Mercury and Dinosaurs

1. **Align with Mercury's Energy**:
   - Use Mercury's influence to enhance your communication skills, embrace adaptability, and explore new ideas. Reflect on how you can apply these traits to your personal and professional life.
2. **Strengthen Mental Agility**:
   - Practice quick thinking and problem-solving. Let Mercury inspire you to approach challenges with curiosity and creativity.
3. **Celebrate Mobility and Exploration**:
   - Embrace opportunities for travel and movement, whether physical or intellectual. Like migratory dinosaurs, seek out new experiences and expand your horizons.

Practical Applications of Mercury's Wisdom

1. **Improve Communication**:
   - Focus on clear and effective communication in your relationships and work. Practice active listening and articulate your ideas with confidence.
2. **Adapt to Dynamic Environments**:
   - Embrace flexibility in the face of change. Learn from Mercury's energy by staying open to new approaches and solutions.
3. **Explore Your World**:
   - Dedicate time to travel or learning new skills. Let Mercury's spirit of curiosity guide your exploration of new places, cultures, or knowledge.
4. **Foster Collaboration**:
   - Work on building strong connections with others. Like social dinosaurs, use teamwork to achieve shared goals and overcome challenges.

In the Dinosaur Zodiac, Mercury represents the dynamic forces of communication, travel, and mental agility that shaped the prehistoric world. By connecting with Mercury's energy, we can learn to adapt, communicate effectively, and embrace the spirit of exploration that defined the lives of dinosaurs. Let Mercury and its influence on dinosaurs inspire you to move forward with curiosity, resilience, and a mind open to endless possibilities.

Chapter 16: Venus and Dinosaur Harmony
Social Bonds and Beauty in the Prehistoric World
Venus's Role in Prehistoric Life

Venus, the planet of love, beauty, and harmony, governs relationships, aesthetics, and the pursuit of connection. In the age of dinosaurs, Venus's energy is reflected in the social bonds that formed between species, the striking physical adaptations that enhanced their survival or attraction, and the cooperative behaviors that allowed entire herds and ecosystems to thrive. Venus embodies the softer, more harmonious aspects of life, emphasizing the importance of unity, balance, and appreciation for the world's beauty.

Dinosaurs lived in a world where relationships—whether between individuals, within herds, or across ecosystems—were critical to survival. From the nurturing care of parental dinosaurs to the collaborative efforts of herds, Venus's influence fostered a sense of connection and interdependence. This chapter explores how Venusian themes manifested in the prehistoric world and what lessons we can draw from them.

Social Bonds Among Dinosaurs

Dinosaurs, like many animals today, formed social structures to enhance their survival and well-being. These bonds reflect Venus's influence over relationships and the interconnectedness of life:

1. **Herd Dynamics**:
   - Many herbivorous dinosaurs, such as the Triceratops and Hadrosaurus, lived in herds for protection against predators. The collective strength and communication within these groups symbolize Venus's emphasis on cooperation and harmony.
   - Herds likely relied on social bonds to raise young, locate food, and protect one another from danger.
2. **Parenting and Nurturing**:
   - Evidence suggests that some dinosaurs, like the Maiasaura (aptly named "Good Mother Lizard"), cared for their young by building nests, protecting eggs, and feeding hatchlings. This nurturing behavior highlights Venus's influence on love and care within family units.
   - The act of raising offspring cooperatively strengthened the bond between individuals, fostering a sense of unity.
3. **Mutual Support**:
   - Dinosaurs often worked together to achieve shared goals, such as securing resources or defending against predators. These acts of mutual support and interdependence reflect Venusian ideals of balance and collaboration.

Beauty and Attraction in Dinosaur Adaptations

Venus governs beauty and aesthetics, which can be seen in the physical adaptations of dinosaurs. These features often served practical purposes while also enhancing their appeal to mates or asserting dominance within their groups.

1. **Colorful Scales and Crests**:
   - While the exact coloration of dinosaurs remains speculative, fossil evidence suggests that some species had vibrant scales or patterns. These displays likely played a role in mating rituals, helping dinosaurs attract partners and assert their vitality.
2. **Elaborate Physical Features**:
   - Dinosaurs like the Parasaurolophus and Lambeosaurus had ornate crests, which may have been used for vocal communication or visual displays. These adaptations symbolize Venus's connection to beauty and its role in fostering connection.
   - The Stegosaurus's iconic plates may have been used for thermoregulation, but they also likely served a social or aesthetic purpose, signaling strength or attractiveness to mates.
3. **Ritualistic Behavior**:
   - Some dinosaurs likely engaged in courtship behaviors, such as posturing, vocalizations, or synchronized movements. These rituals reflect Venus's influence over the art of attraction and the importance of creating bonds through beauty and expression.

Harmony in Prehistoric Ecosystems

Venus not only governs interpersonal relationships but also the broader harmony between living beings and their environments. The age of dinosaurs was a testament to the delicate balance that allowed ecosystems to thrive:

1. **Coexistence Within Ecosystems**:
   - Predators and herbivores played interconnected roles in maintaining ecological balance. Carnivores like the Allosaurus regulated herbivore populations, while herbivores like the Brachiosaurus shaped vegetation patterns.
   - This balance reflects Venus's lesson that harmony requires each individual to play their part within a larger system.
2. **Symbiosis and Mutualism**:
   - Dinosaurs likely engaged in symbiotic relationships with other species. For example, small scavengers may have cleaned wounds or removed parasites from larger dinosaurs, demonstrating Venus's focus on cooperation for mutual benefit.
3. **Adapting to Environmental Cycles**:
   - Dinosaurs adapted to the rhythms of their environments, from seasonal migrations to nesting habits, showing how life can achieve harmony through understanding and working with nature's cycles.

Astrological Symbolism of Venus and Dinosaurs

Astrologically, Venus represents love, beauty, and harmony, which resonate deeply with the behaviors and adaptations of dinosaurs:

1. **Unity Through Connection**:
   - Venus teaches that connection strengthens individuals and communities. Dinosaurs relied on social bonds, whether through herds or parenting, to thrive in their ecosystems.
2. **Beauty as Purpose**:
   - Venus's appreciation for aesthetics is mirrored in the ornate features and behaviors of dinosaurs. These displays remind us that beauty has purpose, whether in attracting mates, asserting dominance, or enhancing survival.
3. **Balance in Relationships**:
   - Venus emphasizes the importance of balance and reciprocity. Dinosaurs demonstrated this balance through mutual support and cooperation, showing how relationships are vital to well-being.
4. **Harmony in Diversity**:
   - Venus celebrates the diversity of life and its ability to coexist harmoniously. The Mesozoic Era's varied ecosystems highlight how different species contributed to a larger, interconnected whole.

Lessons from Venus and Dinosaurs

The influence of Venus on dinosaurs offers timeless lessons about relationships, harmony, and the power of beauty. Here are the key takeaways:

1. **Foster Connection**:
   - Just as dinosaurs relied on social bonds for survival, we can strengthen our lives by building meaningful relationships and working together toward shared goals.
2. **Appreciate Beauty**:
   - Venus reminds us to find beauty in the world around us and within ourselves. Like dinosaurs' colorful displays and graceful movements, we can celebrate and express our individuality through creativity and self-expression.
3. **Value Cooperation**:
   - Dinosaurs thrived by supporting one another, whether in herds or through parenting. Venus teaches us the importance of working harmoniously with others to achieve balance and success.
4. **Seek Harmony in Diversity**:
   - The diverse ecosystems of the Mesozoic Era show the power of coexistence. Venus encourages us to embrace and celebrate differences, finding unity in diversity.

Astrological Reflection for Venus and Dinosaurs

1. **Connect with Venus's Energy:**
   - Reflect on your relationships and how they contribute to your sense of harmony. Use Venus's influence to nurture connections and find balance in your interactions.
2. **Celebrate Aesthetics and Creativity:**
   - Dedicate time to appreciating beauty in your surroundings, whether through art, nature, or personal expression. Let Venus inspire you to find joy in the world's visual and emotional richness.
3. **Cultivate Cooperation and Balance:**
   - Work toward creating harmony in your relationships and environments. Like dinosaurs in their herds, seek to support and uplift those around you.

Practical Applications of Venus's Wisdom

1. **Strengthen Social Bonds:**
   - Focus on building and maintaining meaningful relationships. Practice empathy, active listening, and mutual support in your connections.
2. **Express Yourself Creatively:**
   - Use art, fashion, or other creative outlets to express your individuality. Let Venus inspire you to showcase your unique beauty and personality.
3. **Create Harmony in Your Environment:**
   - Arrange your space to reflect balance and beauty, incorporating natural elements or harmonious designs that bring you peace and joy.
4. **Practice Cooperation and Mutual Support:**
   - Seek opportunities to collaborate with others, emphasizing teamwork and shared success. Reflect on how you can contribute to collective well-being.

In the Dinosaur Zodiac, Venus represents the social bonds, aesthetic beauty, and harmonious connections that shaped the prehistoric world. By connecting with Venus's energy, we can nurture our relationships, celebrate the beauty of life, and create balance in our interactions with others and our environment. Let Venus and the legacy of dinosaurs inspire you to live with love, harmony, and an appreciation for the wonders of connection and creativity.

Chapter 17: Mars and Dinosaur Battles
Strength, Aggression, and Survival Instincts in Prehistoric Times
The Fiery Influence of Mars

Mars, the planet of action, strength, and aggression, governs energy, drive, and the will to survive. In the age of dinosaurs, Mars's influence can be seen in their fierce battles for dominance, survival, and reproduction. From territorial disputes to predator-prey dynamics, the raw power of Mars shaped the behavior and physical evolution of these ancient creatures. Mars's influence highlights the primal instincts that ensured survival in the competitive ecosystems of the Mesozoic Era.

Astrologically, Mars represents assertiveness, courage, and the determination to achieve one's goals. In the Dinosaur Zodiac, Mars reflects the fiery energy and survival instincts that dinosaurs relied upon to navigate their often-hostile world. This chapter explores the role of Mars in shaping dinosaur behaviors, physical adaptations, and their eternal lessons about resilience and strength.

Mars and Dinosaur Battles

The prehistoric world was a place of constant competition, where survival often depended on strength, strategy, and aggression. Mars's influence is evident in the battles that dinosaurs fought to protect territory, secure mates, or hunt for survival.

1. **Territorial Disputes**:
   - Dinosaurs like the Tyrannosaurus Rex likely engaged in fierce battles to assert dominance over hunting grounds. These territorial disputes were displays of Mars's aggressive and assertive energy.
   - Physical adaptations, such as horns, frills, and powerful tails, were used not only for defense but also to establish dominance during confrontations.
2. **Mating Battles**:
   - Male dinosaurs may have fought for the right to mate, similar to modern animals. These contests showcased physical strength and stamina, embodying Mars's influence over competition and reproductive success.
   - Ceratopsians like Triceratops may have clashed their horns in dramatic displays of power to impress potential mates or deter rivals.
3. **Predator-Prey Dynamics**:
   - Carnivorous dinosaurs like the Allosaurus and Velociraptor embodied Mars's hunting energy, using speed, strategy, and raw power to take down prey.
   - Herbivores like the Ankylosaurus and Stegosaurus relied on their Mars-driven defensive instincts, using their armor, spines, and tails to fend off predators.
4. **Group Defense**:
   - Mars also influenced herd dynamics, with some dinosaurs banding together to protect the group from predators. For example, sauropods like the Diplodocus may have used their massive size and whip-like tails to deter threats.

Physical Manifestations of Mars's Energy

Mars's influence is evident in the physical adaptations that equipped dinosaurs for battle. These traits highlight the role of strength, aggression, and resilience in their survival:

1. **Weapons of Defense and Attack**:
    - Dinosaurs like the Stegosaurus had spiked tails, while the Ankylosaurus wielded a club-like tail for powerful defensive strikes. These adaptations reflect Mars's energy as a source of protection and assertiveness.
    - Carnivorous dinosaurs had sharp teeth, claws, and powerful jaws designed for predation, symbolizing Mars's drive for dominance and survival.
2. **Physical Strength and Stamina**:
    - Large predators like the Giganotosaurus possessed immense physical strength, enabling them to overpower prey. This raw power aligns with Mars's association with vitality and determination.
    - Even smaller dinosaurs like the Velociraptor relied on speed and agility, channeling Mars's dynamic and energetic influence.
3. **Display Features for Dominance**:
    - Mars's influence extends to the physical displays used in confrontations. Ceratopsians, with their ornate horns and frills, likely used these features to intimidate rivals or fend off predators.
    - Spinosaurids, with their towering dorsal sails, may have used these structures to appear larger and more intimidating during conflicts.

The Role of Mars in Survival Instincts

Survival instincts were at the core of dinosaur behavior, driven by Mars's fiery energy. These instincts ensured that dinosaurs could adapt to their environments and protect themselves from threats:

1. **Fight-or-Flight Responses:**
   - Mars governs the fight-or-flight instinct, determining whether a dinosaur would stand its ground or flee from danger. Smaller herbivores, like the Hypsilophodon, relied on speed to escape predators, while larger dinosaurs, like the Ankylosaurus, stood firm and fought.
2. **Adaptation to Threats:**
   - Dinosaurs evolved unique defenses to survive in predator-dominated ecosystems. These adaptations, from the spiked plates of the Stegosaurus to the whip-like tails of sauropods, reflect Mars's influence on resilience and strategic survival.
3. **Resilience in Adversity:**
   - Mars imbues creatures with the energy to endure and overcome challenges. Dinosaurs thrived in a world filled with natural disasters, predation, and competition, showcasing their Mars-driven resilience.

Astrological Symbolism of Mars and Dinosaurs

Astrologically, Mars represents action, courage, and the will to assert oneself. In the Dinosaur Zodiac, Mars highlights the lessons dinosaurs offer about strength, survival, and the balance of aggression and strategy:

1. **The Power of Assertiveness:**
   - Mars teaches us to assert our needs and stand our ground. Dinosaurs like the Triceratops, which used its horns to defend against predators, symbolize the importance of protecting what matters.
2. **Courage in the Face of Conflict:**
   - Mars inspires bravery and the willingness to face challenges. Predatory dinosaurs like the Allosaurus demonstrate the courage required to pursue and capture prey in a dangerous world.
3. **Adaptation Through Strength:**
   - Mars encourages us to use our strengths to adapt and thrive. Dinosaurs evolved unique traits that allowed them to dominate their environments, teaching us to harness our own abilities.
4. **Balance of Aggression and Restraint:**
   - While Mars emphasizes aggression, it also teaches the importance of strategic action. Dinosaurs balanced their energy, knowing when to fight and when to flee.

Lessons from Mars and Dinosaurs

The influence of Mars on dinosaurs offers timeless lessons about strength, resilience, and the will to thrive. Here are the key takeaways:

1. **Stand Your Ground**:
    - Mars teaches us to protect our boundaries and assert our needs. Like dinosaurs that defended their territory or herds, we can draw on our inner strength to face challenges.
2. **Channel Aggression Constructively**:
    - Mars reminds us that aggression, when balanced with strategy, can be a powerful force for achieving goals. Use your energy wisely to assert yourself without unnecessary conflict.
3. **Adapt and Evolve**:
    - Just as dinosaurs adapted to their environments, we can use Mars's energy to grow and improve in the face of adversity.
4. **Embrace Resilience**:
    - Mars inspires us to persevere through difficulties. Dinosaurs thrived for millions of years despite natural disasters and competition, demonstrating the power of resilience.

Astrological Reflection for Mars and Dinosaurs

1. **Connect with Mars's Energy**:
    - Reflect on how you assert yourself and face challenges. Use Mars's influence to strengthen your resolve and channel your energy toward meaningful goals.
2. **Cultivate Strength and Vitality**:
    - Focus on building physical and mental resilience. Let Mars inspire you to maintain your health, stamina, and inner drive.
3. **Balance Action with Strategy**:
    - Practice using your energy effectively. Like dinosaurs, balance aggression with planning to achieve the best outcomes.

Practical Applications of Mars's Wisdom

1. **Strengthen Your Inner Warrior**:
    - Build confidence and resilience through practices like physical exercise, meditation, or martial arts. Channel Mars's energy into empowering activities.
2. **Assert Your Boundaries**:
    - Practice standing up for yourself in relationships or at work. Use Mars's influence to communicate your needs clearly and confidently.
3. **Embrace Challenges**:
    - Approach obstacles with courage and determination. Let Mars inspire you to see challenges as opportunities for growth.
4. **Channel Your Energy Productively**:
    - Use your drive to pursue goals and complete tasks. Mars's dynamic energy can help you stay focused and motivated.

In the Dinosaur Zodiac, Mars represents the strength, aggression, and survival instincts that defined the prehistoric world. By connecting with Mars's energy, we can embrace our inner power, face challenges with courage, and thrive in the face of adversity. Let Mars and the legacy of dinosaurs inspire you to channel your strength, adapt to change, and live with determination and resilience.

Chapter 18: Jupiter's Influence on Dinosaur Evolution
Expansion, Luck, and Growth Cycles in Prehistoric Times
Jupiter's Role in Prehistoric Life

Jupiter, the planet of expansion, abundance, and growth, governs cycles of development and opportunities for progress. Its influence is tied to wisdom, exploration, and the boundless potential for greatness. In the prehistoric world, Jupiter's energy is evident in the grand scale of dinosaur evolution, the proliferation of species, and their ability to adapt to diverse ecosystems across millions of years. Jupiter embodies the principles of growth through opportunity, teaching us how abundance and expansion shape life's trajectory.

Dinosaurs, as some of the most successful creatures in Earth's history, exemplify Jupiter's expansive influence. From their dominance over terrestrial, aerial, and aquatic environments to their remarkable diversity, dinosaurs leveraged the opportunities afforded by Jupiter's energy to evolve and flourish. This chapter explores Jupiter's symbolic role in the evolutionary success of dinosaurs and the lessons their legacy offers about growth, luck, and abundance.

The Expansive World of Dinosaurs

The Mesozoic Era, often called the "Age of Dinosaurs," was a time of immense expansion, with life on Earth reaching new heights of diversity and adaptation. Jupiter's energy resonates strongly with this era's themes of growth and exploration.

1. **Diversification of Species**:
   - Dinosaurs evolved into a staggering variety of species, from towering sauropods like Argentinosaurus to feathered theropods like Microraptor. This diversification reflects Jupiter's principle of expansion and the ability to fill every ecological niche.
   - Their adaptations allowed dinosaurs to thrive in environments ranging from deserts to forests, embodying Jupiter's boundless and opportunistic nature.

2. **Global Dominance**:
   - Dinosaurs' success spanned all continents, making them the dominant terrestrial animals for over 160 million years. Jupiter's influence over exploration and expansion is mirrored in their widespread proliferation and adaptability.

3. **Prolific Growth Cycles**:
   - Dinosaurs experienced rapid growth rates, particularly in their juvenile stages, enabling them to reach massive sizes quickly. Jupiter's energy of abundance and acceleration resonates with these cycles of growth.

Jupiter's Luck and Opportunities in Dinosaur Evolution

Jupiter is often associated with luck, fortune, and seizing opportunities for advancement. In the story of dinosaurs, these themes are evident in the evolutionary and environmental factors that shaped their success:

1. **Mass Extinctions and New Beginnings**:
   - The Triassic-Jurassic extinction event cleared the way for dinosaurs to rise to dominance, providing an opportunity for expansion. Jupiter's influence is seen in the fortuitous timing that allowed dinosaurs to capitalize on new ecological niches.
   - Similarly, after the Permian extinction, Earth's ecosystems rebounded, creating fertile ground for new forms of life, including the ancestors of dinosaurs.
2. **Evolutionary Innovations**:
   - Dinosaurs benefited from key evolutionary innovations, such as bipedal locomotion, efficient respiratory systems, and the development of feathers. These traits reflect Jupiter's ability to inspire progress and maximize potential.
   - The emergence of herbivorous dinosaurs coincided with the evolution of flowering plants, a "lucky" alignment that supported their dietary needs and growth.
3. **Environmental Favorability**:
   - Warm, stable climates during much of the Mesozoic Era provided ideal conditions for dinosaurs to thrive. Jupiter's association with environmental abundance and opportunity is evident in these favorable conditions.

Cycles of Growth and Renewal

Jupiter's influence is also tied to cycles of growth and renewal, reflecting the idea that expansion occurs in stages. Dinosaurs' evolutionary history is a testament to the power of these cycles:

1. **Rapid Growth Rates**:
   - Studies of dinosaur bones reveal rapid growth during their juvenile years, followed by slower, more sustained growth as they reached adulthood. This pattern mirrors Jupiter's energy of expansion balanced with stability.
2. **Generational Success**:
   - Dinosaurs passed on their adaptations through successive generations, ensuring the continuity of their evolutionary progress. Jupiter's connection to wisdom and legacy is reflected in this generational growth.
3. **Rise and Fall**:
   - Even in their eventual decline, dinosaurs paved the way for the evolution of modern birds and mammals, demonstrating Jupiter's lesson that growth often leads to renewal and transformation.

Jupiter's Astrological Symbolism and Dinosaurs

Astrologically, Jupiter represents growth, luck, and the quest for knowledge and expansion. These themes resonate deeply with the story of dinosaur evolution, offering insights into their success and survival:

1. **Abundance and Opportunity**:
   - Jupiter's energy of abundance is mirrored in the sheer variety and scale of dinosaur life. Their ability to adapt and thrive across diverse habitats reflects Jupiter's lesson of embracing opportunity.
2. **Exploration and Expansion**:
   - Jupiter inspires exploration and the pursuit of new frontiers. Dinosaurs' global spread and adaptability exemplify this drive to expand and conquer new territories.
3. **Wisdom Through Growth**:
   - Jupiter teaches that growth leads to wisdom and insight. Dinosaurs' evolutionary innovations, such as advanced respiratory systems in theropods, reflect the knowledge gained through adaptation.
4. **Cycles of Expansion and Contraction**:
   - Jupiter governs cycles of growth and renewal, emphasizing that expansion often follows periods of challenge or transformation. Dinosaurs' rise after extinction events and their eventual evolution into birds illustrate these cycles.

Lessons from Jupiter and Dinosaurs

The influence of Jupiter on dinosaur evolution offers profound lessons about growth, opportunity, and embracing abundance. Here are the key takeaways:

1. **Seize Opportunities for Growth**:
   - Just as dinosaurs adapted to new ecological niches, we can embrace opportunities for expansion and improvement in our own lives.
2. **Embrace Diversity**:
   - Jupiter celebrates variety and abundance. Dinosaurs' diverse forms and adaptations remind us to value and cultivate diversity in our perspectives, relationships, and pursuits.
3. **Trust in Cycles of Renewal**:
   - Jupiter's influence teaches that growth is cyclical. Even after setbacks, like mass extinctions, life finds a way to flourish again, offering hope for renewal and progress.
4. **Expand Your Horizons**:
   - Like dinosaurs that explored and adapted to new environments, we can expand our horizons by seeking knowledge, exploring new opportunities, and stepping out of our comfort zones.

Astrological Reflection for Jupiter and Dinosaurs

1. **Connect with Jupiter's Energy**:
   - Reflect on areas of your life where you can embrace growth and abundance. Use Jupiter's influence to pursue opportunities and expand your potential.
2. **Cultivate Wisdom Through Experience**:
   - Like dinosaurs that evolved through cycles of change, embrace life's challenges as opportunities to gain wisdom and insight.
3. **Celebrate Abundance**:
   - Jupiter encourages us to recognize and appreciate the abundance in our lives. Reflect on the blessings and opportunities that have supported your growth.

Practical Applications of Jupiter's Wisdom

1. **Set Ambitious Goals**:
   - Use Jupiter's energy to set expansive, long-term goals. Focus on personal or professional growth that aligns with your highest potential.
2. **Explore New Opportunities**:
   - Embrace Jupiter's spirit of exploration by trying new experiences, traveling, or learning something new. Push beyond your comfort zone to expand your horizons.
3. **Balance Growth with Stability**:
   - Jupiter teaches the importance of sustainable growth. Like dinosaurs that balanced rapid growth with longevity, find ways to expand while maintaining stability.
4. **Trust in Life's Cycles**:
   - Recognize that growth often follows periods of challenge or change. Use Jupiter's influence to stay optimistic and embrace the opportunities that come your way.

In the Dinosaur Zodiac, Jupiter represents the expansive energy, luck, and growth cycles that defined the evolutionary success of dinosaurs. By connecting with Jupiter's influence, we can learn to embrace abundance, seize opportunities, and grow through life's challenges. Let Jupiter and the legacy of dinosaurs inspire you to pursue greatness, celebrate diversity, and trust in the cycles of growth and renewal that shape your journey.

Chapter 19: Saturn and Dinosaur Extinction Lessons
Time, Discipline, and Karmic Cycles in Prehistoric Life
Saturn's Role in Prehistoric Life and Beyond

Saturn, the planet of time, discipline, and karma, governs the cycles of life, death, and rebirth. It represents the hard lessons of limitation, responsibility, and endurance, guiding us through processes of transformation and growth. In the story of dinosaurs, Saturn's influence is most evident in their eventual extinction, a cataclysmic event that reshaped Earth and paved the way for new forms of life to emerge. Saturn reminds us that endings are not just finalities but essential steps in the cycle of renewal and evolution.

The extinction of dinosaurs, while tragic, offers profound lessons about resilience, adaptability, and the inevitability of change. Their dominance spanned over 160 million years, an achievement that exemplifies Saturn's themes of endurance and discipline. Yet their sudden demise, triggered by an asteroid impact and its cascading effects, underscores Saturn's karmic influence—the notion that every rise must eventually lead to transformation. This chapter delves into the Saturnian themes of time, responsibility, and lessons from the extinction of dinosaurs.

Time and the Era of Dinosaurs

Saturn, as the ruler of time, governs the natural cycles of existence, from growth and maturation to decline and renewal. The age of dinosaurs is a testament to these cycles, marked by their long reign and eventual extinction.

1. **The Mesozoic Timeline**:
   - Dinosaurs lived during the Mesozoic Era, which spanned three periods—Triassic, Jurassic, and Cretaceous—over 180 million years. This immense timeline reflects Saturn's influence on longevity and the passage of time.
   - Each period brought evolutionary advancements, demonstrating Saturn's lesson that growth and development require patience and sustained effort.
2. **Gradual Evolution**:
   - The slow, disciplined process of evolution allowed dinosaurs to adapt to diverse environments. Saturn's energy of persistence and steady progress is mirrored in their evolutionary success.
   - Dinosaurs like the Velociraptor and the Brachiosaurus represent the culmination of millions of years of adaptation, showing how time refines and perfects.
3. **The Final Countdown**:
   - The end of the Cretaceous period marked the sudden and dramatic extinction of most dinosaur species. This turning point reflects Saturn's role as the harbinger of transformation, where time signals the end of one cycle to allow for the beginning of another.

Discipline and Survival

Saturn teaches the importance of discipline, structure, and resilience. Dinosaurs embodied these traits in their survival strategies, which allowed them to dominate Earth for millions of years.

1. **Structured Adaptations**:
    - Dinosaurs like the Ankylosaurus developed intricate defensive structures, such as armored plates and clubbed tails, symbolizing Saturn's influence over the disciplined use of resources for survival.
    - Herd behaviors in dinosaurs like Triceratops and Hadrosaurus highlight the importance of cooperation and structure, traits governed by Saturn's energy of organization.
2. **Resilience in Challenging Environments**:
    - Dinosaurs thrived across diverse and often harsh environments, from arid deserts to dense forests. Saturn's influence fostered their resilience, teaching the value of endurance in the face of adversity.
3. **Cycles of Responsibility**:
    - Saturn emphasizes responsibility and the consequences of actions. Dinosaurs' reproductive behaviors, such as nesting and protecting their young, ensured the continuation of their species, reflecting Saturn's lesson of stewardship.

Karmic Cycles and the Extinction Event

The mass extinction event that ended the reign of dinosaurs serves as a stark reminder of Saturn's karmic influence. It highlights the cyclical nature of existence and the necessity of transformation for new growth.

1. **The Asteroid Impact**:
   - Approximately 66 million years ago, a massive asteroid struck Earth near present-day Mexico's Yucatán Peninsula, triggering the Cretaceous-Paleogene (K-Pg) extinction event. The immediate effects included wildfires, tsunamis, and a "nuclear winter" caused by debris blocking sunlight.
   - Saturn's karmic energy is evident in this event, symbolizing the inevitable consequences of living within a system governed by time and cosmic forces.
2. **The Aftermath**:
   - The extinction of dinosaurs made way for the rise of mammals and, eventually, humans. This transformation illustrates Saturn's lesson that endings lead to beginnings, emphasizing the cyclical nature of existence.
   - The asteroid impact reminds us of Saturn's impartiality—it does not punish or reward but enforces the laws of cause and effect.
3. **Adaptation and Survival**:
   - While most dinosaurs perished, some species adapted and evolved into modern birds. This survival demonstrates Saturn's teaching that those who adapt to change can continue to thrive, even after catastrophic events.

Astrological Symbolism of Saturn and Dinosaurs

Astrologically, Saturn represents discipline, structure, and life's harder lessons. In the Dinosaur Zodiac, Saturn's influence is reflected in the endurance, responsibility, and eventual transformation of these creatures:

1. **The Power of Endurance**:
   - Saturn teaches us to endure challenges and embrace responsibility. Dinosaurs' long reign on Earth highlights their resilience and ability to adapt to the demands of their environments.

2. **Cycles of Growth and Decline**:
   - Saturn governs the cycles of life, emphasizing that all things have a beginning, middle, and end. The extinction of dinosaurs illustrates this truth, showing how every cycle contributes to the greater evolution of life.

3. **Lessons from Extinction**:
   - Saturn reminds us that endings are opportunities for transformation. The extinction event that ended the age of dinosaurs paved the way for new forms of life, teaching us to see change as a catalyst for growth.

4. **Responsibility and Consequences**:
   - Saturn emphasizes the importance of responsibility and the consequences of actions. Dinosaurs' ability to maintain ecosystems and adapt to environmental changes reflects their alignment with Saturn's teachings.

Lessons from Saturn and Dinosaurs

The influence of Saturn on dinosaurs offers profound lessons about time, discipline, and transformation. Here are the key takeaways:

1. **Respect the Power of Time**:
   - Saturn teaches us to honor time as a force for growth and change. Like dinosaurs, we can embrace the slow, steady processes that lead to success and adaptation.
2. **Endure and Adapt**:
   - Resilience is key to survival. Dinosaurs thrived for millions of years by adapting to their environments, showing us how to endure and evolve in the face of challenges.
3. **Accept the Cycles of Life**:
   - Saturn's influence reminds us that life operates in cycles. The extinction of dinosaurs teaches us to accept endings as part of the greater cycle of renewal and transformation.
4. **Learn from the Past**:
   - Saturn governs wisdom gained through experience. The legacy of dinosaurs, from their dominance to their extinction, provides valuable lessons about balance, adaptability, and survival.

Astrological Reflection for Saturn and Dinosaurs

1. **Connect with Saturn's Energy**:
   - Reflect on the lessons of time and discipline in your life. Use Saturn's influence to embrace responsibility and navigate challenges with patience and resilience.
2. **Honor Life's Cycles**:
   - Recognize the cyclical nature of life and find peace in endings as opportunities for renewal. Let Saturn inspire you to grow through change and transformation.
3. **Build Endurance and Structure**:
   - Focus on creating a solid foundation for your goals. Saturn's energy can help you develop the discipline and structure needed for lasting success.

Practical Applications of Saturn's Wisdom

1. **Practice Patience and Discipline**:
   ◦ Embrace slow, steady progress in your endeavors. Like dinosaurs that evolved over millions of years, trust in the power of persistence and hard work.
2. **Learn from Challenges**:
   ◦ View obstacles as opportunities for growth. Saturn teaches us that hardship often brings valuable lessons and the chance to build resilience.
3. **Prepare for Transformation**:
   ◦ Accept that change is inevitable and necessary for growth. Use Saturn's energy to embrace transitions with grace and optimism.
4. **Reflect on Responsibility**:
   ◦ Take responsibility for your actions and their consequences. Like dinosaurs that adapted to their environments, strive to live in alignment with your values and surroundings.

In the Dinosaur Zodiac, Saturn represents the enduring lessons of time, discipline, and karmic cycles that defined the rise and fall of these majestic creatures. By connecting with Saturn's influence, we can learn to embrace life's challenges, honor its cycles, and find strength in transformation. Let Saturn and the legacy of dinosaurs inspire you to navigate time with wisdom, resilience, and a deep respect for the interconnectedness of all things.

Chapter 20: Uranus and Dinosaur Adaptability
Revolutionary Changes and Breakthroughs in Prehistoric Life
Uranus's Role in Prehistoric Life

Uranus, the planet of sudden change, innovation, and revolutionary ideas, governs breakthroughs, adaptability, and the power to transform the status quo. Its influence brings upheaval that challenges old systems, but in doing so, it opens doors to unprecedented growth and evolution. In the world of dinosaurs, Uranus's energy resonates in their incredible adaptability, which allowed them to thrive in diverse environments and respond to radical changes over millions of years.

Dinosaurs were pioneers of evolution, showcasing Uranian themes of experimentation and innovation. From the development of feathers to the shift from land to air, their story is one of revolutionary breakthroughs. This chapter explores how Uranus's influence shaped dinosaurs' adaptability, highlighting the evolutionary innovations that ensured their survival in an ever-changing world.

Revolutionary Changes in Dinosaur Evolution

Uranus thrives on disruption and innovation, fostering sudden changes that lead to significant breakthroughs. The evolutionary history of dinosaurs is marked by these Uranian shifts:

1. **The Emergence of Dinosaurs**:
   - Dinosaurs first appeared during the Triassic period, following a mass extinction that cleared the way for new species to dominate. This emergence reflects Uranus's influence, as it often follows dramatic upheavals with opportunities for innovation and growth.
   - Early dinosaurs like Eoraptor were small, bipedal, and agile, showcasing the experimental nature of Uranian energy.

2. **The Feather Revolution**:
   - The evolution of feathers in theropod dinosaurs was a groundbreaking adaptation. Originally developed for insulation or display, feathers later enabled flight, leading to the emergence of birds.
   - This transformative leap reflects Uranus's role in fostering revolutionary changes that redefine possibilities.

3. **Adaptations to New Environments**:
   - Dinosaurs adapted to a wide range of habitats, from the arid deserts of the Triassic to the lush forests of the Cretaceous. Uranus's influence on adaptability and resilience is evident in their ability to thrive in such diverse conditions.
   - Marine reptiles like Plesiosaurs and flying pterosaurs expanded into aquatic and aerial environments, pushing the boundaries of what dinosaurs could achieve.

4. **Mass Extinctions and Rebirth**:
    ◦ Uranus often governs sudden, disruptive events that force transformation. The Triassic-Jurassic extinction and the Cretaceous-Paleogene extinction acted as Uranian catalysts, reshaping ecosystems and allowing new species to emerge in their wake.

Breakthroughs in Dinosaur Adaptability

Uranus inspires innovation, encouraging species to break free from limitations and embrace change. Dinosaurs exemplified this energy through their evolutionary breakthroughs:

1. **Theropod Intelligence and Tool Use**:
    ◦ Theropods like the Velociraptor demonstrated advanced problem-solving abilities and social behaviors, reflecting Uranus's connection to intelligence and innovation.
    ◦ Their sharp claws and cooperative hunting strategies symbolize the ingenuity fostered by Uranus.
2. **Herbivorous Giants and Digestive Adaptations**:
    ◦ Massive sauropods like Brachiosaurus developed long necks to access high vegetation, a revolutionary adaptation that allowed them to thrive in competitive environments.
    ◦ These herbivores also evolved large, complex digestive systems to process tough plant material, showcasing Uranus's influence on practical breakthroughs.
3. **Defensive Innovations**:
    ◦ Dinosaurs like the Ankylosaurus and Stegosaurus developed armor, spikes, and tail clubs to protect themselves from predators. These adaptations reflect Uranus's ability to inspire creative solutions to survival challenges.
4. **Social and Cooperative Behaviors**:
    ◦ Many dinosaurs, such as the Hadrosaurus, lived in herds and developed social behaviors to protect against predators and care for their young. These communal adaptations highlight Uranus's role in fostering collaboration and innovative group dynamics.

Uranus and Sudden Change

Uranus is known for its association with sudden, unexpected events that disrupt the norm. Dinosaurs faced numerous challenges that required rapid adaptation and resilience:

1. **Climate Shifts**:
   - Throughout the Mesozoic Era, climate fluctuations forced dinosaurs to adapt quickly. For instance, arid conditions during the Triassic gave way to more humid environments in the Jurassic, requiring species to evolve new survival strategies.
   - These shifts mirror Uranus's energy, which demands flexibility and a willingness to embrace change.
2. **Mass Extinction Events**:
   - The extinction events that bookended the age of dinosaurs were Uranian in nature, representing sudden and catastrophic changes. While many species perished, some adapted and evolved, leading to the emergence of new life forms.
3. **Geological Transformations**:
   - The breakup of the supercontinent Pangaea during the Mesozoic Era dramatically altered ecosystems, creating new opportunities and challenges for dinosaurs. This geological upheaval reflects Uranus's role in reshaping the physical world.

Astrological Symbolism of Uranus and Dinosaurs

Astrologically, Uranus represents innovation, disruption, and the ability to adapt to revolutionary changes. In the Dinosaur Zodiac, Uranus symbolizes the adaptability and ingenuity that defined the survival and success of these creatures:

1. **The Spirit of Innovation**:
   - Uranus teaches us to embrace creativity and think outside the box. Dinosaurs' evolutionary innovations, such as feathers and flight, highlight the transformative power of Uranian energy.
2. **Adaptation Through Disruption**:
   - Uranus governs sudden changes that challenge the status quo. Dinosaurs' ability to survive mass extinctions and environmental shifts demonstrates their alignment with Uranus's lessons.
3. **Breaking Boundaries**:
   - Uranus inspires us to push beyond limitations. Dinosaurs like the Spinosaurus, which adapted to aquatic environments, embody this spirit of exploration and boundary-breaking.
4. **Collaboration and Progress**:
   - Uranus encourages collective innovation and progress. Dinosaurs' social behaviors, such as herding and cooperative hunting, reflect Uranus's emphasis on collaboration as a tool for survival.

Lessons from Uranus and Dinosaurs

The influence of Uranus on dinosaurs offers timeless lessons about adaptability, resilience, and the power of revolutionary change. Here are the key takeaways:

1. **Embrace Innovation**:
   - Like dinosaurs that evolved feathers or armor, we can use Uranus's energy to find creative solutions and break free from limitations.
2. **Adapt to Change**:
   - Uranus teaches us to thrive in the face of disruption. Dinosaurs' ability to respond to environmental shifts reminds us to remain flexible and open to new possibilities.
3. **Push Boundaries**:
   - Uranus encourages us to explore the unknown and challenge norms. Dinosaurs like the Pteranodon, which took to the skies, inspire us to expand our horizons.
4. **Find Strength in Collaboration**:
   - Many dinosaurs thrived through social and cooperative behaviors. Uranus teaches us that progress often comes from working together and sharing ideas.

Astrological Reflection for Uranus and Dinosaurs

1. **Connect with Uranus's Energy**:
   - Reflect on areas of your life where you can embrace change and innovation. Use Uranus's influence to pursue breakthroughs and embrace new opportunities.
2. **Cultivate Adaptability**:
   - Practice flexibility and resilience in the face of disruption. Like dinosaurs, use Uranus's energy to navigate challenges and emerge stronger.
3. **Explore Revolutionary Ideas**:
   - Seek out new perspectives and unconventional approaches. Uranus inspires us to think creatively and push beyond traditional boundaries.

Practical Applications of Uranus's Wisdom

1. **Embrace Change**:
   - Approach disruptions as opportunities for growth. Use Uranus's energy to find innovative solutions and adapt to new circumstances.
2. **Innovate in Your Field**:
   - Apply creative thinking to your work or personal projects. Let Uranus inspire you to experiment and explore revolutionary ideas.
3. **Collaborate for Progress**:
   - Work with others to achieve collective goals. Like dinosaurs that thrived in herds or packs, find strength in shared efforts and mutual support.
4. **Expand Your Horizons**:

◦ Take risks and explore uncharted territories. Whether through travel, learning, or personal growth, let Uranus guide you toward new frontiers.

In the Dinosaur Zodiac, Uranus represents the adaptability, revolutionary changes, and breakthroughs that defined the prehistoric world. By connecting with Uranus's energy, we can learn to embrace innovation, thrive in the face of disruption, and push beyond our limitations. Let Uranus and the legacy of dinosaurs inspire you to live boldly, adapt creatively, and transform challenges into opportunities for growth.

Chapter 21: Neptune and Dinosaur Mysticism
Dreams, Illusions, and Water-Based Dinosaurs
Neptune's Role in Prehistoric Life

Neptune, the planet of dreams, illusions, and the subconscious, governs intuition, mysticism, and the fluidity of existence. It represents the hidden depths of reality, where imagination and mystery converge to create new possibilities. In the prehistoric world, Neptune's influence is most profoundly reflected in the enigmatic lives of water-based dinosaurs and marine reptiles, whose fluid movements and aquatic environments embody Neptune's essence.

Water-based dinosaurs, though technically rare (as most aquatic reptiles like Plesiosaurs and Mosasaurs were not true dinosaurs), played a critical role in prehistoric ecosystems. Their connection to water—an element tied to Neptune—aligns them with themes of mystery, adaptability, and interconnectedness. This chapter delves into the Neptunian qualities of dreams, illusions, and the fascinating lives of aquatic dinosaurs and reptiles, offering lessons about fluidity, intuition, and the unseen forces that shape existence.

Water: Neptune's Element and Life's Foundation

Water, governed by Neptune, is the essence of life and the medium through which many prehistoric creatures thrived. In the age of dinosaurs, water bodies like oceans, lakes, and rivers were vital ecosystems that nurtured diverse species, including marine reptiles and semi-aquatic dinosaurs.

1. **Life-Giving Properties**:
   - Water was essential for sustaining life, providing habitats for marine reptiles like Plesiosaurs, Ichthyosaurs, and Mosasaurs. These creatures ruled the prehistoric seas, mirroring Neptune's dominion over the mysterious and boundless ocean depths.
   - Semi-aquatic dinosaurs like Spinosaurus depended on water for hunting and survival, embodying Neptune's ability to merge realms—land and sea.

2. **Symbolism of Water**:
   - Water symbolizes intuition, emotion, and transformation, themes central to Neptune's influence. The movements and behaviors of aquatic dinosaurs reflect these qualities, showing fluidity, adaptability, and a deep connection to their environment.

3. **The Ocean as a Mystical Realm**:
   - The prehistoric oceans were vast, uncharted, and teeming with mysterious creatures. This sense of the unknown reflects Neptune's energy, which thrives in ambiguity and depth.

Neptune's Influence on Water-Based Dinosaurs and Marine Reptiles

Neptune's energy is most visible in the behaviors, adaptations, and habitats of water-based dinosaurs and marine reptiles. These creatures embody the mysticism, adaptability, and dreamlike qualities associated with Neptune.

1. **Plesiosaurs: The Graceful Mystics of the Sea**:
   - Plesiosaurs, with their long necks and paddle-like limbs, moved through the water with a fluid, almost ethereal grace. Their elegant movements reflect Neptune's connection to dreams and the subconscious.
   - As apex predators of their time, Plesiosaurs balanced mystery with power, embodying Neptune's dual nature of gentleness and hidden strength.

2. **Ichthyosaurs: The Oceanic Pioneers**:
   - Resembling modern dolphins, Ichthyosaurs were fast, agile swimmers that thrived in prehistoric seas. Their streamlined bodies and ability to dive deep into the ocean mirror Neptune's association with exploration and the unknown.
   - Ichthyosaurs' adaptations for aquatic life, such as large eyes for seeing in dim light, highlight Neptune's focus on intuition and navigating unseen realms.

3. **Spinosaurus: The Bridge Between Land and Water**:
   - Spinosaurus, with its semi-aquatic lifestyle, symbolizes the Neptunian quality of fluidity and transition. Its ability to hunt both on land and in water reflects Neptune's influence over duality and interconnectedness.
   - The enigmatic sail on its back may have been used for thermoregulation or display, adding an element of mystery to this unique predator.

4. **Mosasaurs: Neptune's Apex Hunters**:
   - Mosasaurs were massive marine reptiles that dominated the seas during the Late Cretaceous. Their immense size and predatory prowess reflect Neptune's capacity for both beauty and destruction.
   - As creatures of the ocean, Mosasaurs embody the Neptunian themes of vastness and the interplay between surface appearances and hidden depths.

Mysticism and Illusions in the Prehistoric World

Neptune governs dreams, illusions, and the mystical aspects of life. In the prehistoric world, these themes resonate in the behaviors and habitats of water-based creatures, as well as in the mysteries that still surround them.

1. **The Enigma of the Deep:**
   - The prehistoric oceans were filled with creatures that remain shrouded in mystery. From the bioluminescent adaptations of some deep-sea creatures to the cryptic hunting strategies of marine reptiles, the seas were a realm of illusion and wonder.
   - The fossil record reveals tantalizing glimpses of these creatures but leaves much unknown, reinforcing Neptune's theme of mystery.
2. **Fluidity and Transformation:**
   - Neptune's influence fosters adaptability and the ability to move seamlessly between states. Water-based dinosaurs and marine reptiles embodied this fluidity, adapting to changing environments and thriving in dynamic ecosystems.
3. **Dreamlike Movements:**
   - The graceful, flowing movements of aquatic creatures evoke a dreamlike quality, symbolizing Neptune's connection to the subconscious and the ethereal. These movements suggest a world governed by intuition and instinct rather than rigid structures.
4. **The Illusion of Safety:**
   - Neptune's dual nature—both nurturing and destructive—is reflected in the oceans, which provided life but also harbored danger. Marine reptiles thrived by balancing this duality, relying on both intuition and strength.

Astrological Symbolism of Neptune and Dinosaurs

Astrologically, Neptune represents dreams, illusions, and spiritual connection. In the Dinosaur Zodiac, Neptune's influence is seen in the mysticism and adaptability of water-based dinosaurs and marine reptiles:

1. **Dreams and Intuition**:
   - Neptune governs the realm of dreams and intuition. The behaviors of aquatic dinosaurs, guided by instinct and environmental cues, mirror this connection to the unseen.
2. **Illusions and Mysteries**:
   - Neptune's association with illusions is reflected in the enigmatic nature of prehistoric seas and the creatures that inhabited them. These mysteries remind us of the limits of our understanding and the beauty of the unknown.
3. **Fluidity and Adaptability**:
   - Neptune inspires fluidity and the ability to adapt to changing circumstances. Water-based dinosaurs and marine reptiles, with their seamless integration into aquatic environments, embody this quality.
4. **Interconnectedness**:
   - Neptune emphasizes the unity of all things. The interconnected ecosystems of prehistoric oceans, where every creature played a role, reflect this Neptunian theme.

Lessons from Neptune and Dinosaurs

The influence of Neptune on water-based dinosaurs offers profound lessons about intuition, mystery, and the power of fluidity. Here are the key takeaways:

1. **Trust Your Intuition**:
   - Like aquatic dinosaurs navigating their environments, rely on your instincts to guide you through uncertainty. Neptune teaches us to embrace the wisdom of the subconscious.
2. **Embrace Mystery**:
   - Neptune reminds us that not everything can—or should—be understood. The mysteries of the prehistoric oceans encourage us to find beauty in the unknown.
3. **Adapt to Change**:
   - Neptune inspires us to flow with life's changes. Water-based dinosaurs demonstrate the importance of flexibility and adaptability in thriving within dynamic environments.
4. **Connect with the Ethereal**:
   - Neptune's energy invites us to explore the spiritual and mystical aspects of life. The dreamlike qualities of aquatic dinosaurs remind us to seek wonder and inspiration beyond the physical world.

Astrological Reflection for Neptune and Dinosaurs

1. **Connect with Neptune's Energy**:
   - Reflect on areas of your life where you can embrace mystery and intuition. Use Neptune's influence to explore your dreams and deepen your spiritual connection.
2. **Cultivate Fluidity**:
   - Practice adaptability and resilience. Like water-based dinosaurs, learn to navigate changing circumstances with grace and flexibility.
3. **Explore the Mystical**:
   - Dedicate time to exploring the mystical aspects of life, whether through meditation, dream journaling, or connecting with nature. Let Neptune inspire your spiritual journey.

Practical Applications of Neptune's Wisdom

1. **Embrace Creative Expression**:
   - Use Neptune's energy to fuel your imagination and creativity. Write, paint, or engage in activities that allow you to express your dreams and inner world.
2. **Find Peace in Uncertainty**:
   - Practice mindfulness and acceptance in the face of the unknown. Neptune teaches us to trust the flow of life, even when it feels uncertain.
3. **Connect with Water**:
   - Spend time near water to connect with Neptune's element. Whether swimming, meditating by the sea, or simply enjoying a quiet moment by a lake, let water inspire calm and reflection.

In the Dinosaur Zodiac, Neptune represents the mysticism, dreams, and adaptability of water-based dinosaurs and marine reptiles. By connecting with Neptune's influence, we can embrace intuition, explore the unknown, and navigate life's changes with fluidity and grace. Let Neptune and the legacy of prehistoric seas inspire you to dive deep into your inner world, trust your instincts, and find wonder in the mysteries of life.

Chapter 22: Pluto and Dinosaur Transformation
Endings, Rebirth, and the Mystery of Extinction
Pluto's Role in Prehistoric Life

Pluto, the planet of transformation, endings, and rebirth, governs the cycles of life and death, the power of renewal, and the profound mysteries of existence. Its influence is often associated with deep, irrevocable change, forcing us to confront the impermanence of life and the potential for growth through destruction. In the story of dinosaurs, Pluto's energy is embodied in their extinction, an event that marked the end of an era but also laid the foundation for new forms of life to thrive.

The extinction of dinosaurs, particularly the catastrophic event at the end of the Cretaceous Period, is one of the most profound transformations in Earth's history. This Plutonian moment of destruction reshaped ecosystems, paved the way for the rise of mammals, and ultimately set the stage for humanity's emergence. In this chapter, we explore how Pluto's themes of endings, rebirth, and mystery are reflected in the lives and legacies of dinosaurs.

Pluto's Influence on Dinosaur Extinction

The extinction of the dinosaurs, while devastating, is a quintessential Plutonian event. It symbolizes the profound and often painful transitions that lead to new beginnings.

1. **The Cretaceous-Paleogene Extinction Event**:
   - Approximately 66 million years ago, a massive asteroid struck Earth near the Yucatán Peninsula, triggering the Cretaceous-Paleogene (K-Pg) extinction. This impact caused wildfires, tsunamis, and a "nuclear winter" as dust and debris blocked sunlight. The resulting collapse of ecosystems led to the extinction of nearly 75% of Earth's species, including most dinosaurs.
   - Pluto's energy is evident in this moment of destruction, as it forced a complete reset of life on Earth, ushering in a new era of evolution.

2. **The Mystery of Extinction**:
   - Despite advancements in science, many aspects of dinosaur extinction remain shrouded in mystery. The interplay of volcanic activity, climate change, and the asteroid impact creates a complex narrative that reflects Pluto's enigmatic nature.
   - Pluto governs the unseen and the hidden, reminding us that some truths may never be fully uncovered.

3. **Cycles of Death and Rebirth**:
   - While the extinction of dinosaurs marked the end of their dominance, it also created opportunities for other species to rise. Mammals, which had lived in the dinosaurs' shadow, diversified and flourished, eventually leading to the evolution of humans.
   - This cycle of endings and new beginnings exemplifies Pluto's transformative energy, where death is a precursor to rebirth.

Transformation Through Plutonian Energy

Pluto inspires profound transformations, often through challenging and destructive processes. The extinction and subsequent evolution of life on Earth highlight these themes:

1. **Resilience in the Face of Change**:
   - Some species, such as certain small theropods, adapted to post-extinction conditions and eventually evolved into birds. This transformation reflects Pluto's lesson that resilience and adaptation can lead to new forms of existence.

2. **The Rise of Mammals**:
   - The extinction of dinosaurs allowed mammals to diversify and occupy ecological niches previously dominated by reptiles. Pluto's energy fosters growth through change, demonstrating how destruction creates space for renewal.

3. **Ecosystem Recovery**:
   - After the K-Pg extinction, ecosystems slowly recovered, with plants, animals, and microorganisms evolving to fill the void. This process illustrates Pluto's transformative power, emphasizing regeneration after loss.

4. **The Legacy of Dinosaurs**:
   - Though extinct, dinosaurs continue to influence modern life through their evolutionary descendants (birds) and their impact on our understanding of Earth's history. Pluto's energy ensures that endings are never final but become part of a greater continuum.

The Mystery of Dinosaur Extinction

Pluto governs the mysterious and hidden aspects of life, encouraging us to explore what lies beneath the surface. The extinction of dinosaurs is a puzzle that continues to captivate scientists and the public alike.

1. **Unresolved Questions**:
   - While the asteroid impact is the leading theory for the K-Pg extinction, other factors like volcanic activity in the Deccan Traps and climate change likely contributed. This multifaceted event mirrors Pluto's complexity and the interplay of visible and invisible forces.

2. **The Role of Unseen Forces**:
   - Pluto teaches us that not all causes are immediately apparent. The gradual buildup of ecological pressures before the asteroid impact reflects the hidden dynamics that often precede transformation.

3. **Myth and Symbolism**:
   - Dinosaurs' extinction has inspired myths, stories, and cultural interpretations, turning them into symbols of both power and vulnerability. Pluto's influence on mythology

and the collective subconscious is evident in how we interpret and revere these ancient creatures.

Astrological Symbolism of Pluto and Dinosaurs

Astrologically, Pluto represents transformation, power, and the cycles of life and death. In the Dinosaur Zodiac, Pluto's influence is reflected in the profound changes that shaped the rise and fall of these creatures:

1. **The Power of Endings**:
   ◦ Pluto teaches us that endings are necessary for growth. The extinction of dinosaurs, while tragic, paved the way for new life and evolutionary progress.
2. **Transformation Through Adversity**:
   ◦ Pluto's energy emphasizes the potential for transformation in even the darkest times. Dinosaurs' evolutionary descendants, such as birds, demonstrate the resilience and adaptability fostered by Pluto.
3. **Legacy and Influence**:
   ◦ Pluto governs the unseen impact of the past on the present. Dinosaurs' fossils, evolutionary contributions, and cultural significance highlight their enduring influence on Earth's history.
4. **The Hidden and the Mystical**:
   ◦ Pluto invites us to explore life's mysteries. The story of dinosaur extinction, with its unanswered questions and complex dynamics, reminds us of the beauty in seeking knowledge beyond what is immediately visible.

Lessons from Pluto and Dinosaurs

The influence of Pluto on dinosaurs offers profound lessons about transformation, resilience, and the cycles of life. Here are the key takeaways:

1. **Embrace Transformation**:
   ◦ Like the ecosystems that recovered after the extinction of dinosaurs, we can embrace Pluto's energy to find growth and renewal in times of change.
2. **Accept Endings as Beginnings**:
   ◦ Pluto reminds us that every ending creates space for something new. The extinction of dinosaurs led to the rise of mammals, illustrating the cyclical nature of life.
3. **Explore Life's Mysteries**:
   ◦ Pluto encourages us to delve into the unknown. The story of dinosaur extinction invites us to embrace curiosity and seek deeper understanding.
4. **Find Strength in Resilience**:
   ◦ Even in the face of destruction, life finds a way to adapt and thrive. Pluto teaches us to channel this resilience in our own lives.

Astrological Reflection for Pluto and Dinosaurs

1. **Connect with Pluto's Energy**:
   - Reflect on the transformative cycles in your life. Use Pluto's influence to navigate endings with grace and embrace the opportunities they bring for rebirth.
2. **Honor Life's Impermanence**:
   - Acknowledge that change is inevitable and necessary. Pluto teaches us to accept life's transitions as part of a greater cycle.
3. **Seek Depth and Meaning**:
   - Explore the hidden aspects of your life and the world around you. Pluto's energy encourages us to uncover the truths that lie beneath the surface.

Practical Applications of Pluto's Wisdom

1. **Embrace Change with Courage**:
   - Approach life's challenges as opportunities for growth. Use Pluto's energy to transform adversity into strength.
2. **Reflect on Legacy and Impact**:
   - Consider how your actions today will influence the future. Pluto's lessons about transformation encourage us to leave a meaningful legacy.
3. **Delve into the Mystical**:
   - Explore the spiritual and hidden aspects of life. Whether through meditation, introspection, or studying ancient histories, let Pluto inspire your journey into the unknown.
4. **Rebuild After Loss**:
   - Like ecosystems recovering after the extinction event, focus on rebuilding and regenerating after personal setbacks. Pluto's energy supports renewal and resilience.

In the Dinosaur Zodiac, Pluto represents the endings, transformations, and mysteries that define the legacy of dinosaurs. By connecting with Pluto's influence, we can learn to embrace change, honor life's cycles, and find strength in transformation. Let Pluto and the story of dinosaurs inspire you to navigate life's transitions with resilience, curiosity, and a deep appreciation for the mysteries of existence.

Part 3: **Celestial Events**

Chapter 23: Meteor Showers and Their Impact on Dinosaur Mythology
Cosmic Rain and Historical Parallels
The Cosmic Spectacle of Meteor Showers

Meteor showers, often referred to as "cosmic rain," are among the most awe-inspiring celestial phenomena. These showers occur when Earth passes through trails of debris left by comets or asteroids, resulting in streaks of light across the night sky. Throughout history, meteor showers have been shrouded in mystery, inspiring myths and legends about divine intervention, cosmic messages, and transformative events.

In the world of dinosaurs, meteor showers take on an even more profound meaning. While regular meteor showers likely illuminated the skies of the Mesozoic Era, the catastrophic asteroid impact that marked the end of the Cretaceous Period is often conflated with cosmic rain in modern interpretations. This chapter explores how meteor showers have influenced our mythology about dinosaurs, drawing historical parallels and highlighting their symbolic resonance as agents of change and transformation.

Meteor Showers in the Prehistoric Sky

During the Mesozoic Era, the skies were just as dynamic as they are today, with meteor showers likely gracing the heavens with their fleeting brilliance. These celestial events would have been part of the natural cycles experienced by dinosaurs, shaping their environments and ecosystems in subtle ways.

1. **Prehistoric Meteor Activity**:
    - Meteor showers occurred regularly during the age of dinosaurs, as Earth passed through comet debris trails. While these events were not catastrophic, they may have influenced atmospheric phenomena and even minor ecological shifts.
    - Larger meteors, occasionally striking Earth, could have caused localized destruction, reminding us of the unpredictable power of cosmic forces.
2. **The Great Impact Event**:
    - The asteroid impact at the end of the Cretaceous Period often overshadows the regular meteor activity of prehistoric times. This collision, which left the Chicxulub Crater in modern-day Mexico, unleashed devastation on a global scale.
    - In hindsight, this event is often mythologized as the ultimate "cosmic rain," merging scientific understanding with the dramatic imagery of a meteor shower heralding an era's end.
3. **Celestial Cycles and Environmental Influence**:
    - Meteor activity may have subtly influenced atmospheric conditions, contributing to long-term ecological changes. These cycles reflect the interconnectedness of cosmic and terrestrial systems, a recurring theme in mythology.

Dinosaur Mythology and Meteor Showers

Meteor showers have become a symbolic bridge between the heavens and Earth in stories about dinosaurs, inspiring interpretations that blend science with myth. These narratives often focus on transformation, divine intervention, and the enduring legacy of cosmic forces.

1. **The Meteor as a Harbinger**:
   - In modern retellings, the asteroid impact that ended the dinosaurs' reign is often portrayed as a celestial warning or a divine reckoning. Meteor showers, with their dramatic and fleeting nature, amplify this imagery, representing cosmic forces delivering fateful messages.
2. **Cosmic Renewal and Rebirth**:
   - Meteor showers are frequently associated with renewal, as their fiery trails symbolize destruction followed by rebirth. The dinosaurs' extinction is often framed as a necessary sacrifice for the rise of new species, aligning with myths that view meteors as agents of transformation.
3. **Guardians of the Skies**:
   - In speculative mythology, some envision dinosaurs interpreting celestial phenomena, such as meteor showers, as part of their environment's natural cycles. This imagined perspective fosters a sense of continuity between prehistoric creatures and modern humanity's fascination with the cosmos.
4. **Dinosaurs in the Stars**:
   - Meteor showers are often connected to constellations, many of which feature creatures resembling dinosaurs. The imagery of dinosaurs among the stars reinforces their mythical status as both ancient and eternal beings.

Historical Parallels and Cultural Myths

Throughout human history, meteor showers have inspired myths, many of which align with themes of transformation and divine influence. These parallels provide a deeper context for understanding the symbolic impact of meteor showers on dinosaur mythology.

1. **Myths of Cosmic Judgment**:
   - Cultures around the world have interpreted meteors as signs of divine wrath or intervention. The dinosaurs' extinction, attributed to an asteroid impact, echoes these themes, symbolizing the cleansing power of cosmic forces.
2. **Stories of Renewal**:
   - Meteor showers have often been linked to cycles of destruction and rebirth. In Native American myths, meteors are seen as the sparks of creation, aligning with the idea that the dinosaurs' end paved the way for mammals and humanity.
3. **Connection to Ancestral Spirits**:
   - Some myths view meteors as spirits or souls returning to Earth. The dinosaurs, often imagined as ancestral guardians of the planet, could be seen as cosmic presences returning through meteor showers.
4. **Celestial Portents**:
   - Meteor showers have historically been interpreted as omens, signaling great change. The asteroid impact that ended the Cretaceous Period is a literal manifestation of this belief, marking a turning point in Earth's history.

Astrological Symbolism of Meteor Showers and Dinosaurs

Astrologically, meteor showers symbolize sudden insights, inspiration, and transformation. In the Dinosaur Zodiac, they represent the moments of upheaval and renewal that defined the dinosaurs' legacy:

1. **Agents of Change**:
   - Meteor showers bring sudden and transformative energy, reflecting the impact of the asteroid that reshaped life on Earth. Dinosaurs' extinction symbolizes the dramatic shifts often associated with meteor symbolism.
2. **Cosmic Messages**:
   - Meteors are seen as messengers from the universe, delivering insights and warnings. The asteroid impact can be interpreted as a cosmic message about the fragility of dominance and the necessity of adaptation.
3. **Symbol of Continuity**:
   - Meteor showers, occurring regularly, remind us of the enduring cycles of the cosmos. Dinosaurs' connection to meteor mythology reinforces their place in Earth's ongoing story.
4. **Illumination of the Unknown**:
   - Just as meteors briefly illuminate the night sky, they symbolize the fleeting moments of understanding in the vast unknown. The dinosaurs' story invites us to reflect on the mysteries of existence and our place in the universe.

Lessons from Meteor Showers and Dinosaurs

The influence of meteor showers on dinosaur mythology offers profound lessons about transformation, resilience, and cosmic connection. Here are the key takeaways:

1. **Embrace Change as a Catalyst**:
   - Like the asteroid impact that ended the dinosaurs' reign, transformative events often pave the way for renewal and growth. Meteor showers remind us to welcome change as a necessary part of life.
2. **Find Meaning in the Fleeting**:
   - Meteor showers are brief but impactful, symbolizing the power of transient moments. Dinosaurs' legacy, though cut short, continues to inspire and teach us about resilience and adaptation.
3. **Connect with the Cosmos**:
   - Meteor showers link us to the universe's greater cycles. Dinosaurs' story reminds us of our connection to the cosmos and the importance of understanding our place within it.
4. **Honor the Mystery of Existence**:
   - Both meteor showers and the dinosaurs' extinction invite us to reflect on life's mysteries. Embrace curiosity and the search for meaning in the unknown.

Astrological Reflection for Meteor Showers and Dinosaurs

1. **Meditate on Cosmic Connections**:
   - Use meteor showers as a time to reflect on your connection to the universe. Let their energy inspire transformation and renewal.
2. **Seek Sudden Inspiration**:
   - Like the fleeting brilliance of meteors, embrace moments of insight and creativity. Use them to spark new ideas and approaches.
3. **Honor Cycles of Change**:
   - Recognize the cycles of destruction and rebirth in your life. Meteor showers and the dinosaurs' extinction teach us to navigate these transitions with grace.

Practical Applications of Meteor Shower Wisdom

1. **Watch Meteor Showers Mindfully**:
   - Observe meteor showers as opportunities for reflection. Consider how their transient beauty mirrors the fleeting but meaningful moments in your life.
2. **Journal About Transformation**:
   - Use the energy of meteor showers to explore changes in your life. Write about how you've grown through past transitions and how you can embrace future transformations.
3. **Celebrate Renewal**:
   - Meteor showers remind us of life's capacity for renewal. Engage in rituals or practices that honor rebirth and fresh starts.
4. **Explore Celestial Mysteries**:
   - Study the science and mythology of meteor showers to deepen your understanding of their significance. Let them inspire your sense of wonder and connection to the universe.

In the Dinosaur Zodiac, meteor showers represent the cosmic forces of transformation and renewal that defined the age of dinosaurs and their enduring legacy. By connecting with the symbolism of meteor showers, we can learn to embrace change, honor the fleeting beauty of life, and find meaning in the mysteries of existence. Let the cosmic rain and the story of dinosaurs inspire you to seek transformation, celebrate renewal, and connect with the boundless universe.

Chapter 24: Eclipses in the Prehistoric Era
Solar and Lunar Eclipses in Dinosaur Lore

Eclipses: Celestial Mysteries Through Time

Eclipses, both solar and lunar, are among the most dramatic celestial events observable from Earth. These rare occurrences, where the Sun, Moon, and Earth align, have fascinated and mystified life on our planet for eons. In human history, eclipses have inspired myths and rituals, often symbolizing moments of transformation, cosmic balance, or foreboding omens. During the prehistoric era, these phenomena would have had a profound yet unknowable impact on the creatures that roamed the Earth, including dinosaurs.

In modern times, eclipses have become symbolic events in dinosaur lore, blending scientific curiosity with imaginative myth-making. The mystery and majesty of these celestial alignments resonate with themes of power, change, and the interconnectedness of all life. This chapter explores how solar and lunar eclipses might have influenced the prehistoric world and how they've been woven into our interpretations of dinosaur mythology.

Eclipses During the Mesozoic Era

The Mesozoic Era, spanning approximately 180 million years, was a time of dynamic geological and atmospheric conditions, with the skies playing a significant role in shaping ecosystems. Eclipses, though brief, would have been unforgettable phenomena, creating unique atmospheric effects and altering the behaviors of creatures below.

1. **Solar Eclipses:**
   - **What Happens During a Solar Eclipse**: A solar eclipse occurs when the Moon passes between the Earth and the Sun, temporarily blocking sunlight. During totality, daylight transforms into eerie twilight, temperatures drop, and shadows distort, creating a surreal environment.
   - **Impact on Dinosaurs**:
     - The sudden darkness and cooling during a solar eclipse might have startled dinosaurs, causing temporary disruptions in their behaviors. Herbivores could have paused foraging, while predators might have been spurred into action, taking advantage of confusion.
     - Nocturnal dinosaurs, like small theropods potentially active during twilight, may have interpreted the event as an early nightfall, adjusting their routines accordingly.
   - **Environmental Effects**: The drop in temperature during a solar eclipse could have influenced the behavior of cold-blooded dinosaurs, which relied on external heat sources

for thermoregulation. Such events might have triggered a chain of responses within ecosystems.

2. **Lunar Eclipses**:
   - **What Happens During a Lunar Eclipse**: A lunar eclipse occurs when Earth passes between the Sun and the Moon, casting a reddish shadow over the Moon. This event, visible only at night, creates an otherworldly appearance in the sky.
   - **Impact on Dinosaurs**:
     - Lunar eclipses likely had less direct impact on dinosaur behavior compared to solar eclipses but may have altered the activity patterns of nocturnal species.
     - The reddish hue of the Moon might have triggered alarm or curiosity among dinosaurs, especially those relying on moonlight for navigation or hunting.

3. **Cycles and Patterns**:
   - Dinosaurs, like modern animals, were likely attuned to natural cycles, such as day and night, seasons, and lunar phases. Eclipses, disrupting these cycles, may have served as rare but significant celestial markers, influencing behaviors in subtle ways.

Eclipses and Dinosaur Mythology

Eclipses have been powerful symbols in human mythology, often associated with transformation, divine intervention, and the balance between light and darkness. When imagined within the context of dinosaurs, these celestial events take on a mythical dimension, blending science with storytelling.

1. **Eclipses as Omens**:
   - In modern dinosaur mythology, eclipses are often imagined as omens of significant events, such as battles, migrations, or the rise and fall of species. This aligns with human interpretations of eclipses as signs of cosmic upheaval or change.

2. **The Predator's Advantage**:
   - Eclipses might be mythologized as moments when predatory dinosaurs gained an edge, using the sudden darkness of a solar eclipse or the dim light of a lunar eclipse to stalk prey. These stories highlight the adaptability and cunning of dinosaurs, reinforcing their role as dominant creatures.

3. **Celestial Balance and Dinosaur Lore**:
   - The interplay of light and shadow during eclipses mirrors the balance of power within ecosystems, where herbivores and predators coexisted in a delicate equilibrium. Eclipses, as cosmic expressions of balance, symbolize this dynamic in dinosaur mythology.

4. **Eclipses as Portals**:
   - Some myths imagine eclipses as portals to other worlds or dimensions, linking dinosaurs to cosmic mysteries. These stories draw on the awe-inspiring nature of eclipses, suggesting that dinosaurs were not only creatures of Earth but also connected to the universe's greater forces.

Scientific Parallels and Eclipses' Effects on Prehistoric Life

While eclipses are short-lived, their atmospheric effects and potential influence on ecosystems provide a scientific basis for imagining their impact on prehistoric life:

1. **Behavioral Responses**:
   - Sudden darkness and cooling during solar eclipses likely caused shifts in behavior across species. Birds and mammals today exhibit altered activity patterns during eclipses, suggesting dinosaurs may have responded similarly, pausing or redirecting their behaviors.
2. **Environmental Impact**:
   - Large-scale atmospheric changes caused by prolonged volcanic activity or asteroid impacts (both linked to extinction events) share some parallels with the temporary effects of solar eclipses, such as cooling and reduced sunlight. These parallels reinforce the idea of eclipses as harbingers of significant change.
3. **Cycles of Light and Life**:
   - Eclipses disrupt the natural cycles of light and darkness that govern life's rhythms. For dinosaurs, this disruption might have provided rare opportunities for adaptation or highlighted their reliance on celestial patterns.

Astrological Symbolism of Eclipses and Dinosaurs

Astrologically, eclipses symbolize transformation, revelation, and moments of profound change. In the Dinosaur Zodiac, eclipses represent the pivotal events and cosmic forces that shaped the prehistoric world:

1. **Solar Eclipses: Turning Points**:
   - Solar eclipses symbolize dramatic shifts and turning points, much like the asteroid impact that marked the end of the Cretaceous Period. They remind us of the sudden, transformative events that redefine existence.
2. **Lunar Eclipses: Reflection and Shadow**:
   - Lunar eclipses represent introspection and the unveiling of hidden truths. In dinosaur mythology, they might symbolize the mystery of extinction and the secrets preserved in the fossil record.
3. **Cosmic Cycles and Balance**:
   - Eclipses embody the balance between opposites—light and darkness, life and death. Dinosaurs' existence and extinction align with these cosmic cycles, teaching us to embrace the ebb and flow of life.

Lessons from Eclipses and Dinosaurs

The influence of eclipses on dinosaur mythology offers timeless lessons about change, balance, and cosmic connection. Here are the key takeaways:

1. **Embrace Transformation**:
   - Like the sudden darkness of a solar eclipse, life's turning points can be unsettling but necessary for growth. Eclipses remind us to welcome change as part of the cosmic order.
2. **Find Balance in Opposites**:
   - Eclipses show us the harmony between light and shadow, teaching us to appreciate the balance in life's dualities.
3. **Honor the Mysteries of the Cosmos**:
   - Eclipses, like the dinosaurs' story, invite us to marvel at the universe's mysteries and seek meaning in its patterns.
4. **Adapt to Disruption**:
   - Just as eclipses temporarily disrupt natural rhythms, life often brings unexpected challenges. Dinosaurs' resilience inspires us to adapt and thrive in the face of change.

Astrological Reflection for Eclipses and Dinosaurs

1. **Meditate on Cosmic Cycles**:
   - Use eclipses as moments to reflect on your own cycles of change and transformation. Let their energy guide you through transitions with grace and clarity.
2. **Seek Balance in Your Life**:
   - Eclipses remind us of the importance of harmony. Evaluate areas where you can bring more balance to your relationships, work, and personal growth.
3. **Explore the Hidden**:
   - Lunar eclipses invite introspection and uncovering truths. Use this energy to explore your subconscious and connect with your inner self.

Practical Applications of Eclipse Wisdom

1. **Observe Eclipses as Sacred Events**:
    ◦ Watch eclipses with a sense of reverence and wonder. Use them as opportunities to reflect on your connection to the cosmos.
2. **Align Your Goals with Eclipse Cycles**:
    ◦ Solar eclipses are ideal times for setting intentions and initiating change, while lunar eclipses are perfect for letting go of what no longer serves you.
3. **Celebrate Cosmic Unity**:
    ◦ Host gatherings or rituals to honor eclipses, drawing inspiration from their ability to unite people across cultures and eras.

In the Dinosaur Zodiac, eclipses represent the profound changes and cosmic forces that shaped the prehistoric world. By connecting with the symbolism of solar and lunar eclipses, we can learn to embrace transformation, find balance, and honor the mysteries of the universe. Let the story of eclipses and dinosaurs inspire you to navigate life's cycles with resilience, wonder, and a deep appreciation for the interconnectedness of all things.

Chapter 25: The Nodes and Prehistoric Destiny
North and South Nodes' Karmic Implications
The Nodes: Cosmic Markers of Destiny

In astrology, the North and South Nodes are celestial points where the Moon's orbit intersects the ecliptic (the Sun's apparent path through the sky). These points hold profound karmic significance, representing life's journey of growth and evolution. The North Node symbolizes destiny, aspirations, and the future we are meant to embrace, while the South Node reflects past lives, inherited patterns, and lessons learned. Together, they guide us through a cosmic narrative of transformation and purpose.

In the context of the prehistoric world, the Nodes take on an intriguing symbolic dimension. They offer a lens to view the rise, dominance, and eventual extinction of dinosaurs as part of Earth's karmic story. From the lessons of their reign to the legacy they left behind, the Nodes illuminate the interplay of past and future in shaping prehistoric destiny.

The South Node: Dinosaur Legacy and Lessons

The South Node represents the past, carrying the wisdom, patterns, and habits that form the foundation of existence. For dinosaurs, this energy is reflected in their evolutionary legacy and the lessons humanity has drawn from their time on Earth.

1. **Inherited Strengths**:
   - Dinosaurs' incredible adaptability and dominance over diverse ecosystems illustrate the strengths carried by their symbolic South Node. Their ability to evolve and thrive offers lessons in resilience and innovation.
   - Their advanced respiratory systems, social behaviors, and physical adaptations have influenced modern life, particularly through their evolutionary descendants, birds.

2. **Patterns of Survival and Extinction**:
   - The South Node also carries patterns that can limit growth. Dinosaurs, for all their success, were deeply reliant on environmental stability. The sudden disruption caused by the asteroid impact revealed the fragility of their dominance, highlighting the karmic lesson of adaptability.
   - The cyclical rise and fall of species echo the South Node's theme of revisiting and reworking past behaviors.

3. **The Fossil Record as Memory**:
   - Fossils serve as a physical manifestation of the South Node, preserving the history and legacy of dinosaurs. These remnants remind us of the interconnectedness of past and present, offering insights into the Earth's evolutionary trajectory.

The North Node: Evolutionary Destiny and Renewal
The North Node symbolizes the future, pointing toward growth, evolution, and the new paths we are meant to explore. For dinosaurs, this energy is embodied in their transformative impact on Earth and the life that emerged after their extinction.

1. **Transforming Earth's Ecosystems**:
   - The extinction of dinosaurs cleared the way for mammals to rise and eventually for humanity to evolve. This pivotal event reflects the North Node's energy of transformation and the forward momentum of destiny.
   - Dinosaurs' evolutionary adaptations, such as feathers and bipedal locomotion, influenced the development of modern birds, carrying their legacy into the future.
2. **Lessons in Adaptation**:
   - The North Node teaches that growth requires stepping out of comfort zones and embracing change. Dinosaurs that adapted to new environments or challenges, such as theropods evolving into birds, exemplify this principle.
   - The asteroid impact that ended the Mesozoic Era serves as a North Node moment for Earth itself, catalyzing a new phase of life's journey.
3. **The Evolutionary Ripple Effect**:
   - The changes initiated by dinosaurs' extinction continue to shape Earth's ecosystems. The North Node invites us to consider how present actions ripple into the future, creating legacies that transcend immediate lifetimes.

The Nodes and Earth's Karmic Story
The interplay of the Nodes in the prehistoric era reveals a larger karmic narrative, where the rise and fall of dinosaurs serve as chapters in Earth's journey of evolution and transformation.

1. **Cycles of Life and Death**:
   - The Nodes emphasize the cyclical nature of existence. Dinosaurs' dominance and extinction reflect these cycles, reminding us that endings are not final but part of a larger process of renewal.
2. **Karmic Balancing**:
   - The South Node's lessons must be integrated to move toward the North Node's aspirations. Dinosaurs' reign demonstrates the importance of balance—between innovation and stability, adaptation and reliance on the environment.
3. **Earth's Evolutionary Growth**:
   - The Nodes symbolize the growth of Earth itself, as life continuously evolves and adapts to new challenges. The transition from the age of dinosaurs to the age of mammals reflects this upward spiral of progress.

Astrological Symbolism of the Nodes and Dinosaurs

Astrologically, the Nodes represent the tension between past and future, urging growth while honoring the lessons of history. In the Dinosaur Zodiac, they highlight the karmic implications of dinosaurs' existence and their enduring impact:

1. **South Node: The Wisdom of the Past**:
   - The South Node's energy is seen in the dinosaurs' evolutionary strengths and the lessons they left behind. Their legacy offers guidance for navigating challenges in the present and future.
2. **North Node: The Path of Growth**:
   - The North Node calls for transformation and embracing the unknown. Dinosaurs' extinction and the rise of new life forms illustrate the potential for growth through change and adaptation.
3. **Balance Between Nodes**:
   - The Nodes remind us to balance the wisdom of the past with the opportunities of the future. Dinosaurs' story teaches us to honor their legacy while striving for progress and innovation.

Lessons from the Nodes and Dinosaurs

The influence of the Nodes on prehistoric destiny offers profound lessons about growth, balance, and the interconnectedness of life. Here are the key takeaways:

1. **Honor the Past**:
   - Like the South Node, the dinosaurs' legacy reminds us to learn from history and carry its wisdom into the future.
2. **Embrace the Future**:
   - The North Node calls us to step into the unknown and pursue growth. Dinosaurs' extinction teaches us to see change as an opportunity for renewal.
3. **Balance Stability and Innovation**:
   - The Nodes highlight the importance of balance. Dinosaurs thrived through their strengths but ultimately needed greater adaptability to face sudden challenges.
4. **Recognize Cycles of Growth**:
   - The Nodes remind us that life evolves in cycles. The rise and fall of dinosaurs demonstrate the ongoing journey of transformation and progress.

Astrological Reflection for the Nodes and Dinosaurs

1. **Connect with the South Node**:
   - Reflect on your inherited strengths and patterns. What lessons from the past can guide your growth in the present?
2. **Pursue Your North Node**:
   - Identify your aspirations and the areas where you seek growth. Use the North Node's energy to move toward your destiny with courage and curiosity.
3. **Balance Past and Future**:
   - Honor the wisdom of the past while embracing the possibilities of the future. The Nodes teach us to integrate both energies for a harmonious journey.

Practical Applications of the Nodes' Wisdom

1. **Reflect on Legacy and Purpose**:
   - Consider how your actions contribute to your legacy and impact future generations. Let the Nodes inspire you to live with intention and purpose.
2. **Embrace Change as Growth**:
   - Use the North Node's energy to view change as an opportunity for progress. Like Earth after the dinosaurs, find ways to thrive in new circumstances.
3. **Honor Life's Cycles**:
   - Recognize the cyclical nature of growth and transformation. Celebrate milestones and embrace transitions as part of your journey.
4. **Balance Reflection and Aspiration**:
   - Spend time reflecting on the past while setting goals for the future. The Nodes remind us to move forward while staying grounded in what we've learned.

In the Dinosaur Zodiac, the Nodes represent the karmic balance between past and future, legacy and growth. By connecting with the symbolism of the Nodes, we can learn to honor history, embrace transformation, and navigate life's journey with wisdom and purpose. Let the story of the Nodes and dinosaurs inspire you to pursue your destiny while carrying the lessons of the past into a brighter future.

Chapter 26: Comets and Dinosaur Tales
Ancient Travelers and Their Spiritual Significance
Comets: Messengers of the Cosmos

Comets, often referred to as "cosmic travelers," have long captured the imagination of humanity as harbingers of change, transformation, and divine messages. With their radiant tails and unpredictable appearances, comets evoke wonder and mystery, embodying the spiritual and physical connection between Earth and the cosmos. In prehistoric times, comets would have graced the skies as rare and spectacular events, their luminous trails illuminating the night and inspiring an aura of the unknown.

In dinosaur lore, comets are often tied to tales of transformation, extinction, and celestial guidance. Their symbolic role as bringers of both destruction and renewal aligns with the dramatic evolutionary shifts that shaped the age of dinosaurs. This chapter explores the spiritual significance of comets, their impact on the prehistoric world, and their role in shaping modern interpretations of dinosaur mythology.

Comets in the Prehistoric Sky

During the Mesozoic Era, comets would have been visible to dinosaurs, just as they are to us today. Their presence in the skies might have had subtle but profound effects on prehistoric life.

1. **Cosmic Visitors of the Mesozoic Era:**
    - Comets passing near Earth during the Mesozoic would have been awe-inspiring events, their glowing tails streaking across the night sky. While dinosaurs lacked the cognitive awareness to interpret these phenomena, comets might have indirectly influenced their environments.
    - Dust and debris from comet trails occasionally enter Earth's atmosphere, creating meteor showers. These cosmic particles could have subtly altered atmospheric conditions, contributing to the ever-changing ecosystems of the prehistoric world.
2. **The Great Impact Connection:**
    - While comets and asteroids differ, the catastrophic event that ended the Cretaceous Period is often linked to celestial bodies. If a comet had been responsible for the extinction of the dinosaurs, it would have underscored their dual nature as both awe-inspiring travelers and agents of transformation.
    - Modern interpretations often conflate comets with the asteroid impact, weaving them into tales of cosmic intervention and karmic rebalancing.
3. **Symbolic Resonance with Evolution:**
    - Comets, with their elliptical orbits and transient appearances, symbolize cycles of return and renewal. These qualities align with the evolutionary journey of dinosaurs, marked by periods of dominance, adaptation, and eventual transformation.

Comets in Dinosaur Mythology

In modern dinosaur mythology, comets are imbued with spiritual significance, blending scientific understanding with imaginative storytelling. These narratives explore themes of guidance, destiny, and the interconnectedness of all life.

1. **Harbingers of Change**:
   - Comets are often imagined as cosmic omens, signaling significant events in the age of dinosaurs. Their sudden and luminous appearances mirror the dramatic shifts that defined the prehistoric world, from mass extinctions to evolutionary breakthroughs.
   - In mythological tales, comets might be seen as celestial warnings of impending environmental changes or the rise of new species.
2. **Guides to the Celestial Realm**:
   - Some stories portray comets as spiritual guides, connecting Earth to the cosmos. Dinosaurs, as ancient and majestic beings, are often depicted as attuned to these cosmic messengers, drawing inspiration or guidance from their appearances.
3. **Agents of Transformation**:
   - In narratives about dinosaur extinction, comets are often cast as agents of transformation, bringing destruction but also paving the way for renewal. This dual role highlights their symbolic connection to cycles of life, death, and rebirth.
4. **Guardians of the Stars**:
   - Comets are sometimes imagined as guardians or carriers of dinosaur spirits, traveling across the cosmos to preserve their legacy. These tales emphasize the timelessness of dinosaurs and their enduring connection to the universe.

Spiritual Significance of Comets

Comets hold a profound spiritual resonance, representing themes of impermanence, transformation, and the mysteries of existence. Their symbolic qualities align closely with the story of dinosaurs and their role in Earth's history.

1. **Messengers of the Unknown**:
   - Comets are often viewed as messengers from the cosmos, delivering divine insights or warnings. In the context of dinosaurs, they symbolize the unpredictable forces that shaped their existence and ultimate extinction.
2. **Cycles of Return**:
   - The elliptical orbits of comets, which bring them back to Earth's vicinity after long periods, reflect cycles of return and renewal. This mirrors the evolutionary journey of dinosaurs, whose legacy continues through their descendants, modern birds.
3. **Agents of Purification**:
   - In many cultures, comets are seen as agents of purification, sweeping away the old to make way for the new. The extinction of dinosaurs, often tied to celestial phenomena, exemplifies this role, marking the end of an era and the beginning of another.
4. **Guides to the Divine**:
   - Comets' luminous trails and celestial origins connect them to the divine. They serve as reminders of the vastness of the universe and the interconnectedness of all life, from dinosaurs to humanity.

Astrological Symbolism of Comets and Dinosaurs

Astrologically, comets represent sudden insights, transformative events, and cosmic guidance. In the Dinosaur Zodiac, comets symbolize the dynamic forces that shaped the prehistoric world and the lessons they offer for modern life:

1. **Catalysts of Change**:
   - Comets embody the power of transformation, reflecting the dramatic shifts that defined the age of dinosaurs. Their symbolism reminds us to embrace change as a necessary part of growth.
2. **Illuminators of Destiny**:
   - Comets are seen as beacons of light, guiding us toward our purpose. In dinosaur mythology, they represent the alignment of celestial forces that shaped Earth's evolutionary path.
3. **Eternal Travelers**:
   - The cyclical nature of comets, returning after long intervals, mirrors the enduring legacy of dinosaurs. Their story continues to inspire curiosity and wonder, much like the cosmic travelers that grace our skies.
4. **Bridge Between Realms**:
   - Comets symbolize the connection between the physical and spiritual realms. In dinosaur lore, they serve as bridges between the ancient past and the cosmic future.

Lessons from Comets and Dinosaurs

The influence of comets on dinosaur mythology offers profound lessons about transformation, interconnectedness, and the mysteries of the cosmos. Here are the key takeaways:

1. **Embrace Transformation**:
   - Like comets that bring change, we must learn to adapt and evolve. Dinosaurs' extinction teaches us to see transformation as an opportunity for renewal and growth.
2. **Recognize Cosmic Connections**:
   - Comets remind us of our connection to the universe and its cycles. Dinosaurs, as ancient beings, symbolize this interconnectedness, inspiring us to honor the past while embracing the future.
3. **Find Meaning in the Ephemeral**:
   - The fleeting brilliance of comets parallels the transience of life. Dinosaurs' reign, though vast in time, serves as a reminder to appreciate the present and create lasting legacies.
4. **Seek Guidance from the Cosmos**:
   - Comets are seen as celestial guides, illuminating our path forward. Their symbolism encourages us to seek wisdom and inspiration from the universe's greater forces.

Astrological Reflection for Comets and Dinosaurs

1. **Connect with Cosmic Energy**:
   - Reflect on the symbolism of comets as messengers of transformation. Use their energy to guide you through periods of change and growth.
2. **Embrace Cycles of Return**:
   - Recognize the cycles of life and evolution in your own journey. Like comets and dinosaurs, find strength in your ability to adapt and renew.
3. **Honor the Mystery of the Universe**:
   - Comets inspire awe and curiosity. Use their symbolism to deepen your connection to the cosmos and explore life's mysteries.

Practical Applications of Comet Wisdom

1. **Observe Comets Mindfully**:
   - Watch for comets as opportunities for reflection. Let their appearances inspire you to consider the cycles of change in your life.
2. **Journal About Transformation**:
   - Use comet symbolism to explore your personal growth. Write about the changes you've experienced and how they've shaped your journey.
3. **Celebrate Cosmic Events**:
   - Honor celestial phenomena like comets with rituals or gatherings that connect you to the universe's energy and cycles.
4. **Seek Inspiration in the Sky**:
   - Let comets remind you of the beauty and mystery of existence. Use their symbolism to inspire creativity and wonder in your daily life.

In the Dinosaur Zodiac, comets represent the ancient travelers and cosmic forces that shaped the prehistoric world. By connecting with the symbolism of comets, we can learn to embrace transformation, honor our connection to the universe, and find meaning in life's cycles. Let the story of comets and dinosaurs inspire you to navigate change with resilience, seek cosmic guidance, and marvel at the mysteries of existence.

Part 4: **Moon Phases**

Chapter 27: The New Moon and Dinosaur Beginnings
Fresh Starts and Evolutionary Insights
The New Moon: A Symbol of Beginnings

The New Moon, a time when the Moon is completely dark and invisible from Earth, represents a fresh start, renewal, and the potential for growth. In astrology, it is the phase associated with planting seeds for the future, setting intentions, and initiating new cycles. This symbolism resonates deeply with the evolutionary journey of dinosaurs, whose emergence marked a groundbreaking chapter in Earth's history.

Dinosaurs first appeared during the Triassic Period, rising after one of the most devastating mass extinction events in Earth's history: the Permian-Triassic Extinction. This event wiped out approximately 90% of life, creating a blank slate for new species to rise and evolve. The emergence of dinosaurs during this transformative era mirrors the themes of the New Moon—overcoming darkness to bring forth renewal and evolution.

This chapter explores the connection between the New Moon and the early days of dinosaurs, examining the evolutionary breakthroughs that defined their beginnings and the lessons we can draw from their story of resilience and potential.

The Mesozoic Era: A New Moon for Life

The Mesozoic Era, spanning the Triassic, Jurassic, and Cretaceous periods, is often referred to as the "Age of Dinosaurs." However, this age began with the metaphorical darkness of the Permian extinction, much like the New Moon marks the beginning of a lunar cycle.

1. **The Permian-Triassic Extinction as the Dark Phase**:
    - Before dinosaurs, Earth faced its darkest period, with widespread extinction that cleared ecosystems of life. This extinction event, akin to the "darkness" of the New Moon, created the conditions for new life to emerge.
    - The barren landscapes that followed were fertile ground for evolutionary innovation, setting the stage for the rise of dinosaurs.
2. **The Triassic Period: Seeds of Dinosaur Evolution**:
    - The Triassic Period saw the first dinosaurs emerge, including early species like *Eoraptor* and *Herrerasaurus*. These small, agile creatures represented the first sparks of dinosaur evolution, much like the first sliver of light after a New Moon.
    - Dinosaurs began to diversify rapidly, experimenting with new physical traits and behaviors that would define their reign for millions of years.
3. **Fresh Starts for Ecosystems**:
    - Alongside dinosaurs, other groups like early mammals and reptiles began to flourish, creating new and dynamic ecosystems. This period of renewal underscores the New Moon's theme of fresh starts and infinite potential.

Evolutionary Insights from Dinosaur Beginnings

The emergence of dinosaurs offers profound evolutionary insights, reflecting the themes of the New Moon—adaptability, innovation, and the courage to grow from the void.

1. **Innovation in Anatomy and Movement**:
   - Early dinosaurs developed traits that set them apart, such as upright posture, bipedal locomotion, and efficient respiratory systems. These innovations allowed them to exploit new ecological niches and outcompete other species.
   - The New Moon inspires similar innovation, encouraging us to explore new approaches and embrace change.
2. **Diversification and Experimentation**:
   - The first dinosaurs were relatively small and lightweight, but they quickly diversified into herbivorous, carnivorous, and omnivorous species. This period of experimentation highlights the importance of adaptability in uncertain times.
   - Like the New Moon, which signifies planting seeds for growth, the early days of dinosaurs were about exploring possibilities and finding what worked in a new world.
3. **Resilience in the Face of Adversity**:
   - Dinosaurs emerged in a challenging environment, where volcanic activity, fluctuating climates, and scarce resources created immense pressure. Their success underscores the New Moon's lesson that growth often begins in moments of hardship.
   - Resilience and adaptability were their greatest strengths, enabling them to dominate ecosystems for over 160 million years.

The New Moon and Dinosaur Mythology

In modern interpretations of dinosaur mythology, the New Moon serves as a powerful symbol for their beginnings and the evolutionary forces that shaped their legacy.

1. **The Spark of Life**:
   - The New Moon's invisible phase represents the hidden potential of life, much like the early days of dinosaurs. Their emergence reminds us that even in darkness, seeds of greatness are planted.
   - Mythological tales often frame the rise of dinosaurs as a cosmic act of renewal, with the New Moon symbolizing the fertile ground from which they sprang.
2. **Cycles of Renewal**:
   - The New Moon's association with cycles aligns with the evolutionary journey of dinosaurs. From their humble beginnings in the Triassic to their dominance in the Jurassic and Cretaceous, they embody the continuous process of growth and renewal.
   - These cycles mirror the lunar phases, reminding us of the interconnectedness of life's rhythms.
3. **The Birth of Giants**:
   - The New Moon is often seen as a moment of gestation and preparation. The small, agile dinosaurs of the Triassic laid the foundation for the gigantic sauropods and apex predators of later periods. This progression reflects the New Moon's role in nurturing potential and leading to eventual greatness.

Spiritual Lessons from the New Moon and Dinosaurs

The New Moon's connection to beginnings and growth offers profound lessons when viewed through the lens of dinosaur evolution:

1. **Embrace the Void**:
   - Just as the New Moon begins in darkness, the story of dinosaurs teaches us to embrace moments of uncertainty and see them as opportunities for growth. The Permian extinction was a void that allowed new life to flourish.
   - In our own lives, periods of challenge can be fertile ground for creativity and transformation.

2. **Plant Seeds for the Future**:
   - The New Moon encourages intention-setting and planting seeds for future growth. Dinosaurs, through their adaptability and innovation, laid the groundwork for ecosystems that would thrive for millions of years.
   - This reminds us to take deliberate steps toward our goals, trusting that they will bear fruit in time.

3. **Adapt and Experiment**:
   - The early days of dinosaurs were marked by experimentation and diversification. Similarly, the New Moon inspires us to explore new possibilities and adapt to changing circumstances.
   - Flexibility and openness to change are key to thriving in an evolving world.

4. **Trust the Process**:
   - The New Moon's cycle reminds us that growth takes time and begins with small steps. The rise of dinosaurs from small, early species to towering giants illustrates the power of steady progress.
   - By trusting the process, we can achieve great things even from humble beginnings.

Astrological Symbolism of the New Moon and Dinosaurs

Astrologically, the New Moon represents beginnings, potential, and the courage to start anew. In the Dinosaur Zodiac, it symbolizes the transformative energy of the Triassic Period and the evolutionary breakthroughs that defined their early days:

1. **Potential for Growth**:
   - The New Moon reminds us that even the smallest beginnings hold immense potential. Dinosaurs' emergence after the Permian extinction demonstrates the power of starting fresh and embracing new opportunities.
2. **Cycles of Renewal**:
   - The New Moon's cycle of darkness and light mirrors the evolutionary cycles of life on Earth. Dinosaurs' story reflects the continuous journey of growth, adaptation, and transformation.
3. **Hidden Strengths**:
   - The New Moon represents hidden potential and unseen forces. Dinosaurs' early innovations, such as their efficient respiratory systems, highlight the importance of laying strong foundations for future success.

Practical Applications of the New Moon's Wisdom

1. **Set Intentions**:
   - Use the energy of the New Moon to set clear goals and intentions for your personal and professional growth. Reflect on the lessons of dinosaurs' adaptability and resilience.
2. **Embrace New Beginnings**:
   - Start new projects or ventures during the New Moon phase. Draw inspiration from the dinosaurs' ability to thrive after the void of extinction.
3. **Reflect and Plan**:
   - The New Moon is a time for quiet reflection and preparation. Consider how you can build strong foundations for your future, much like the early dinosaurs paved the way for their descendants.
4. **Stay Resilient**:
   - In moments of challenge or uncertainty, remember that even the darkest times can lead to renewal and growth. Trust in your ability to adapt and evolve, just as dinosaurs did.

In the Dinosaur Zodiac, the New Moon represents the fresh starts, potential, and evolutionary insights that defined the beginning of the dinosaurs' reign. By connecting with the symbolism of the New Moon, we can learn to embrace change, set intentions, and trust in the cycles of growth that shape our lives. Let the story of the New Moon and dinosaurs inspire you to find strength in new beginnings and the courage to explore your potential.

Chapter 28: The Waxing Crescent Moon and Growth
Symbolism of Progress and Survival
The Waxing Crescent Moon: A Symbol of Growth

The Waxing Crescent Moon, the phase following the New Moon, symbolizes growth, progress, and the first steps toward achieving potential. It is the stage of the lunar cycle where intentions set during the New Moon begin to take shape, encouraging effort, resilience, and incremental advancement. In prehistoric times, this phase metaphorically aligns with the evolutionary journey of dinosaurs as they emerged, adapted, and began their ascent to dominance during the Triassic and Jurassic periods.

For dinosaurs, the Waxing Crescent symbolizes survival through growth—incremental adaptations that allowed them to overcome challenges, expand into new ecosystems, and refine the traits that defined their success. This chapter explores the symbolism of the Waxing Crescent Moon, its connection to dinosaur evolution, and the lessons it offers about progress, survival, and resilience.

Dinosaurs' Growth and the Waxing Crescent

The Waxing Crescent phase is about taking initial steps toward a vision or goal. For dinosaurs, this phase is mirrored in their rise during the Triassic Period and their steady expansion into various niches and habitats.

1. **The First Steps After Emergence**:
    - After their initial appearance during the Triassic, early dinosaurs like *Coelophysis* and *Plateosaurus* began to diversify, slowly spreading across continents and experimenting with new ecological roles.
    - This period of growth represents the Waxing Crescent's energy of building momentum—small but significant steps toward broader dominance.

2. **Incremental Adaptations**:
    - The Waxing Crescent reminds us that growth happens gradually, with steady progress toward a greater goal. Dinosaurs exhibited this through the evolution of traits like better locomotion, more efficient metabolism, and social behaviors that enhanced survival.
    - For example, theropods like *Herrerasaurus* refined their hunting strategies, while early herbivores adapted to exploit new plant life, showcasing resilience and adaptability.

3. **Expansion and Exploration**:
    - During the Triassic and Jurassic periods, dinosaurs expanded into diverse environments, from arid deserts to lush forests. This phase of exploration aligns with the Waxing Crescent's symbolism of outward growth and discovery.
    - Their ability to adapt to varying conditions demonstrates the Waxing Crescent's message: progress requires effort, exploration, and the willingness to embrace new opportunities.

Symbolism of Progress and Survival

The Waxing Crescent Moon embodies themes of progress, resilience, and the determination to survive. These themes resonate with the evolutionary strategies that allowed dinosaurs to flourish:

1. **Progress Through Effort**:
   - The Waxing Crescent encourages action and perseverance. Dinosaurs, as early pioneers of the Mesozoic ecosystems, exemplified this through their incremental adaptations and survival strategies.
   - Small evolutionary changes, such as the development of stronger limbs or sharper teeth, contributed to their gradual but unstoppable rise.
2. **Survival in a Competitive World**:
   - The Waxing Crescent is also about resilience and determination. Dinosaurs thrived in a world filled with competition, predation, and environmental challenges. Their survival depended on their ability to innovate and persist.
   - Herbivores developed defensive adaptations like armored plates and herding behaviors, while predators honed their speed and agility, embodying the Waxing Crescent's drive for growth.
3. **Embracing Potential**:
   - The Waxing Crescent reminds us that potential must be nurtured through effort and intention. Dinosaurs' evolutionary journey reflects this principle, as they steadily refined their traits to maximize their success in various niches.

Lessons from Dinosaur Growth

The Waxing Crescent phase offers valuable lessons about growth and survival, drawn from the evolutionary history of dinosaurs:

1. **Take Incremental Steps**:
   - Dinosaurs' rise to dominance was not instantaneous; it was a gradual process of adaptation and experimentation. The Waxing Crescent teaches us to focus on steady progress, knowing that small steps can lead to significant outcomes.
2. **Embrace Resilience**:
   - Dinosaurs faced numerous challenges, from environmental changes to competition with other species. Their survival demonstrates the Waxing Crescent's lesson that resilience and persistence are essential for growth.
3. **Explore Opportunities**:
   - The Waxing Crescent encourages exploration and the willingness to take risks. Dinosaurs' expansion into new environments highlights the importance of embracing opportunities for growth.
4. **Build on Strengths**:
   - Like dinosaurs refining their traits, we can use the Waxing Crescent's energy to build on our strengths and enhance our potential. This phase reminds us that growth is an ongoing process.

The Waxing Crescent Moon in Dinosaur Mythology

In modern interpretations of dinosaur mythology, the Waxing Crescent represents the early stages of their evolutionary journey, marked by progress, innovation, and resilience.

1. **The Pioneer Spirit**:
   - The Waxing Crescent is often associated with pioneering efforts and new beginnings. Dinosaurs, as the dominant species of their era, symbolize the courage and determination required to forge new paths.
2. **Cycles of Growth**:
   - Dinosaur mythology often highlights the cyclical nature of life, with the Waxing Crescent symbolizing the growth phase of their reign. This phase reminds us that progress is part of a larger journey, guided by cosmic rhythms.
3. **Hope and Aspiration**:
   - The Waxing Crescent inspires hope and aspiration, much like the early days of dinosaurs' evolution. Their ability to rise from humble beginnings to dominate the Earth reflects the Waxing Crescent's promise of potential.

Spiritual Lessons from the Waxing Crescent and Dinosaurs

The Waxing Crescent Moon offers spiritual insights that align with the evolutionary journey of dinosaurs. These lessons inspire us to embrace growth, resilience, and the courage to take the first steps toward our goals.

1. **Commit to Growth**:
   - The Waxing Crescent reminds us that growth requires commitment and effort. Dinosaurs' steady rise teaches us to focus on progress, even when the path is uncertain.
2. **Stay Resilient in Challenges**:
   - The Waxing Crescent encourages resilience in the face of obstacles. Dinosaurs adapted to shifting climates, competition, and predation, demonstrating the power of persistence.
3. **Focus on the Journey**:
   - Growth is a journey, not a destination. The Waxing Crescent's energy mirrors the evolutionary journey of dinosaurs, reminding us to celebrate each step forward.
4. **Embrace Change as Opportunity**:
   - The Waxing Crescent teaches us to see change as an opportunity for growth. Dinosaurs' adaptability highlights the importance of remaining open to new possibilities.

Astrological Symbolism of the Waxing Crescent and Dinosaurs

Astrologically, the Waxing Crescent represents growth, effort, and the courage to pursue potential. In the Dinosaur Zodiac, it symbolizes the early stages of dinosaurs' dominance and the evolutionary progress that defined their reign:

1. **Momentum Toward Greatness**:
   - The Waxing Crescent's energy of building momentum aligns with dinosaurs' gradual rise to dominance. Their journey reminds us that progress requires consistent effort.
2. **Resilience and Adaptability**:
   - The Waxing Crescent inspires resilience in the face of challenges. Dinosaurs' ability to adapt to new environments and circumstances embodies this energy.
3. **Exploration and Discovery**:
   - The Waxing Crescent encourages exploration, much like dinosaurs expanding into diverse habitats. This phase reminds us to seek out opportunities for growth and learning.

Practical Applications of the Waxing Crescent's Wisdom

1. **Set Short-Term Goals**:
   ◦ Use the Waxing Crescent's energy to focus on small, achievable goals that build momentum toward larger aspirations. Like dinosaurs refining their traits, progress happens incrementally.
2. **Practice Resilience**:
   ◦ Embrace challenges as opportunities to grow stronger. The Waxing Crescent teaches us to persist, even when progress feels slow.
3. **Celebrate Progress**:
   ◦ Acknowledge and celebrate each step forward. The Waxing Crescent reminds us to appreciate the journey of growth, no matter how small the victories.
4. **Explore New Opportunities**:
   ◦ Use this phase to take calculated risks and explore new possibilities. Like dinosaurs expanding into new habitats, growth often comes from stepping outside your comfort zone.

In the Dinosaur Zodiac, the Waxing Crescent Moon represents the progress, resilience, and survival strategies that defined the early days of dinosaurs' evolution. By connecting with the symbolism of the Waxing Crescent, we can learn to embrace growth, focus on progress, and navigate challenges with determination. Let the story of the Waxing Crescent and dinosaurs inspire you to take bold steps toward your potential, celebrate your journey, and thrive in the face of change.

Chapter 29: The First Quarter Moon and Dinosaur Challenges
Strength and Decision-Making Moments
The First Quarter Moon: A Turning Point

The First Quarter Moon marks a pivotal moment in the lunar cycle, a time of challenge and decision-making. It represents the phase where the initial intentions set during the New Moon, and the early progress made during the Waxing Crescent, are tested. Astrologically, this phase encourages action, strength, and the courage to overcome obstacles. It is a time for decisive choices, where the effort to push forward meets resistance, demanding resilience and clarity of purpose.

In the story of dinosaurs, the First Quarter Moon symbolizes the challenges they faced during their rise and dominance, as well as their ability to adapt, innovate, and persevere. From environmental shifts to predatory dynamics, dinosaurs navigated countless decision-making moments that defined their evolutionary success. This chapter delves into the connection between the First Quarter Moon and the challenges faced by dinosaurs, offering insights into their strength, adaptability, and the lessons we can draw from their journey.

Dinosaur Challenges and Turning Points

Dinosaurs thrived for over 160 million years, but their dominance was far from guaranteed. Their journey was marked by challenges that tested their resilience and required crucial adaptations. These turning points mirror the energy of the First Quarter Moon, where strength and decision-making are paramount.

1. **Environmental Shifts**:
   - **Climate Changes**:
     - Throughout the Mesozoic Era, dinosaurs faced significant climate fluctuations, from the arid conditions of the Triassic to the lush forests of the Jurassic and the more dynamic weather patterns of the Cretaceous. These shifts tested their adaptability, requiring them to evolve or perish.
     - Dinosaurs like *Stegosaurus* developed thermoregulatory adaptations, while sauropods like *Brachiosaurus* thrived in diverse environments, reflecting the First Quarter Moon's challenge to adapt or falter.
   - **Geological Transformations**:
     - The breakup of the supercontinent Pangaea created new ecosystems and isolated habitats. This geological upheaval forced dinosaurs to migrate, adapt, and compete in unfamiliar territories.
     - Herbivores like *Triceratops* adapted to evolving vegetation patterns, while predators like *Allosaurus* expanded their ranges, illustrating strength in navigating change.
2. **Predator-Prey Dynamics**:
   - The balance between predators and prey was a constant test of survival. Carnivorous dinosaurs like *Tyrannosaurus rex* had to develop advanced hunting strategies, while herbivores like *Ankylosaurus* evolved defensive mechanisms to withstand attacks.
   - These interactions mirror the First Quarter Moon's theme of confrontation, where success often depends on quick thinking and decisive action.
3. **Competition Within Species**:
   - Dinosaurs also faced competition within their own groups, particularly for resources, territory, and mates. Such rivalries often led to significant evolutionary advancements, as the fittest individuals passed on their traits.
   - The First Quarter Moon reflects these moments of tension and decision-making, where choices determine future success.
4. **Mass Extinction Events**:
   - Smaller extinction events during the Mesozoic Era, such as the Triassic-Jurassic extinction, created periods of upheaval that forced dinosaurs to adapt or risk extinction.

These moments of crisis align with the First Quarter Moon's energy of resilience and the need to push through adversity.

Decision-Making in the Prehistoric World

The First Quarter Moon emphasizes the importance of decisive action, a theme echoed in the behaviors and adaptations of dinosaurs. Their ability to make survival-driven decisions often determined the course of their evolution.

1. **Adapting to Predators**:
   - Herbivorous dinosaurs made crucial decisions about when to flee, fight, or band together. Herding behaviors in species like *Hadrosaurus* and *Iguanodon* reflect their strategic responses to predation.
   - Defensive adaptations, such as the tail spikes of *Stegosaurus* or the armored plates of *Ankylosaurus*, were evolutionary decisions that enhanced survival.
2. **Resource Allocation**:
   - Dinosaurs had to make decisions about how to allocate their energy and resources, particularly during periods of scarcity. This is evident in the migratory behaviors of some species, as they sought new food sources and water during droughts.
   - The First Quarter Moon's lesson of assessing priorities is mirrored in these survival strategies.
3. **Reproductive Choices**:
   - Parental care, seen in species like *Maiasaura*, represents a decision to invest energy in protecting and nurturing offspring, increasing the chances of survival for the next generation.
   - These decisions highlight the balance between immediate survival and long-term success, a key theme of the First Quarter Moon.

Strength and Resilience in Dinosaur Evolution

The First Quarter Moon teaches us to harness strength and resilience in the face of challenges. Dinosaurs exemplified these qualities through their ability to overcome adversity and thrive in dynamic environments.

1. **Physical Strength:**
   - Dinosaurs like *Tyrannosaurus rex* and *Spinosaurus* relied on their physical power to dominate their ecosystems. Their strength allowed them to adapt to the challenges of hunting, competition, and environmental changes.
   - This mirrors the First Quarter Moon's call for physical and emotional strength in navigating life's obstacles.
2. **Mental Resilience:**
   - Behavioral adaptations, such as the pack-hunting strategies of raptors or the nesting behaviors of *Maiasaura*, demonstrate the mental resilience required to survive in challenging environments.
   - The First Quarter Moon encourages us to develop similar resilience, using intelligence and adaptability to overcome obstacles.
3. **Collaborative Efforts:**
   - Dinosaurs often relied on cooperation to survive, whether through herding, nesting, or pack hunting. These collaborative efforts reflect the importance of unity and shared strength during times of difficulty, a key lesson of the First Quarter Moon.

The First Quarter Moon in Dinosaur Mythology

In modern interpretations of dinosaur mythology, the First Quarter Moon symbolizes the challenges that shaped their legacy and the strength they demonstrated in overcoming them.

1. **The Warrior Spirit:**
   - The First Quarter Moon is often associated with the warrior archetype, representing courage and determination. Dinosaurs, as apex creatures, embody this spirit through their dominance and survival strategies.
2. **Moments of Transformation:**
   - The First Quarter Moon's theme of decision-making aligns with key evolutionary moments in dinosaur history, such as the development of feathers in theropods or the emergence of massive sauropods. These transformative choices define their mythology as creatures of strength and innovation.
3. **Lessons in Resilience:**
   - Dinosaur mythology often emphasizes their resilience in the face of extinction events and environmental changes. The First Quarter Moon symbolizes their ability to push through adversity and thrive.

Spiritual Lessons from the First Quarter Moon and Dinosaurs

The First Quarter Moon offers profound spiritual lessons about strength, resilience, and the importance of decisive action, inspired by the challenges faced by dinosaurs.

1. **Face Challenges with Courage**:
    - Like dinosaurs navigating a competitive and dynamic world, the First Quarter Moon encourages us to confront challenges with determination and bravery.
2. **Make Decisive Choices**:
    - The First Quarter Moon reminds us that progress often requires clear, decisive action. Dinosaurs' survival depended on their ability to adapt and respond to changing circumstances.
3. **Harness Strength and Resilience**:
    - Strength, whether physical, mental, or emotional, is essential for overcoming obstacles. The First Quarter Moon teaches us to draw on our inner resources and persevere.
4. **Collaborate for Success**:
    - Just as dinosaurs relied on herding and pack behaviors, the First Quarter Moon emphasizes the power of collaboration and shared strength in navigating challenges.

Astrological Symbolism of the First Quarter Moon and Dinosaurs

Astrologically, the First Quarter Moon represents action, decision-making, and resilience. In the Dinosaur Zodiac, it symbolizes the challenges that shaped their evolution and the strength they demonstrated in overcoming adversity:

1. **Turning Points and Growth**:
    - The First Quarter Moon reflects the critical moments in dinosaur evolution where resilience and adaptability determined their success.
2. **Strength Through Challenge**:
    - This phase emphasizes the importance of strength in navigating obstacles, mirroring the physical and mental resilience of dinosaurs.
3. **Decisive Action**:
    - The First Quarter Moon teaches us to make decisive choices, much like the survival strategies of dinosaurs in competitive environments.

Practical Applications of the First Quarter Moon's Wisdom

1. **Take Decisive Action**:
    - Use the First Quarter Moon's energy to make clear, intentional choices that propel you forward. Reflect on how dinosaurs adapted to challenges and applied similar strategies in your life.
2. **Embrace Resilience**:
    - Develop mental and emotional resilience to navigate obstacles. The First Quarter Moon reminds us that strength comes from perseverance.
3. **Collaborate for Success**:
    - Seek support and collaboration during challenging times. Just as dinosaurs relied on herds or packs, the First Quarter Moon encourages shared strength.
4. **Focus on Progress**:
    - Recognize that challenges are opportunities for growth. Use the First Quarter Moon's energy to push through resistance and stay focused on your goals.

In the Dinosaur Zodiac, the First Quarter Moon represents the strength, decision-making, and resilience that defined dinosaurs' journey through evolution. By connecting with the symbolism of the First Quarter Moon, we can learn to face challenges with courage, make decisive choices, and harness our inner strength. Let the story of the First Quarter Moon and dinosaurs inspire you to overcome obstacles, embrace resilience, and thrive in the face of adversity.

Chapter 30: The Waxing Gibbous Moon and Preparation
Refinement and Adaptation Strategies
The Waxing Gibbous Moon: A Time for Preparation

The Waxing Gibbous Moon is a phase of refinement, growth, and preparation. It follows the challenges of the First Quarter Moon, offering an opportunity to evaluate progress, make adjustments, and fine-tune efforts before the culmination of the Full Moon. This phase symbolizes the importance of adaptability and strategic planning to achieve success.

For dinosaurs, the Waxing Gibbous Moon mirrors their ability to refine survival strategies and adapt to dynamic ecosystems. As they approached the peak of their dominance during the Jurassic and Cretaceous periods, dinosaurs optimized their physical traits, behaviors, and ecological roles. This chapter explores how the Waxing Gibbous Moon's themes of refinement and preparation align with the evolutionary strategies of dinosaurs, providing insights into their adaptability and the lessons we can apply to our own lives.

Dinosaur Adaptation Strategies

Dinosaurs were masters of adaptation, using refined strategies to thrive in diverse environments and overcome challenges. These adaptations align with the Waxing Gibbous Moon's energy of preparation and optimization.

1. **Physical Refinements**:
   - Dinosaurs evolved a wide range of physical traits that enhanced their survival and ecological success:
     - **Efficient Locomotion**: Theropods like *Velociraptor* developed powerful legs and claws for speed and precision in hunting.
     - **Defensive Innovations**: Herbivores like *Stegosaurus* evolved tail spikes and protective plates, refining their ability to ward off predators.
     - **Size and Strength**: Sauropods like *Brachiosaurus* grew to enormous sizes, leveraging their scale to deter predators and access high vegetation.
   - These traits were not immediate; they were honed over millions of years, reflecting the Waxing Gibbous Moon's message of refinement through time.

2. **Behavioral Adaptations**:
   - Beyond physical traits, dinosaurs refined their behaviors to increase their chances of survival:
     - **Herding and Social Structures**: Dinosaurs like *Triceratops* formed herds, creating safety in numbers and coordinated defense strategies.
     - **Parental Care**: Species such as *Maiasaura* demonstrated nurturing behaviors, protecting and feeding their young, ensuring the continuation of their species.
     - **Hunting Strategies**: Predators like *Allosaurus* adapted to hunting in packs or targeting weak or isolated prey, optimizing their efforts for success.

3. **Ecological Niche Optimization**:
   - Dinosaurs diversified into highly specialized roles within ecosystems, reducing competition and ensuring mutual survival:
     - **Herbivores** refined their diets to include specific types of vegetation, from low-lying ferns to the tops of trees.
     - **Carnivores** targeted prey based on size, behavior, and availability, maximizing their efficiency in hunting.
   - This specialization reflects the Waxing Gibbous Moon's theme of fine-tuning and preparation for peak performance.

Refinement Before the Peak

The Waxing Gibbous Moon encourages reflection and refinement to ensure success during the Full Moon phase. Dinosaurs embodied this principle as they prepared for the challenges and opportunities of their environments.

1. **Adapting to Environmental Changes**:
   - Dinosaurs faced significant environmental shifts, including volcanic activity, climate changes, and the breakup of Pangaea. Their ability to adapt to these changes was critical to their survival:
     - **Thermoregulation**: Dinosaurs like *Stegosaurus* may have used their plates for thermoregulation, adjusting to temperature fluctuations.
     - **Migration**: Some dinosaurs migrated seasonally, refining their movement patterns to access resources and avoid harsh climates.
2. **Improving Predatory and Defensive Strategies**:
   - The constant evolutionary arms race between predators and prey led to the refinement of strategies on both sides:
     - Predators developed sharper teeth, stronger jaws, and better hunting tactics.
     - Prey evolved camouflage, tougher armor, and cooperative behaviors.
   - These adaptations mirror the Waxing Gibbous Moon's message of continuous improvement before critical moments.
3. **Balancing Growth and Efficiency**:
   - Dinosaurs optimized their energy use, balancing growth, reproduction, and survival. For example:
     - Large herbivores like *Diplodocus* developed efficient digestive systems to extract maximum nutrients from tough plant material.
     - Small predators like *Compsognathus* relied on speed and agility, conserving energy for quick bursts of action.

Lessons from Dinosaur Preparation

The Waxing Gibbous Moon offers valuable lessons about preparation and refinement, drawn from the adaptive strategies of dinosaurs:

1. **Focus on Incremental Improvement:**
   - Dinosaurs didn't achieve dominance overnight; their success came from gradual, incremental changes. The Waxing Gibbous Moon reminds us that small adjustments lead to big results.
2. **Prepare for Peak Performance:**
   - Just as dinosaurs optimized their traits and behaviors before challenges, we can use the Waxing Gibbous phase to prepare for important milestones or events.
3. **Adapt to Changing Circumstances:**
   - Dinosaurs thrived by adapting to new environments and challenges. The Waxing Gibbous Moon encourages us to remain flexible and adjust our strategies as needed.
4. **Refine Strengths and Address Weaknesses:**
   - Dinosaurs honed their strengths while evolving to overcome vulnerabilities. This phase reminds us to focus on refining what we do well and addressing areas for improvement.

The Waxing Gibbous Moon in Dinosaur Mythology

In modern interpretations of dinosaur mythology, the Waxing Gibbous Moon symbolizes the preparation and refinement that allowed dinosaurs to flourish. It is a phase of hope, growth, and the courage to keep improving.

1. **The Builders of Greatness:**
   - The Waxing Gibbous represents the builders—the species that laid the groundwork for the ecological balance of the Mesozoic Era. Dinosaurs like *Apatosaurus* and *Iguanodon* symbolize this steady progress.
2. **Cycles of Improvement:**
   - Dinosaur mythology often emphasizes their adaptability and gradual refinement. The Waxing Gibbous phase reflects this ongoing journey of growth.
3. **Preparation for Greatness:**
   - The Waxing Gibbous Moon represents the final steps before reaching full potential. Dinosaurs, as symbols of resilience and adaptability, embody this phase of preparation.

Spiritual Lessons from the Waxing Gibbous and Dinosaurs

The Waxing Gibbous Moon offers profound spiritual lessons about growth, preparation, and the importance of continuous refinement, inspired by the adaptability of dinosaurs.

1. **Refine and Optimize:**
   - The Waxing Gibbous teaches us to focus on incremental improvements. Dinosaurs' evolutionary journey reminds us that refinement is key to long-term success.
2. **Prepare for the Future:**
   - This phase encourages thoughtful preparation. Like dinosaurs adapting to environmental changes, we can use this time to plan for future challenges and opportunities.
3. **Balance Growth with Efficiency:**
   - The Waxing Gibbous reminds us to grow strategically, balancing effort and resources. Dinosaurs' efficient energy use offers a model for sustainable progress.
4. **Stay Resilient and Adaptable:**
   - The Waxing Gibbous teaches us to embrace change and remain flexible. Dinosaurs' adaptability highlights the importance of staying open to new possibilities.

Astrological Symbolism of the Waxing Gibbous and Dinosaurs

Astrologically, the Waxing Gibbous Moon represents refinement, preparation, and the final push toward achievement. In the Dinosaur Zodiac, it symbolizes the strategies and adaptations that allowed dinosaurs to thrive:

1. **Optimizing Potential:**
   - The Waxing Gibbous reflects the process of optimizing traits and behaviors for success, much like the evolutionary refinements of dinosaurs.
2. **Resilience Through Preparation:**
   - This phase emphasizes resilience, mirroring dinosaurs' ability to prepare for and navigate challenges.
3. **Growth Toward Fulfillment:**
   - The Waxing Gibbous symbolizes growth toward the Full Moon's culmination, much like dinosaurs' steady rise to ecological dominance.

Practical Applications of the Waxing Gibbous Moon's Wisdom

1. **Evaluate and Adjust**:
   - Use this phase to evaluate your progress and make necessary adjustments. Reflect on how dinosaurs refined their strategies and apply similar practices to your goals.
2. **Focus on Preparation**:
   - Prepare for upcoming challenges or milestones with intention and care. The Waxing Gibbous reminds us that preparation is key to success.
3. **Refine Your Strengths**:
   - Identify your strengths and focus on enhancing them. Use this phase to address weaknesses and improve efficiency.
4. **Embrace Adaptability**:
   - Be open to change and ready to adapt your plans as needed. The Waxing Gibbous teaches us to remain flexible and responsive.

In the Dinosaur Zodiac, the Waxing Gibbous Moon represents the refinement, preparation, and adaptability that defined dinosaurs' evolutionary journey. By connecting with the symbolism of the Waxing Gibbous, we can learn to embrace growth, optimize our strategies, and prepare for success. Let the story of the Waxing Gibbous and dinosaurs inspire you to refine your efforts, adapt to challenges, and move confidently toward your goals.

Chapter 31: The Full Moon and Dinosaur Prosperity
Energy Peaks and Collective Power
The Full Moon: A Symbol of Prosperity and Peak Energy

The Full Moon represents the culmination of the lunar cycle, a moment when the Moon's light fully illuminates the night sky, symbolizing peak energy, completion, and abundance. Astrologically, it is a time of celebration, manifestation, and collective power. It encourages us to reap the rewards of our efforts, enjoy the fruits of our labor, and reflect on the journey that brought us to this point.

For dinosaurs, the Full Moon aligns with the height of their reign during the Jurassic and Cretaceous periods. This era was their peak of prosperity, marked by unparalleled diversity, ecological dominance, and collective balance within the ecosystems they inhabited. The Full Moon represents the collective power of dinosaurs as they thrived across continents, influencing every aspect of life on Earth. This chapter explores the connection between the Full Moon and dinosaur prosperity, examining their energy peaks, collective power, and the lessons we can draw from their reign.

Dinosaur Prosperity During the Jurassic and Cretaceous

The Jurassic and Cretaceous periods were the golden ages of dinosaur life, where these ancient creatures reached their peak in size, diversity, and ecological influence.

1. **Unparalleled Diversity**:
   - The Full Moon's energy of abundance is reflected in the vast diversity of dinosaurs during these periods:
     - **Herbivores**: Massive sauropods like *Diplodocus* and *Brachiosaurus* roamed in herds, shaping ecosystems by consuming vast amounts of vegetation.
     - **Carnivores**: Apex predators like *Tyrannosaurus rex* and *Allosaurus* thrived, balancing the food chain with their predatory roles.
     - **Smaller Species**: Agile dinosaurs like *Velociraptor* and *Protoceratops* filled critical ecological niches, contributing to the overall stability of their environments.
   - This explosion of diversity mirrors the Full Moon's symbolism of collective energy and abundance.

2. **Ecological Balance**:
   - Dinosaurs' prosperity was marked by a delicate balance within ecosystems:
     - Predators and prey coexisted in dynamic relationships, maintaining the health and stability of their habitats.
     - Plant-eating dinosaurs helped regulate vegetation growth, while carnivores prevented overpopulation.
   - This balance reflects the Full Moon's theme of harmony and interconnectedness.

3. **Global Dominance**:
   - Dinosaurs were not confined to one region; they thrived on every continent, from lush tropical forests to arid deserts.

- Their adaptability and resilience allowed them to dominate diverse ecosystems, showcasing the peak energy and expansive reach symbolized by the Full Moon.

Collective Power in Dinosaur Communities

The Full Moon emphasizes the power of collective energy and collaboration. Dinosaurs demonstrated this through their social behaviors, herd dynamics, and ecological influence.

1. **Herding and Cooperation**:
   - Many herbivorous dinosaurs, such as *Triceratops* and *Iguanodon*, lived in herds, using collective power to protect against predators and ensure survival.
   - Herd dynamics created safety in numbers, allowing these dinosaurs to thrive even in predator-rich environments.
   - This collective strength reflects the Full Moon's energy of unity and shared power.
2. **Parental Care and Social Bonds**:
   - Species like *Maiasaura* exhibited nurturing behaviors, protecting and raising their young in groups.
   - These social bonds enhanced the survival of offspring and strengthened the cohesion of dinosaur communities, mirroring the Full Moon's emphasis on collective prosperity.
3. **Ecosystem Engineers**:
   - Dinosaurs were instrumental in shaping their environments:
     - Sauropods cleared forests and dispersed seeds through their feeding habits, promoting plant diversity.
     - Predators like *Spinosaurus* maintained balance in aquatic ecosystems by regulating fish populations.
   - Their influence highlights the Full Moon's theme of abundance and interconnectedness, where every part of the whole contributes to its prosperity.

Energy Peaks in Dinosaur Evolution

The Full Moon represents the peak of energy and achievement, a time to celebrate milestones and reflect on the journey. Dinosaurs' golden age during the Jurassic and Cretaceous embodies this energy peak.

1. **Physical Magnificence**:
   - Dinosaurs reached extraordinary sizes and physical adaptations during this period:
     - *Argentinosaurus*, one of the largest known dinosaurs, exemplifies the sheer scale of their evolutionary achievements.
     - Predators like *Tyrannosaurus rex* developed powerful jaws and keen senses, representing the peak of predatory evolution.
   - These advancements reflect the Full Moon's energy of maximized potential and achievement.
2. **Evolutionary Innovation**:
   - Dinosaurs continued to innovate during their peak, with theropods developing feathers that would later give rise to birds.
   - Their ability to evolve and refine their traits during their reign mirrors the Full Moon's theme of reaching one's fullest potential.
3. **Global Influence**:
   - Dinosaurs' dominance influenced not only their ecosystems but also the evolutionary paths of other species.
   - Their legacy, preserved in the fossil record, continues to inspire awe and curiosity, embodying the Full Moon's lasting illumination and impact.

The Full Moon in Dinosaur Mythology

In modern interpretations of dinosaur mythology, the Full Moon symbolizes their prosperity, collective power, and peak energy.

1. **The Zenith of Life**:
   - The Full Moon represents the pinnacle of existence, much like the height of dinosaur dominance during the Jurassic and Cretaceous.
   - Dinosaurs' abundance and diversity reflect the Full Moon's energy of celebration and fulfillment.
2. **Unity and Collaboration**:
   - The Full Moon emphasizes collective strength, mirroring the social behaviors and ecosystem roles of dinosaurs.
   - Myths often depict dinosaurs as guardians of balance, embodying the harmony of the Full Moon.
3. **Illumination of Legacy**:
   - Just as the Full Moon lights up the night, dinosaurs' legacy continues to illuminate our understanding of Earth's history and evolution.

◦ Their story serves as a reminder of the interconnectedness of all life.

Spiritual Lessons from the Full Moon and Dinosaurs

The Full Moon offers profound spiritual lessons about prosperity, collective power, and the importance of celebrating achievements, inspired by the reign of dinosaurs.

1. **Celebrate Milestones**:
   ◦ The Full Moon teaches us to acknowledge and celebrate our successes. Dinosaurs' peak prosperity reminds us to reflect on our achievements and honor the journey that brought us here.
2. **Embrace Collective Power**:
   ◦ Just as dinosaurs thrived through collaboration and balance, the Full Moon encourages us to harness collective energy and work together toward shared goals.
3. **Maximize Potential**:
   ◦ The Full Moon symbolizes reaching one's fullest potential. Dinosaurs' physical and ecological achievements inspire us to strive for greatness and embrace our strengths.
4. **Recognize Interconnectedness**:
   ◦ The Full Moon emphasizes harmony and unity. Dinosaurs' role in shaping ecosystems reminds us of the interconnectedness of all life and the importance of contributing to the greater good.

Astrological Symbolism of the Full Moon and Dinosaurs

Astrologically, the Full Moon represents culmination, abundance, and collective energy. In the Dinosaur Zodiac, it symbolizes the prosperity and peak energy of their reign:

1. **Culmination of Efforts**:
   ◦ The Full Moon reflects the culmination of the evolutionary journey that brought dinosaurs to their peak. Their success demonstrates the rewards of perseverance and growth.
2. **Energy Peaks**:
   ◦ The Full Moon's peak energy aligns with the height of dinosaur diversity and dominance, symbolizing achievement and fulfillment.
3. **Collective Prosperity**:
   ◦ The Full Moon emphasizes unity and shared power, mirroring dinosaurs' role as both individuals and contributors to thriving ecosystems.

Practical Applications of the Full Moon's Wisdom

1. **Celebrate Achievements**:
   - Use the Full Moon as an opportunity to reflect on your accomplishments and express gratitude for your progress. Let dinosaurs' prosperity inspire you to honor your successes.
2. **Harness Collective Energy**:
   - Collaborate with others to amplify your efforts and achieve shared goals. The Full Moon reminds us that collective power leads to greater prosperity.
3. **Maximize Your Potential**:
   - Focus on reaching your peak potential during this phase. Draw inspiration from dinosaurs' evolutionary achievements to strive for your best.
4. **Reflect on Interconnectedness**:
   - Take time to appreciate the interconnectedness of your relationships, community, and environment. The Full Moon encourages harmony and unity.

In the Dinosaur Zodiac, the Full Moon represents the prosperity, energy peaks, and collective power that defined the golden age of dinosaurs. By connecting with the symbolism of the Full Moon, we can learn to celebrate achievements, embrace unity, and maximize our potential. Let the story of the Full Moon and dinosaurs inspire you to thrive, honor your journey, and contribute to the greater balance of life.

Chapter 32: The Waning Gibbous Moon and Reflection
Wisdom and Legacy of the Prehistoric Era
The Waning Gibbous Moon: A Time for Reflection

The Waning Gibbous Moon follows the Full Moon, marking the transition from the peak of energy to a quieter phase of reflection and understanding. It symbolizes gratitude for achievements, the sharing of wisdom, and the consideration of legacy. Astrologically, this phase encourages introspection, learning from experiences, and refining one's understanding of the journey so far.

For dinosaurs, the Waning Gibbous Moon reflects the legacy they left behind after their golden age of prosperity. Their extinction does not symbolize failure but instead serves as a poignant reminder of impermanence and the cycles of life. Dinosaurs' story continues to teach us about resilience, adaptation, and the interconnectedness of all life. This chapter explores the connection between the Waning Gibbous Moon and the reflection on dinosaurs' wisdom and legacy, offering insights into their enduring influence on Earth's history and evolution.

Dinosaurs' Legacy: The Wisdom of the Prehistoric Era

Dinosaurs dominated Earth for over 160 million years, and their reign provides profound lessons about adaptation, survival, and ecological balance. Their legacy, preserved in fossils and ecosystems, offers enduring wisdom.

1. **The Gift of Resilience**:
   - Dinosaurs thrived in diverse environments, adapting to challenges ranging from climate shifts to ecological competition:
     - *Theropods* evolved into birds, demonstrating the power of transformation and survival.
     - Herbivores like *Diplodocus* and *Triceratops* maintained balance in their ecosystems through their roles as grazers and seed dispersers.
   - Their resilience highlights the importance of flexibility and innovation, reflecting the Waning Gibbous Moon's message of learning from the past.
2. **Cycles of Dominance and Transition**:
   - The extinction of dinosaurs, brought about by the asteroid impact and subsequent environmental changes, marked the end of their era but paved the way for mammals to rise.
   - This transition illustrates the cyclical nature of life, a key theme of the Waning Gibbous Moon, which emphasizes endings as precursors to new beginnings.
3. **The Power of Ecosystem Engineering**:
   - Dinosaurs were instrumental in shaping prehistoric ecosystems:
     - Sauropods cleared forests, promoting biodiversity.
     - Predators like *Allosaurus* controlled herbivore populations, maintaining ecological balance.

- Their role as ecosystem engineers reflects the interconnectedness of all life and the importance of leaving a positive impact, a lesson echoed by the Waning Gibbous Moon.

Reflection on Dinosaur Wisdom

The Waning Gibbous Moon encourages us to reflect on the lessons learned and share them with others. Dinosaurs' story offers timeless wisdom that continues to inspire curiosity and learning.

1. **Adaptation is Key to Survival**:
   - Dinosaurs' ability to adapt to changing environments was central to their success:
     - Feathered theropods adapted to flight, giving rise to modern birds.
     - Semi-aquatic dinosaurs like *Spinosaurus* thrived in diverse habitats, showcasing the importance of versatility.
   - This adaptability reminds us to remain open to change and to evolve with our circumstances.
2. **Balance and Interdependence**:
   - The delicate balance maintained by dinosaurs within their ecosystems highlights the importance of collaboration and interdependence:
     - Predators and prey coexisted in dynamic relationships that ensured the health of their habitats.
     - Herbivores' feeding behaviors promoted plant diversity and ecosystem resilience.
   - The Waning Gibbous Moon invites us to reflect on our own roles within our communities and the impact we have on others.
3. **Legacy Through Transformation**:
   - Dinosaurs' evolutionary journey, culminating in the rise of birds, demonstrates the enduring power of transformation and legacy.
   - Their story encourages us to consider how our actions today shape the future, a central theme of the Waning Gibbous Moon.

Lessons from the Waning Gibbous Moon and Dinosaurs

The Waning Gibbous Moon offers profound lessons about reflection, wisdom, and legacy, inspired by the prehistoric era.

1. **Learn from the Past**:
    ◦ The Waning Gibbous Moon encourages introspection and learning from experiences. Dinosaurs' story reminds us to draw wisdom from history and use it to guide future decisions.
2. **Honor the Cycle of Life**:
    ◦ The Waning Gibbous Moon symbolizes the cycles of growth, culmination, and transition. Dinosaurs' extinction and the rise of new species highlight the beauty of these natural cycles.
3. **Share Knowledge and Insights**:
    ◦ This phase is a time to share wisdom with others. Dinosaurs' legacy, preserved through fossils and research, continues to educate and inspire, emphasizing the importance of passing on knowledge.
4. **Consider Your Legacy**:
    ◦ The Waning Gibbous Moon invites us to reflect on the impact we leave behind. Dinosaurs' enduring influence on Earth's history encourages us to consider how our actions shape the future.

The Waning Gibbous Moon in Dinosaur Mythology

In modern interpretations of dinosaur mythology, the Waning Gibbous Moon represents reflection on their wisdom and the enduring impact of their reign.

1. **Guardians of Earth's History**:
    ◦ The Waning Gibbous Moon emphasizes dinosaurs' role as custodians of Earth's ancient story, preserving lessons about resilience, balance, and transformation.
2. **Symbols of Endurance**:
    ◦ Dinosaurs, despite their extinction, remain symbols of endurance and adaptability. The Waning Gibbous Moon reflects their ability to leave a lasting legacy.
3. **Teachers of Evolutionary Wisdom**:
    ◦ Myths often portray dinosaurs as wise beings whose story holds the secrets of Earth's past. This aligns with the Waning Gibbous Moon's message of learning and sharing wisdom.

Astrological Symbolism of the Waning Gibbous and Dinosaurs

Astrologically, the Waning Gibbous Moon represents reflection, gratitude, and the sharing of knowledge. In the Dinosaur Zodiac, it symbolizes the wisdom and legacy of the prehistoric era:

1. **Reflection on Achievements**:
   - The Waning Gibbous Moon reflects on the prosperity and accomplishments of dinosaurs during their reign, encouraging us to appreciate their contributions to Earth's history.
2. **Gratitude for Lessons Learned**:
   - This phase emphasizes gratitude for the lessons and wisdom gained. Dinosaurs' story teaches us to value resilience, adaptability, and balance.
3. **Sharing Knowledge and Impact**:
   - The Waning Gibbous Moon encourages the sharing of knowledge. Dinosaurs' legacy, preserved through fossils and scientific research, continues to enlighten and inspire.

Practical Applications of the Waning Gibbous Moon's Wisdom

1. **Reflect on Your Journey**:
   - Use this phase to reflect on your achievements, challenges, and lessons learned. Consider how dinosaurs' story of resilience and adaptation can inspire your own growth.
2. **Share Wisdom with Others**:
   - Take the opportunity to share your knowledge and experiences with those around you. The Waning Gibbous Moon reminds us of the importance of passing on wisdom.
3. **Express Gratitude**:
   - Show appreciation for the journey and the milestones you've reached. The Waning Gibbous Moon encourages gratitude for the efforts that brought you to this point.
4. **Consider Your Legacy**:
   - Reflect on the impact you want to leave behind. Dinosaurs' lasting influence reminds us to think about how our actions shape the world for future generations.

In the Dinosaur Zodiac, the Waning Gibbous Moon represents the wisdom, reflection, and legacy of the prehistoric era. By connecting with the symbolism of the Waning Gibbous, we can learn to honor the past, embrace gratitude, and consider our role in shaping the future. Let the story of the Waning Gibbous and dinosaurs inspire you to reflect on your journey, share your wisdom, and leave a lasting legacy.

Chapter 33: The Last Quarter Moon and Letting Go
Release and Transformation
The Last Quarter Moon: A Time for Release

The Last Quarter Moon is a phase of transition, marking the waning of the lunar cycle. It is a time for letting go, reflection, and preparation for the new cycle ahead. This phase symbolizes release—of old habits, unproductive patterns, or unfinished business—and transformation, as we shed what no longer serves us to create space for renewal. Astrologically, it is a time of surrender, acceptance, and trust in the cycles of life.

For dinosaurs, the Last Quarter Moon aligns with the profound transformation that occurred at the end of their reign. Their extinction, caused by the asteroid impact approximately 66 million years ago, was a dramatic and unavoidable transition. Yet, it also paved the way for new life to flourish, including mammals and eventually humans. The Last Quarter Moon embodies the lessons of release and transformation that dinosaurs' story offers: the inevitability of change, the beauty of letting go, and the potential for renewal.

The Extinction of Dinosaurs: A Lesson in Letting Go

The end of the Cretaceous Period was marked by one of the most significant extinction events in Earth's history. While it resulted in the loss of most dinosaur species, it also set the stage for a new era of life. This transition mirrors the themes of the Last Quarter Moon, emphasizing release and transformation.

1. **The Asteroid Impact and Its Effects**:
   - A 10-kilometer-wide asteroid struck near the Yucatán Peninsula, triggering catastrophic events:
     - **Immediate Destruction**: The impact caused massive wildfires, tsunamis, and an "impact winter" as dust and debris blocked sunlight.
     - **Long-Term Consequences**: The cooling and loss of sunlight disrupted ecosystems, leading to the collapse of food chains.
   - This event symbolizes the sudden and transformative power of the Last Quarter Moon, which often requires dramatic change for renewal.
2. **The End of an Era**:
   - Dinosaurs had dominated Earth for over 160 million years. Their extinction marked the end of their reign but also highlighted the cyclical nature of life.
   - The Last Quarter Moon teaches us to accept endings as a natural part of existence, paving the way for new beginnings.
3. **Seeds of Transformation**:
   - While the asteroid impact brought destruction, it also created opportunities for mammals and other species to rise.

- Dinosaurs' extinction reminds us that release is often a prerequisite for transformation and growth.

The Role of Transformation in the Last Quarter Moon

The Last Quarter Moon emphasizes the importance of transformation, encouraging us to embrace change and trust in the process of renewal. Dinosaurs' story provides powerful examples of this principle:

1. **The Evolutionary Legacy of Dinosaurs**:
   - While most dinosaurs went extinct, their evolutionary legacy continues through birds, which are their modern descendants.
   - This transformation illustrates the Last Quarter Moon's lesson that even in endings, there is continuity and potential for growth.
2. **The Adaptability of Life**:
   - After the extinction event, Earth's ecosystems gradually recovered, leading to the rise of mammals, flowering plants, and new biodiversity.
   - The Last Quarter Moon reminds us that life is resilient and adaptable, capable of thriving even after significant disruption.
3. **The Gift of Change**:
   - Dinosaurs' extinction created a world where new species could evolve and flourish.
   - This transition highlights the Last Quarter Moon's message that letting go of the old can make space for the new.

Lessons from the Last Quarter Moon and Dinosaurs

The Last Quarter Moon offers profound lessons about release, transformation, and the cycles of life, inspired by the story of dinosaurs.

1. **Embrace Endings as Beginnings**:
   - The Last Quarter Moon teaches us that endings are not final but are part of a larger cycle of renewal. Dinosaurs' extinction reminds us that transformation often begins with letting go.
2. **Trust the Process of Change**:
   - Letting go can be challenging, but the Last Quarter Moon encourages us to trust in the natural cycles of life. Dinosaurs' story demonstrates the resilience and adaptability of life, even in the face of profound change.
3. **Release What No Longer Serves You**:
   - Just as ecosystems adapted to the absence of dinosaurs, we can release old patterns or habits that no longer serve us. The Last Quarter Moon invites us to reflect on what we need to let go of to grow.
4. **Honor the Cycles of Life**:

- The Last Quarter Moon reminds us to honor the cycles of life and death, growth and decay. Dinosaurs' legacy highlights the beauty of these cycles and the potential they hold for transformation.

The Last Quarter Moon in Dinosaur Mythology

In modern interpretations of dinosaur mythology, the Last Quarter Moon represents their extinction and the transformation that followed. It is a phase of surrender, acceptance, and renewal.

1. **Symbols of Transition**:
   - The Last Quarter Moon emphasizes the transition from one era to another, much like the extinction of dinosaurs marked the shift to the age of mammals.
2. **Guardians of Change**:
   - Dinosaurs are often seen as guardians of Earth's history, embodying the lessons of impermanence and transformation.
   - Myths often portray them as symbols of resilience and continuity, reminding us of the enduring cycles of life.
3. **Lessons in Renewal**:
   - The Last Quarter Moon highlights the potential for renewal that comes from letting go. Dinosaurs' extinction paved the way for the evolution of new species, emphasizing the creative power of transformation.

Astrological Symbolism of the Last Quarter Moon and Dinosaurs

Astrologically, the Last Quarter Moon represents release, reflection, and transformation. In the Dinosaur Zodiac, it symbolizes the profound changes brought about by their extinction and the lessons we can draw from their story:

1. **The Necessity of Letting Go**:
   - The Last Quarter Moon reminds us that holding onto the past can hinder growth. Dinosaurs' extinction teaches us to release what no longer serves us to create space for renewal.
2. **Transformation Through Change**:
   - This phase emphasizes the transformative power of change. Dinosaurs' story highlights the resilience of life and its ability to adapt and thrive.
3. **Cycles of Renewal**:
   - The Last Quarter Moon symbolizes the cycles of life, death, and rebirth. Dinosaurs' extinction and the rise of new species reflect these natural rhythms.

Practical Applications of the Last Quarter Moon's Wisdom

1. **Let Go of the Past**:
   - Use this phase to release old habits, patterns, or relationships that no longer serve you. Reflect on what you can let go of to create space for new opportunities.
2. **Embrace Transformation**:
   - View change as an opportunity for growth and renewal. Let dinosaurs' story inspire you to see transformation as a natural and necessary part of life.
3. **Reflect on Your Journey**:
   - Take time to reflect on your experiences and the lessons they've taught you. The Last Quarter Moon encourages introspection and understanding.
4. **Prepare for Renewal**:
   - Use this phase to prepare for the new cycle ahead. Like ecosystems recovering after dinosaurs' extinction, focus on building a foundation for growth and success.

In the Dinosaur Zodiac, the Last Quarter Moon represents the release, transformation, and renewal that defined the end of their era. By connecting with the symbolism of the Last Quarter Moon, we can learn to embrace change, let go of the past, and trust in the cycles of life. Let the story of the Last Quarter Moon and dinosaurs inspire you to release what no longer serves you, honor transformation, and prepare for new beginnings.

Chapter 34: The Waning Crescent Moon and Rest
Healing and the Cycle's End
The Waning Crescent Moon: A Time for Rest and Renewal

The Waning Crescent Moon, the final phase of the lunar cycle, symbolizes the quieting of energy and the preparation for renewal. It is a time for introspection, healing, and surrendering to the natural cycles of life. Often called the "Balsamic Moon," this phase encourages rest, letting go of lingering burdens, and embracing stillness before the next New Moon begins a new journey.

For dinosaurs, the Waning Crescent Moon metaphorically represents the aftermath of their extinction—a period of healing and transformation for Earth as it began to recover from the catastrophic events of the asteroid impact. This phase also aligns with the long arc of Earth's history, where the lessons and legacies of dinosaurs became part of the planet's evolutionary memory. In this chapter, we explore the symbolism of the Waning Crescent Moon, the healing of Earth after the dinosaurs' reign, and the lessons of rest and reflection that their story offers.

The End of an Era and the Healing of Earth

The extinction of dinosaurs marked not just an end, but also a period of healing and renewal for the planet. The destruction caused by the asteroid impact left Earth scarred, but over time, new life emerged, and ecosystems began to recover. This mirrors the Waning Crescent Moon's themes of rest and preparation for rebirth.

1. **The Aftermath of Extinction**:
     ◦ The asteroid impact that ended the Cretaceous Period caused widespread devastation:
         ▪ **Global Cooling**: Dust and debris blocked sunlight, leading to a "nuclear winter" that disrupted photosynthesis and collapsed ecosystems.
         ▪ **Loss of Biodiversity**: Entire species vanished, including nearly all non-avian dinosaurs, leaving behind empty ecological niches.
     ◦ This destruction parallels the Waning Crescent Moon's quiet and introspective energy, where the focus shifts from action to rest and recovery.
2. **Earth's Healing Process**:
     ◦ Over millions of years, Earth healed and new life began to thrive:
         ▪ Plants regrew, stabilizing the atmosphere and creating habitats for emerging species.
         ▪ Mammals, birds (the descendants of theropod dinosaurs), and flowering plants diversified, forming the foundation of modern ecosystems.
     ◦ The slow but steady renewal reflects the Waning Crescent Moon's message of healing through rest and patience.
3. **The Role of Fossils in Earth's Memory**:
     ◦ Fossils preserved the story of dinosaurs, embedding their legacy into the Earth's history.
     ◦ This preservation mirrors the Waning Crescent Moon's introspective energy, where the focus shifts to reflection and understanding.

Healing Through Rest: Lessons from Dinosaurs

The Waning Crescent Moon emphasizes the importance of rest and renewal, a theme echoed in the planet's recovery after the age of dinosaurs. Their story offers profound lessons about healing and the cycles of life.

1. **The Importance of Rest in Cycles**:
   - Just as Earth needed time to recover after the asteroid impact, the Waning Crescent Moon reminds us that rest is an essential part of any cycle.
   - This phase teaches us to honor moments of stillness and trust that they are necessary for future growth.
2. **Surrendering to Change**:
   - The Waning Crescent encourages us to release control and surrender to the natural flow of life. Dinosaurs' extinction, while devastating, allowed new species to rise and ecosystems to evolve.
   - Letting go, even of dominant structures, creates space for renewal and transformation.
3. **Reflection on Legacies**:
   - The quiet energy of the Waning Crescent Moon invites us to reflect on the legacies left behind. Dinosaurs' story continues to teach us about resilience, adaptation, and the interconnectedness of life.
   - This phase encourages us to consider the impact of our own actions and how they shape the future.

The Waning Crescent Moon in Dinosaur Mythology

In modern interpretations of dinosaur mythology, the Waning Crescent Moon symbolizes the peaceful conclusion of their era and the healing that followed. It is a phase of acceptance, wisdom, and preparation for renewal.

1. **Symbols of Rest and Healing**:
   - The Waning Crescent represents the stillness after the storm, a time to heal and prepare for the next cycle. Dinosaurs' extinction mirrors this energy, marking a transition from dominance to quiet reflection.
2. **Guardians of Earth's Memory**:
   - Dinosaurs are often seen as custodians of Earth's ancient story, embodying the wisdom gained from millions of years of evolution.
   - This aligns with the Waning Crescent's message of honoring the past and integrating its lessons.
3. **The Beauty of Quiet Transitions**:
   - The Waning Crescent emphasizes the quiet beauty of transitions. Dinosaurs' extinction paved the way for new forms of life, demonstrating the grace of letting go.

Spiritual Lessons from the Waning Crescent and Dinosaurs

The Waning Crescent Moon offers spiritual insights about rest, healing, and the preparation for renewal, inspired by the story of dinosaurs and Earth's recovery.

1. **Honor the Need for Rest**:
   ◦ The Waning Crescent teaches us that rest is not a sign of weakness but a necessary part of growth. Earth's recovery after the extinction event demonstrates the power of patience and renewal.
2. **Release What is No Longer Needed**:
   ◦ This phase encourages us to let go of what no longer serves us, just as Earth released old ecosystems to create space for new ones.
   ◦ Dinosaurs' story reminds us that release is a natural and essential part of life's cycles.
3. **Trust in the Cycles of Life**:
   ◦ The Waning Crescent Moon symbolizes trust in the natural rhythms of existence. Dinosaurs' extinction highlights the resilience of life and its ability to adapt and thrive.
4. **Reflect and Prepare for Renewal**:
   ◦ Use this phase to reflect on your journey and prepare for the next cycle. Like Earth after the dinosaurs, moments of quiet can set the stage for profound transformation.

Astrological Symbolism of the Waning Crescent and Dinosaurs

Astrologically, the Waning Crescent Moon represents rest, healing, and the end of a cycle. In the Dinosaur Zodiac, it symbolizes the peaceful transition after their extinction and the lessons of renewal and preparation:

1. **Rest and Healing**:
   ◦ The Waning Crescent emphasizes the need for rest and recovery, mirroring Earth's healing after the asteroid impact.
2. **Acceptance and Letting Go**:
   ◦ This phase encourages acceptance of endings and the release of the past. Dinosaurs' extinction serves as a reminder of the transformative power of letting go.
3. **Preparation for Renewal**:
   ◦ The Waning Crescent invites us to prepare for the next phase of growth. Dinosaurs' story highlights the potential for renewal that follows even the most profound transitions.

Practical Applications of the Waning Crescent Moon's Wisdom

1. **Prioritize Rest and Healing**:
    - Use this phase to rest, recharge, and focus on self-care. Reflect on how Earth's recovery after the dinosaurs mirrors the importance of taking time to heal.
2. **Let Go of the Past**:
    - Release old patterns, habits, or attachments that no longer serve you. The Waning Crescent reminds us that letting go creates space for new beginnings.
3. **Reflect on Your Journey**:
    - Take time to reflect on your experiences and the lessons they've taught you. Consider how dinosaurs' legacy continues to influence the present.
4. **Prepare for Renewal**:
    - Use this phase to prepare for the next cycle of growth and opportunity. Trust that rest and reflection are necessary steps toward transformation.

In the Dinosaur Zodiac, the Waning Crescent Moon represents the healing, rest, and preparation that followed the dinosaurs' extinction. By connecting with the symbolism of the Waning Crescent, we can learn to embrace stillness, release the past, and trust in the cycles of life. Let the story of the Waning Crescent and dinosaurs inspire you to rest, heal, and prepare for the renewal that lies ahead.

Part 5: **Astrological Cycles and Special Events**

Chapter 35: Retrogrades and Dinosaur Survival Instincts
How Retrogrades Align with Adaptability
Retrogrades: Cosmic Calls for Reflection and Adaptation

In astrology, retrogrades occur when a planet appears to move backward in its orbit from the perspective of Earth. These periods are often associated with challenges, delays, and the need for reevaluation. Rather than viewing retrogrades as inherently negative, they can be seen as opportunities to pause, reassess, and adapt. Retrogrades emphasize the importance of internal growth, adaptability, and resilience, urging us to reflect on past actions and prepare for future success.

Dinosaurs, as some of the most adaptable creatures in Earth's history, faced countless metaphorical "retrogrades" throughout their reign. From shifting continents to drastic climate changes, dinosaurs had to continuously adjust their behaviors, habitats, and survival strategies. Their ability to adapt and thrive for over 160 million years showcases their instinctual alignment with the lessons of retrogrades: persistence, flexibility, and reflection.

Retrogrades and the Challenges of Dinosaur Survival

Retrogrades symbolize periods of disruption, where progress may seem stalled, and challenges arise. Dinosaurs encountered these moments in their evolutionary journey, responding with remarkable adaptability.

1. **Environmental Retrogrades: Shifting Continents and Climate Change**
   - **The Breakup of Pangaea**:
     - During the Mesozoic Era, the supercontinent Pangaea fragmented into the continents we recognize today. This tectonic shift drastically altered ecosystems, creating new barriers and opening migration routes.
     - Dinosaurs adapted by expanding into new territories, evolving traits suited to varied climates and environments. Herbivores diversified their diets to match changing vegetation, while predators honed hunting strategies to navigate new terrains.
     - This mirrors the lesson of retrogrades: when forward progress seems disrupted, adaptability is key to survival.
   - **Drastic Climate Events**:
     - Climate fluctuations, including periods of global warming and cooling, forced dinosaurs to adjust. For example, theropods evolved feathers, likely for thermoregulation, as climates cooled during certain periods.
     - These adaptations reflect the importance of resilience during retrogrades, finding innovative solutions to unexpected challenges.

2. **Predator-Prey Dynamics: Survival as a Two-Way Adaptation**
   - Retrogrades often highlight imbalances that require recalibration, much like the dynamic relationship between predators and prey in dinosaur ecosystems:
     - Predators such as *Tyrannosaurus rex* developed keen senses and ambush strategies to counter evolving defensive traits in prey.
     - Herbivores like *Ankylosaurus* responded with physical defenses, including armor and tail clubs, creating an evolutionary "arms race."
   - These interactions demonstrate how challenges can drive innovation, mirroring the reflective and adaptive energy of retrogrades.

3. **Mass Extinction Events: Resetting the Balance**
   - Smaller extinction events during the Mesozoic Era acted as planetary retrogrades, forcing species to reevaluate their ecological roles:
     - Dinosaurs that could adapt to new environments or diets, such as omnivorous theropods, thrived while others perished.
     - These extinction events created opportunities for diversification, aligning with retrogrades' call to pause, reassess, and pivot.

Survival Instincts in a Retrograde Framework

Dinosaurs' survival instincts closely parallel the themes of retrogrades, emphasizing the importance of reflection, adaptability, and strategic action during challenging periods.

1. **Reflection on Behavior**:
    ◦ Retrogrades encourage introspection, much like dinosaurs had to adjust their behaviors to survive environmental or ecological shifts:
        ▪ Migratory species like *Hadrosaurus* likely evaluated seasonal patterns to locate food and water.
        ▪ Pack hunters like *Velociraptor* adapted their strategies based on the behavior of prey, refining techniques for success.
2. **Adaptation to New Challenges**:
    ◦ Retrogrades often bring unforeseen obstacles, requiring flexibility. Dinosaurs demonstrated this through:
        ▪ **Dietary Adaptation**: Herbivores diversified their diets as plant life evolved, consuming everything from ferns to flowering plants.
        ▪ **Physical Adaptations**: Predators like *Spinosaurus* evolved semi-aquatic lifestyles to exploit new food sources in aquatic environments.
    ◦ These adaptations highlight the importance of embracing change and finding creative solutions during retrogrades.
3. **Persistence Through Disruption**:
    ◦ Retrogrades test resilience, much like the challenges dinosaurs faced:
        ▪ Some species, like *Iguanodon*, adapted to changing ecosystems by developing robust limbs for both grazing and defending against predators.
        ▪ The evolution of avian dinosaurs during periods of environmental instability demonstrates persistence and the ability to capitalize on shifting conditions.

Retrogrades as Catalysts for Dinosaur Evolution
Retrogrades often act as catalysts for growth and transformation, much like the challenges that drove dinosaurs' evolutionary success.

1. **Catalyzing Innovation**:
    - Just as retrogrades encourage reevaluation, periods of disruption led to innovative adaptations in dinosaurs:
        - The development of feathers in theropods was not only a response to cooling climates but also a precursor to flight in avian species.
        - The emergence of complex social behaviors, such as herding in *Triceratops*, provided collective protection and resource-sharing.
2. **Creating Opportunities**:
    - Retrogrades often force us to slow down and discover hidden opportunities, much like dinosaurs did during environmental shifts:
        - Carnivorous dinosaurs like *Deinonychus* refined cooperative hunting techniques, turning challenges into advantages.
        - Herbivores exploited niche environments, thriving in areas where competition was minimal.
3. **Fostering Resilience**:
    - Retrogrades strengthen resilience by challenging existing patterns. Dinosaurs' ability to endure millions of years of change demonstrates the power of adaptability and persistence.

Lessons from Retrogrades and Dinosaur Survival Instincts

The alignment between retrogrades and dinosaur survival instincts offers timeless lessons about adaptability, resilience, and the potential for growth during challenging times.

1. **Reflect and Reassess**:
   - Retrogrades teach us to pause and evaluate our actions. Dinosaurs' ability to adapt their behaviors and strategies reflects the importance of reflection during periods of disruption.
2. **Embrace Change as Growth**:
   - Challenges often present opportunities for innovation. Dinosaurs thrived by embracing change, from evolving new physical traits to adapting to shifting environments.
3. **Cultivate Resilience**:
   - Retrogrades remind us to persist through setbacks. Dinosaurs' survival instincts highlight the power of resilience in overcoming obstacles and thriving in uncertainty.
4. **Find Strength in Adaptability**:
   - Flexibility is key to navigating retrogrades. Dinosaurs' ability to adjust to new conditions demonstrates the importance of staying open to change and finding creative solutions.

Retrogrades in Dinosaur Mythology

In modern interpretations of dinosaur mythology, retrogrades symbolize periods of challenge and transformation, highlighting their adaptability and survival instincts.

1. **The Teachers of Resilience**:
   - Dinosaurs are often seen as symbols of resilience, embodying the ability to thrive through disruption and change. Retrogrades reflect this enduring strength.
2. **Navigators of Change**:
   - The challenges dinosaurs faced align with retrogrades' themes of recalibration and transformation. Myths often portray dinosaurs as wise beings, adapting to cosmic cycles and earthly challenges.
3. **Catalysts of Evolution**:
   - Retrogrades emphasize the potential for growth through challenge. Dinosaurs' evolutionary journey serves as a testament to the power of adaptability and persistence.

Astrological Symbolism of Retrogrades and Dinosaurs

Astrologically, retrogrades represent periods of reflection, adaptation, and growth. In the Dinosaur Zodiac, they symbolize the challenges and transformations that shaped dinosaurs' evolutionary success:

1. **Reflection and Reevaluation**:
    - Retrogrades encourage introspection, much like the adaptive behaviors of dinosaurs during periods of disruption.
2. **Adaptability Through Challenges**:
    - This phase highlights the importance of flexibility. Dinosaurs' ability to evolve in response to changing conditions mirrors retrogrades' call for adaptability.
3. **Transformation and Growth**:
    - Retrogrades serve as catalysts for growth, aligning with the transformative power of dinosaurs' survival instincts and evolutionary innovations.

Practical Applications of Retrograde Wisdom

1. **Pause and Reflect**:
    - Use retrograde periods to evaluate your progress and reassess your goals. Reflect on how dinosaurs adapted to their challenges and apply similar strategies to your life.
2. **Embrace Change**:
    - View disruptions as opportunities for growth. Like dinosaurs, find innovative solutions to navigate obstacles and seize new possibilities.
3. **Strengthen Resilience**:
    - Use retrogrades to cultivate resilience. Focus on persistence and adaptability, drawing inspiration from dinosaurs' survival instincts.
4. **Reframe Challenges as Opportunities**:
    - Retrogrades encourage us to see challenges as catalysts for growth. Let dinosaurs' story inspire you to transform setbacks into stepping stones for success.

In the Dinosaur Zodiac, retrogrades represent the adaptability, resilience, and transformative power of dinosaurs' survival instincts. By connecting with the symbolism of retrogrades, we can learn to reflect on challenges, embrace change, and harness the potential for growth. Let the story of retrogrades and dinosaurs inspire you to navigate disruptions with wisdom, adaptability, and strength.

Chapter 36: Solstices and Dinosaur Cycles
Summer and Winter Solstices in Their World
Solstices: Markers of Celestial Cycles

Solstices, the longest and shortest days of the year, are moments when the Sun reaches its highest or lowest point in the sky relative to the equator. These astronomical events, occurring twice a year, mark the changing seasons and have profound implications for life on Earth. In astrology, solstices symbolize transitions, renewal, and the cyclical nature of existence, representing extremes of light and darkness.

For dinosaurs, the solstices were critical markers of ecological and behavioral cycles. From the intense heat of the summer solstice to the challenges of the colder, darker winter solstice, these celestial events influenced everything from migration and feeding patterns to reproduction and survival strategies. This chapter explores how solstices shaped the prehistoric world, their role in dinosaur life cycles, and the lessons we can draw from their enduring influence.

The Summer Solstice: The Apex of Light

The summer solstice, marking the longest day and shortest night of the year, represents the height of solar energy and abundance. During the Mesozoic Era, this period would have been crucial for dinosaurs, particularly in regions with dramatic seasonal changes.

1. **Peak Abundance and Activity**
   - The summer solstice brought extended daylight and warmer temperatures, creating a period of ecological abundance:
     - **Vegetation Growth**: Long days and high solar energy fueled the growth of plants, providing ample food for herbivorous dinosaurs like *Apatosaurus* and *Stegosaurus*.
     - **Predatory Opportunities**: Carnivorous dinosaurs such as *Tyrannosaurus rex* took advantage of the increased prey activity, feeding on herbivores drawn to lush feeding grounds.
2. **Reproductive Cycles**
   - Many dinosaurs likely timed their reproductive cycles to coincide with the summer solstice, ensuring that hatchlings emerged during periods of maximum food availability:
     - Nesting sites discovered in fossil records, such as those of *Maiasaura*, suggest coordinated breeding and nurturing efforts during this season.
     - Warm temperatures and abundant resources increased the survival rate of offspring, highlighting the solstice's role in the continuation of species.
3. **Behavioral Patterns**
   - During the summer solstice, dinosaurs may have displayed increased social and migratory behaviors:
     - Herding species like *Iguanodon* traveled to areas with optimal grazing conditions, forming massive groups to ensure safety and resource access.
     - Predators adapted their hunting strategies to match the changing distribution of prey, demonstrating the dynamic interplay of light, energy, and behavior.

The Winter Solstice: The Depth of Darkness

The winter solstice, marking the shortest day and longest night of the year, represents a time of scarcity, reflection, and survival. For dinosaurs, this period brought significant challenges, particularly in regions with harsh climates or limited resources.

1. **Resource Scarcity**
   - The winter solstice heralded a period of reduced sunlight and colder temperatures, limiting the availability of food:
     - Herbivores like *Triceratops* adapted by foraging for tougher, low-nutrient plants, such as conifers and cycads, which persisted through winter.
     - Carnivores faced greater difficulty locating prey, as many herbivores migrated or entered periods of reduced activity.

2. **Adaptations to Cold Climates**
   - Some dinosaurs developed physical and behavioral adaptations to survive the colder months:
     - Feathered theropods, such as *Velociraptor*, used their plumage for insulation, retaining body heat during frigid nights.
     - Fossil evidence suggests that certain species may have hibernated or entered torpor-like states, conserving energy during periods of extreme cold.

3. **Symbolism of Survival**
   - The winter solstice tested the resilience of dinosaurs, serving as a reminder of the cyclical nature of life:
     - Those that survived the darkness emerged stronger, prepared for the renewal of spring and the abundance of the summer solstice.
     - This period of hardship reflects the solstice's astrological theme of endurance and transformation.

Solstices and Dinosaur Migration

Solstices likely played a significant role in the migratory patterns of dinosaurs, guiding their movements across vast landscapes in search of optimal conditions.

1. **Summer Migration**
   - During the summer solstice, dinosaurs followed the abundance of resources to fertile feeding grounds:
     - Herding dinosaurs like *Hadrosaurus* traveled to regions with dense vegetation and freshwater sources, forming seasonal migration routes.
     - Fossilized trackways reveal evidence of large-scale movements, suggesting coordinated group behaviors tied to solstice-driven cycles.
2. **Winter Retreats**
   - The winter solstice prompted migrations to warmer, more hospitable climates:
     - Dinosaurs living in high-latitude regions, such as *Edmontosaurus*, likely migrated southward during winter months to escape harsh conditions.
     - These movements highlight the adaptability of dinosaurs in responding to the challenges posed by seasonal extremes.

Ecological Impact of Solstices

Solstices shaped not only the behaviors of dinosaurs but also the dynamics of their ecosystems, influencing biodiversity and resource distribution.

1. **Ecosystem Productivity**
   - The summer solstice fueled ecosystem productivity, supporting a wide range of species:
     - Plants flourished under extended daylight, creating habitats and food sources for herbivores and their predators.
     - Wetlands, forests, and riverbanks became hubs of activity, sustaining diverse prehistoric life forms.
2. **Winter Adaptations in Ecosystems**
   - The winter solstice brought dormancy and reduced activity, requiring ecosystems to adapt to lower energy inputs:
     - Deciduous plants shed leaves to conserve resources, while evergreens provided limited sustenance for herbivores.
     - Predator-prey dynamics shifted, with opportunistic scavenging becoming more prevalent among carnivores.

Spiritual Lessons from Solstices and Dinosaurs

The solstices offer profound spiritual lessons about cycles, transitions, and the balance of light and darkness, reflected in the life cycles of dinosaurs.

1. **Embrace Cycles of Light and Darkness**
   - The solstices remind us that life is cyclical, with periods of abundance and scarcity, growth and rest. Dinosaurs' ability to thrive through these cycles teaches us to honor both the highs and lows of our journey.
2. **Adapt to Change**
   - The solstices emphasize the importance of adaptability. Dinosaurs' responses to seasonal changes highlight the resilience needed to navigate life's transitions.
3. **Celebrate Abundance and Persevere Through Hardship**
   - The summer solstice symbolizes celebration and gratitude, while the winter solstice represents resilience and endurance. Dinosaurs' behaviors during these periods inspire us to appreciate moments of prosperity and persevere through challenges.
4. **Balance Growth and Rest**
   - The solstices teach us to balance growth with rest, mirroring the rhythms of nature. Dinosaurs' seasonal behaviors reflect the wisdom of aligning with natural cycles for long-term survival.

Astrological Symbolism of Solstices and Dinosaurs

Astrologically, solstices represent transitions and extremes, offering lessons in balance, adaptability, and the cyclical nature of life. In the Dinosaur Zodiac, they symbolize the rhythms of survival and prosperity:

1. **Summer Solstice: Abundance and Energy**
   - The summer solstice reflects the peak of activity and growth, aligning with dinosaurs' behaviors during periods of abundance.
2. **Winter Solstice: Reflection and Resilience**
   - The winter solstice symbolizes endurance and adaptation, mirroring the strategies dinosaurs used to survive challenging conditions.
3. **Balance and Transition**
   - Solstices emphasize the balance of light and darkness, growth and rest. Dinosaurs' cycles of activity and dormancy demonstrate the importance of harmonizing with natural rhythms.

Practical Applications of Solstice Wisdom

1. **Honor Seasonal Cycles**
    - Use the solstices as opportunities to reflect on your own cycles of growth and rest. Let dinosaurs' alignment with natural rhythms inspire you to live in harmony with the seasons.
2. **Celebrate Abundance**
    - During the summer solstice, express gratitude for the abundance in your life. Focus on growth, creativity, and connection.
3. **Cultivate Resilience**
    - During the winter solstice, embrace rest and reflection. Use this time to build resilience and prepare for the renewal of spring.
4. **Adapt to Transitions**
    - Solstices teach us to navigate transitions with grace. Like dinosaurs responding to seasonal changes, stay flexible and open to new opportunities.

In the Dinosaur Zodiac, solstices represent the cycles of abundance, challenge, and renewal that defined the prehistoric world. By connecting with the symbolism of solstices, we can learn to honor life's rhythms, celebrate its highs, and persevere through its lows. Let the story of solstices and dinosaurs inspire you to embrace the cycles of nature, adapt to change, and find balance in all aspects of life.

Chapter 37: Equinoxes and Dinosaur Migration Patterns
Cosmic Balance and Earth's Changes
Equinoxes: The Balance of Light and Dark

Equinoxes occur twice a year when the Sun crosses the celestial equator, resulting in nearly equal lengths of day and night across the globe. The vernal (spring) and autumnal (fall) equinoxes symbolize balance and transition, marking the changing of seasons and the equilibrium between light and darkness. Astrologically, equinoxes represent harmony, shifts in energy, and the opportunity to adapt to Earth's natural rhythms.

For dinosaurs, equinoxes played a significant role in shaping migration patterns, ecological dynamics, and survival strategies. The balance of light and dark during these periods, coupled with seasonal shifts, influenced their movement, reproduction, and behavior. This chapter explores the cosmic balance of the equinoxes, their impact on Earth's changes, and how these transitions shaped dinosaur migration patterns and life cycles.

The Role of Equinoxes in Dinosaur Migration

Migration, the large-scale movement of species in response to environmental changes, was a critical survival strategy for many dinosaurs. Equinoxes, as markers of seasonal transitions, guided these movements and ensured access to resources.

1. **Spring Equinox: The Awakening of Life**
   - The vernal equinox signaled the arrival of spring, bringing longer days, warmer temperatures, and the renewal of ecosystems:
     - **Return to Fertile Grounds**: Herbivorous dinosaurs like *Hadrosaurus* migrated to regions with fresh vegetation, following the seasonal growth patterns triggered by increased sunlight.
     - **Breeding and Nesting**: Many dinosaurs synchronized their reproductive cycles with the spring equinox, ensuring that hatchlings would benefit from the abundance of food and mild weather.
     - **Social Dynamics**: Herding species such as *Iguanodon* displayed heightened social behaviors, forming large groups during migrations to optimize protection and resource access.
2. **Autumn Equinox: Preparation for Scarcity**
   - The autumnal equinox marked the transition to shorter days and cooler temperatures, prompting preparations for the challenges of winter:
     - **Journey to Warmer Climates**: Dinosaurs in temperate regions migrated southward to avoid harsh winters and maintain access to food.
     - **Resource Gathering**: Herbivores focused on consuming and storing energy, feeding intensively on the last remnants of seasonal vegetation.

- **Behavioral Shifts**: Predators like *Tyrannosaurus rex* adapted their hunting strategies to capitalize on prey migrations and dwindling food sources.

Ecological Changes During Equinoxes

Equinoxes heralded significant ecological changes, influencing the behavior and survival strategies of dinosaurs.

1. **Plant Growth and Decay**
   - The spring equinox triggered a burst of plant growth, providing abundant food for herbivores:
     - Ferns, cycads, and conifers flourished in the warmer temperatures and longer daylight hours, creating lush feeding grounds.
   - The autumn equinox, in contrast, marked the decline of vegetation, requiring herbivores to adapt to sparser and tougher plant material.
2. **Water Availability**
   - Seasonal shifts during equinoxes affected water sources, influencing migration routes:
     - During spring, melting snow and increased rainfall replenished rivers and lakes, attracting dinosaurs to areas with reliable water supplies.
     - In autumn, drier conditions forced dinosaurs to seek remaining water sources, often leading to congregation near shrinking rivers and ponds.
3. **Predator-Prey Dynamics**
   - Equinoxes altered predator-prey relationships, creating opportunities and challenges:
     - Predators exploited the predictable movements of prey during migrations, refining their hunting strategies to match seasonal behaviors.
     - Herbivores, in turn, relied on collective strength and vigilance to navigate dangerous landscapes during these transitions.

Cosmic Balance and Dinosaur Adaptations

The balance of light and dark during equinoxes mirrors the equilibrium dinosaurs maintained within their ecosystems. Their adaptations reflect the need for harmony and resilience in response to changing conditions.

1. **Physical Adaptations**
   - Dinosaurs evolved traits to cope with the challenges of seasonal transitions:
     - Feathered theropods, such as *Deinonychus*, used plumage for both insulation during cooler months and display during breeding seasons.
     - Herbivores like *Camarasaurus* developed robust digestive systems to process a variety of plant material, ensuring survival across different seasons.
2. **Behavioral Adaptations**
   - Behavioral flexibility allowed dinosaurs to thrive during equinox-driven transitions:
     - Herding species formed tighter groups to navigate long migrations, providing safety in numbers.
     - Carnivores adapted their hunting techniques to take advantage of prey vulnerabilities during migrations or seasonal scarcity.
3. **Ecological Contributions**
   - Dinosaurs played an active role in maintaining ecosystem balance:
     - Their grazing and seed dispersal behaviors during migrations helped shape the distribution of plant life.
     - Predatory species regulated herbivore populations, preventing overgrazing and supporting ecological diversity.

Lessons from Equinoxes and Dinosaur Migration

The equinoxes offer timeless lessons about balance, adaptability, and the interconnectedness of life, as demonstrated by the migration patterns and survival strategies of dinosaurs.

1. **Adapt to Transitions**
   - Equinoxes remind us that change is inevitable and often brings opportunities for growth. Dinosaurs' ability to navigate seasonal shifts highlights the importance of flexibility and preparation.
2. **Find Balance in Movement**
   - Just as dinosaurs balanced their needs for food, safety, and reproduction during migrations, equinoxes teach us to seek harmony in our actions and decisions.
3. **Prepare for Cycles of Abundance and Scarcity**
   - The equinoxes symbolize the ebb and flow of resources. Dinosaurs' seasonal behaviors reflect the wisdom of preparing for both times of plenty and periods of challenge.
4. **Embrace Collective Strength**
   - Migration required cooperation and coordination among dinosaurs, illustrating the power of collective effort. Equinoxes inspire us to work together during transitions, drawing strength from our communities.

The Equinoxes in Dinosaur Mythology

In modern interpretations of dinosaur mythology, the equinoxes symbolize their migrations, the balance of their ecosystems, and the harmony of life's cycles.

1. **Guardians of Balance**
   - Dinosaurs are often portrayed as guardians of ecological balance, embodying the harmony of light and dark celebrated during equinoxes.
2. **Navigators of Change**
   - The equinoxes highlight dinosaurs' ability to navigate Earth's changing conditions, serving as symbols of adaptability and resilience.
3. **Symbols of Interconnectedness**
   - Myths often depict dinosaurs as part of a larger cosmic cycle, emphasizing their role in maintaining the balance of their ecosystems.

Astrological Symbolism of Equinoxes and Dinosaurs

Astrologically, the equinoxes represent balance, transitions, and the harmony of opposites. In the Dinosaur Zodiac, they symbolize the migratory patterns and seasonal adaptations that defined their survival:

1. **Balance of Light and Dark**
   - The equinoxes reflect the equilibrium between abundance and scarcity, mirroring dinosaurs' ability to thrive through seasonal cycles.
2. **Transitions and Growth**
   - These periods of change emphasize adaptability and renewal, aligning with dinosaurs' responses to shifting conditions.
3. **Harmony with Nature**
   - The equinoxes inspire alignment with natural rhythms, much like dinosaurs' migrations maintained ecological balance.

Practical Applications of Equinox Wisdom

1. **Seek Balance in Your Life**
   - Use the equinoxes as opportunities to reflect on areas of imbalance and make adjustments. Let dinosaurs' harmonious adaptations inspire you to align with natural cycles.
2. **Prepare for Transitions**
   - Plan for periods of change by anticipating challenges and opportunities. Like dinosaurs during migrations, approach transitions with resilience and flexibility.
3. **Celebrate Interconnectedness**
   - Recognize the ways in which your actions affect others and your environment. The equinoxes remind us of the importance of collective harmony.
4. **Honor Cycles of Nature**
   - Embrace the rhythms of growth and rest in your life, aligning your efforts with the natural flow of energy.

In the Dinosaur Zodiac, the equinoxes represent cosmic balance, seasonal transitions, and the migratory patterns that defined dinosaurs' survival. By connecting with the symbolism of the equinoxes, we can learn to adapt to change, find harmony in our actions, and embrace the cycles of nature. Let the story of equinoxes and dinosaurs inspire you to navigate transitions with grace, align with life's rhythms, and celebrate the balance of light and dark.

Part 6: **Dinosaur Lore and Astrology**

Chapter 38: Fossil Zodiac Signs
Connecting Modern Discoveries with Celestial Wisdom
Fossils and the Eternal Connection to the Cosmos

Fossils, the preserved remains of ancient life, are time capsules that connect us to Earth's distant past. These remnants of prehistoric creatures, particularly dinosaurs, not only offer insights into the physical world but also evoke a deeper sense of wonder about our connection to the cosmos. Just as fossils reveal the evolutionary history of life on Earth, the zodiac maps the celestial forces that influence our lives. Together, they create a bridge between ancient terrestrial wisdom and the mysteries of the universe.

The concept of Fossil Zodiac Signs emerges from this intersection, connecting specific dinosaur fossils and their characteristics to the archetypal energy of each zodiac sign. This chapter explores how fossils, as symbols of endurance, transformation, and timeless wisdom, align with celestial archetypes to form the Fossil Zodiac. Through these connections, we can gain insights into how ancient life continues to shape modern perspectives.

Fossils and Their Symbolism

Fossils hold profound symbolic meaning, representing endurance, transformation, and the passage of time. These qualities mirror the energies of the zodiac, making fossils a natural counterpart to celestial archetypes.

1. **Endurance Across Time**
    - Fossils are symbols of survival and permanence, preserving the story of life long after the creatures themselves have vanished.
    - This mirrors the zodiac's role in preserving celestial wisdom, offering timeless guidance through the cycles of life.
2. **Transformation Through Preservation**
    - The process of fossilization transforms organic material into stone, symbolizing alchemical change and the preservation of essence.
    - Similarly, the zodiac transforms cosmic patterns into archetypes, guiding us through personal and collective evolution.
3. **Connection to Ancestral Wisdom**
    - Fossils connect us to the Earth's ancient history, reminding us of our place within the larger narrative of life.
    - The zodiac connects us to the rhythms of the cosmos, offering insights into our relationship with the universe.

The Fossil Zodiac Signs

Each zodiac sign corresponds to specific traits, energies, and celestial influences. By aligning these signs with notable dinosaur fossils, we can create a symbolic Fossil Zodiac that bridges ancient life and celestial archetypes. Here is a detailed exploration of each Fossil Zodiac Sign:

1. Aries: The Allosaurus Fossil

Traits: Bold, determined, pioneering

- The Allosaurus, a fierce theropod predator, embodies the Aries spirit of courage and initiative. Known for its agility and hunting prowess, this dinosaur symbolizes the fearless energy and competitive nature of Aries.
- **Celestial Connection**: The fiery determination of Aries aligns with the Allosaurus's role as a dominant predator, forging paths in its ecosystem.

2. Taurus: The Triceratops Fossil

Traits: Reliable, patient, grounded

- The Triceratops, with its iconic horns and sturdy build, represents Taurus's steadfast and protective nature. As a herbivore that thrived in herds, it embodies stability and the nurturing energy of this earth sign.
- **Celestial Connection**: Taurus's grounded nature resonates with the Triceratops's role in maintaining balance within its ecosystem.

3. Gemini: The Velociraptor Fossil

Traits: Curious, communicative, versatile

- The Velociraptor, a highly intelligent and social predator, captures Gemini's quick-witted and adaptable energy. Its cooperative hunting strategies reflect Gemini's duality and ability to thrive in partnerships.
- **Celestial Connection**: The Velociraptor's agility and resourcefulness mirror Gemini's intellectual curiosity and versatility.

4. Cancer: The Camarasaurus Fossil

Traits: Nurturing, intuitive, protective

- The Camarasaurus, a gentle sauropod known for its herding behavior, symbolizes Cancer's maternal and community-oriented qualities. Its reliance on group dynamics reflects Cancer's protective instincts.
- **Celestial Connection**: The Camarasaurus's nurturing role within herds aligns with Cancer's emotional depth and care for others.

5. Leo: The Tyrannosaurus Rex Fossil
Traits: Charismatic, bold, leader-like

- The Tyrannosaurus rex, often called the "king of dinosaurs," embodies Leo's regal and commanding energy. Its dominance and powerful presence mirror Leo's confidence and leadership.
- **Celestial Connection**: The T. rex's role as an apex predator resonates with Leo's desire to shine and inspire.

6. Virgo: The Ankylosaurus Fossil
Traits: Analytical, detail-oriented, practical

- The Ankylosaurus, with its armored body and club-like tail, represents Virgo's meticulous and protective nature. Its adaptations for survival reflect Virgo's focus on preparation and practicality.
- **Celestial Connection**: The Ankylosaurus's resilience and methodical defense mechanisms align with Virgo's precision and care.

7. Libra: The Stegosaurus Fossil
Traits: Harmonious, diplomatic, balanced

- The Stegosaurus, with its iconic plates and calm demeanor, embodies Libra's quest for balance and harmony. Its peaceful nature and cooperative behavior reflect Libra's social grace.
- **Celestial Connection**: The Stegosaurus's ability to balance defense with tranquility mirrors Libra's diplomatic approach to relationships.

8. Scorpio: The Spinosaurus Fossil
Traits: Intense, transformative, mysterious

- The Spinosaurus, a semi-aquatic predator with a striking sail, captures Scorpio's intense and enigmatic energy. Its adaptability to both land and water symbolizes Scorpio's transformative power.
- **Celestial Connection**: The Spinosaurus's dominance in diverse environments aligns with Scorpio's resourcefulness and depth.

9. Sagittarius: The Brachiosaurus Fossil
Traits: Adventurous, expansive, optimistic

- The Brachiosaurus, one of the tallest dinosaurs, represents Sagittarius's far-reaching and visionary nature. Its ability to access high vegetation reflects Sagittarius's thirst for exploration and growth.
- **Celestial Connection**: The Brachiosaurus's expansive presence mirrors Sagittarius's adventurous spirit and philosophical outlook.

10. Capricorn: The Iguanodon Fossil
Traits: Disciplined, ambitious, determined

- The Iguanodon, a versatile herbivore with efficient locomotion, embodies Capricorn's practicality and work ethic. Its ability to thrive in varied environments reflects Capricorn's determination to succeed.
- **Celestial Connection**: The Iguanodon's adaptability and endurance align with Capricorn's ambition and resilience.

11. Aquarius: The Parasaurolophus Fossil
Traits: Innovative, independent, visionary

- The Parasaurolophus, known for its unique crest and social intelligence, symbolizes Aquarius's inventive and forward-thinking energy. Its use of vocalizations reflects Aquarius's communication skills.
- **Celestial Connection**: The Parasaurolophus's innovative adaptations align with Aquarius's quest for originality and progress.

12. Pisces: The Plesiosaurus Fossil
Traits: Compassionate, imaginative, intuitive

- The Plesiosaurus, an aquatic dinosaur with graceful movements, captures Pisces's dreamy and intuitive nature. Its connection to water aligns with Pisces's emotional depth and fluidity.
- **Celestial Connection**: The Plesiosaurus's ability to navigate underwater realms mirrors Pisces's spiritual insight and creativity.

Fossil Zodiac: Connecting Earth and Sky

The Fossil Zodiac bridges the ancient wisdom of dinosaurs with celestial archetypes, offering unique insights into our relationship with the Earth and the cosmos.

1. **Honoring the Past**
   - The Fossil Zodiac reminds us to honor the legacy of prehistoric life and its influence on modern ecosystems and consciousness.
2. **Integrating Earthly and Celestial Wisdom**
   - By connecting fossils to zodiac signs, we integrate the tangible history of Earth with the intangible forces of the cosmos.
3. **Symbolic Guidance**
   - The Fossil Zodiac provides symbolic guidance, offering lessons in resilience, adaptability, and harmony from the ancient world.

Practical Applications of the Fossil Zodiac

1. **Discover Your Fossil Sign**
   - Align your zodiac sign with its corresponding fossil to explore how prehistoric traits resonate with your personality and life journey.
2. **Reflect on Ancient Wisdom**
   - Use the Fossil Zodiac to reflect on the enduring lessons of dinosaurs, integrating their resilience and adaptability into your daily life.
3. **Connect with Nature and the Cosmos**
   - Let the Fossil Zodiac inspire a deeper connection to Earth's history and the celestial forces that shape our world.

In the Dinosaur Zodiac, Fossil Zodiac Signs offer a unique perspective on how ancient life aligns with celestial wisdom. By exploring these connections, we can uncover new layers of meaning in both the prehistoric and cosmic realms, celebrating the enduring legacy of dinosaurs and their role in the universal story of life.

Chapter 39: Dinosaurs and Constellations
Celestial Bodies Named After Dinosaurs or Their Mythology
The Intersection of Dinosaurs and the Cosmos

Dinosaurs, as symbols of endurance, evolution, and the mysteries of Earth's ancient past, captivate human imagination. Similarly, constellations and celestial bodies represent the universe's vastness and our connection to it. Over time, scientific discoveries and cultural mythologies have intertwined these two realms, leading to the naming of asteroids, stars, and even informal constellations after dinosaurs or their mythical significance. This chapter explores the fascinating relationship between dinosaurs and the stars, delving into celestial bodies named after these prehistoric giants and the stories behind them.

1. Dinosaurs in Celestial Nomenclature

Modern science has honored dinosaurs by naming celestial bodies—such as asteroids and minor planets—after these magnificent creatures. These cosmic tributes highlight the enduring legacy of dinosaurs and their connection to humanity's fascination with discovery.

Asteroids Named After Dinosaurs

1. **Asteroid 9951 Tyrannosaurus**
   - Discovered in 1990, this asteroid is named after *Tyrannosaurus rex*, one of the most iconic and fearsome dinosaurs. Its naming celebrates the T. rex's role as a symbol of power and dominance.
   - **Astronomical Significance**: Like its namesake, this asteroid symbolizes strength and survival, qualities that resonate across space and time.

2. **Asteroid 6223 Stégosaurus**
   - Named after *Stegosaurus*, this asteroid reflects the dinosaur's distinctive back plates and role in prehistoric ecosystems.
   - **Symbolic Connection**: Its celestial naming honors the balance and resilience of herbivorous dinosaurs.

3. **Asteroid 1865 Ceratops**
   - This asteroid pays tribute to the *Ceratopsidae* family, including *Triceratops*, known for their iconic horns and frills.
   - **Cultural Impact**: Its name highlights the enduring popularity of horned dinosaurs in both science and popular culture.

Stars with Dinosaur-Inspired Names
While stars themselves are not officially named after dinosaurs, their mythological or symbolic associations sometimes overlap with the characteristics of these ancient creatures. For instance:

1. **The Dinosaur Egg Nebula (PK 3-4.1)**
   - This planetary nebula resembles the shape of a dinosaur egg, symbolizing the beginnings of life and creation.
   - **Astronomical Significance**: Located in the constellation Cygnus, this nebula connects the idea of dinosaur origins with cosmic creation.
2. **Proposed Star Names by Dinosaur Discoverers**
   - Astronomers and paleontologists occasionally suggest star names inspired by dinosaurs or prehistoric life, weaving a connection between Earth's past and the cosmos.

2. Dinosaur Mythology and Constellations
Many constellations in ancient cultures are tied to myths that echo the power, mystery, and grandeur of dinosaurs, even if directly unknown to ancient stargazers.
The Dragon Connection
Dinosaurs are often associated with dragons in mythology, as their fossilized remains inspired legends of these mythical beasts. Several dragon-related constellations can be indirectly linked to dinosaurs:

1. **Draco (The Dragon)**
   - **Mythological Roots**: Representing a serpent-like dragon guarding treasures in Greek mythology, Draco's celestial imagery parallels how dinosaurs are perceived as ancient guardians of Earth's history.
   - **Symbolism**: Draco embodies the strength and mystery attributed to creatures like *Spinosaurus* or *Allosaurus*.
2. **Hydra (The Water Serpent)**
   - **Connection to Aquatic Dinosaurs**: The constellation Hydra aligns with the imagery of marine reptiles like *Plesiosaurus*, which dominated prehistoric seas.
   - **Mythological Parallel**: Just as Hydra's many heads regenerated, the evolutionary adaptability of dinosaurs ensured their long reign on Earth.

Phoenix: A Symbol of Rebirth

- While the constellation Phoenix represents the mythical bird rising from its ashes, it also resonates with the evolutionary rebirth of dinosaurs into modern birds.
- **Connection to Dinosaurs**: Phoenix symbolizes transformation, much like feathered theropods transitioning into avian species.

3. Dinosaur-Inspired Asterisms and Patterns

Asterisms, unofficial star patterns, offer opportunities to honor dinosaurs in the night sky. Some modern enthusiasts have created dinosaur-inspired star groupings.

1. **The Dinosaur Asterism**
   - Amateur astronomers have identified unofficial star groupings that resemble the shape of a dinosaur, often modeled after the iconic *Tyrannosaurus rex.*
   - **Educational Uses**: These asterisms are used to engage students and the public in astronomy, connecting Earth's ancient history with the wonders of the cosmos.
2. **The Sauropod Pattern**
   - Asterisms resembling long-necked dinosaurs like *Brachiosaurus* or *Diplodocus* are popular in stargazing communities.
   - **Symbolism**: These patterns emphasize the majesty and scale of sauropods, paralleling the grandeur of the universe.

4. Thematic Overlap: Dinosaurs and Celestial Archetypes

Dinosaurs and celestial bodies share thematic overlaps that make their connection even more profound. Both evoke a sense of awe, mystery, and timelessness.

1. **Timelessness**
   - Fossils and stars both endure across eons, reminding us of the vastness of time.
   - Dinosaurs, preserved in stone, and celestial bodies, burning in the cosmos, inspire similar feelings of eternity.
2. **Discovery and Curiosity**
   - The exploration of fossils and space reflects humanity's drive to uncover the unknown.
   - Both dinosaurs and celestial bodies fuel scientific and imaginative pursuits.
3. **Transformation and Evolution**
   - Just as stars go through life cycles of birth, death, and rebirth, dinosaurs underwent evolutionary transformations that continue through their avian descendants.

5. Dinosaurs and Planetary Systems

In addition to asteroids, scientists have drawn inspiration from dinosaurs when naming planetary systems or features.

1. **Exoplanets with Prehistoric Names**
   - Some exoplanetary systems are informally nicknamed after prehistoric creatures due to their unique characteristics, such as rocky compositions or extreme climates resembling Earth's Mesozoic Era.
2. **Craters and Surface Features**
   - Certain craters on planets and moons are named after prehistoric creatures, linking the study of paleontology with planetary science.

Conclusion: The Cosmic Legacy of Dinosaurs

Dinosaurs and celestial bodies are united by their ability to spark wonder and connect us to larger narratives. The naming of asteroids, stars, and asterisms after dinosaurs bridges the ancient and cosmic realms, highlighting humanity's enduring fascination with both the Earth's past and the universe's mysteries.

Lessons from Dinosaurs and Constellations

1. **Celebrate Connections**
   - Recognize how the stories of dinosaurs and the stars intersect, enriching our understanding of life and the cosmos.
2. **Find Inspiration in the Universe**
   - Use the celestial naming of dinosaurs as a reminder of humanity's creative spirit and our connection to Earth's ancient history.
3. **Explore the Unknown**
   - Just as paleontologists uncover fossils and astronomers map the stars, let the legacy of dinosaurs and constellations inspire you to explore uncharted territories in your own life.

In the Dinosaur Zodiac, constellations and celestial bodies named after dinosaurs or their mythology symbolize the enduring connection between Earth and the cosmos. By exploring these links, we can honor the legacy of dinosaurs and celebrate the universal quest for understanding our place in the universe.

Chapter 40: Prehistoric Star Gazing
Imagining the Ancient Skies and Their Impact
The Prehistoric Skies: A Vast and Untouched Canvas

Long before human civilization and the advent of telescopes, the skies of prehistoric Earth stretched vast and unpolluted, providing a perfect view of the cosmos. For dinosaurs, the stars, planets, and celestial events like eclipses and meteor showers likely held no conscious meaning, yet they profoundly impacted their environment and survival. As we imagine these ancient skies, we connect with a world untainted by modern light and urbanization—a world where the stars played a silent but essential role in shaping life on Earth.

This chapter explores the prehistoric skies, how celestial phenomena influenced the lives of dinosaurs, and the ways in which imagining their interactions with the cosmos can inspire our modern understanding of astronomy, mythology, and the interconnectedness of life and the universe.

The Ancient Skies of the Mesozoic Era

The Mesozoic Era (roughly 252 to 66 million years ago), encompassing the Triassic, Jurassic, and Cretaceous periods, was a time of profound change not only on Earth but also in the cosmos. The skies of the dinosaurs were vastly different from ours today due to the shifting positions of stars, galaxies, and the configuration of continents.

1. **A Dynamic Celestial Landscape**
   - **Galactic Position**:
     - During the Mesozoic Era, the solar system was located in a slightly different position within the Milky Way galaxy. As Earth orbited through different stellar regions, the constellations would have appeared altered compared to today.
   - **Bright Starfields**:
     - Without light pollution, the prehistoric skies were likely dazzling with stars, the Milky Way a prominent, glowing band across the heavens.
   - **Visible Phenomena**:
     - Meteor showers, auroras, and cometary displays were likely even more vivid, offering stunning visual displays in the untouched night sky.
2. **Shifting Continents and Celestial Perspectives**
   - The breakup of Pangaea during the Mesozoic altered the orientation of landmasses, influencing the position of celestial bodies as viewed from Earth. Dinosaurs living in different regions of the supercontinent would have experienced unique views of the stars.
   - As continents drifted, new skies emerged over millions of years, reflecting the dynamic relationship between Earth and the cosmos.
3. **Planetary Alignments and Celestial Events**
   - Just as today, the prehistoric skies witnessed planetary alignments, eclipses, and other celestial phenomena. These events might have influenced the behaviors of prehistoric creatures in subtle but meaningful ways.

Celestial Events and Their Impact on Dinosaur Life

Though dinosaurs were not aware of celestial phenomena in the way humans are, these events likely influenced their environment and behaviors in significant ways.

1. **Meteor Showers and Impacts**
   - **Frequent Meteor Activity**:
     - The Mesozoic Era saw heightened meteor activity, as Earth passed through denser regions of cosmic debris. Bright meteor showers would have illuminated the night skies, creating awe-inspiring light displays.
   - **Meteor Impacts**:
     - While most meteors burned harmlessly in the atmosphere, occasional impacts—like the Chicxulub asteroid—altered ecosystems dramatically. Such events underline the interplay between celestial phenomena and life on Earth.
2. **Solar and Lunar Eclipses**
   - **Dramatic Shadows**:
     - Solar eclipses, with their sudden dimming of sunlight, could have temporarily disrupted dinosaur behaviors, particularly in diurnal species that relied on light cues.
   - **Lunar Cycles**:
     - The waxing and waning of the Moon likely influenced migration, reproduction, and feeding cycles, much like they do for modern animals.
3. **Auroras and Atmospheric Displays**
   - Enhanced auroras, caused by solar activity, would have been visible closer to the equator during periods of strong geomagnetic storms. These shimmering lights may have influenced nocturnal activity patterns or served as natural markers of environmental shifts.

Theoretical Dinosaur Behaviors Under Ancient Skies

While we cannot know for certain how dinosaurs reacted to celestial phenomena, we can hypothesize based on their known behaviors and the impact of similar events on modern animals.

1. **Response to Lunar Cycles**
   - Herbivores like *Apatosaurus* may have used the light of the full Moon to graze more safely at night, taking advantage of improved visibility.
   - Predators like *Velociraptor* might have coordinated hunting efforts around moonlight, maximizing their stealth and efficiency.
2. **Reaction to Eclipses**
   - Sudden darkness during solar eclipses may have caused confusion or shifts in behavior, similar to the way modern birds and mammals react by seeking shelter or becoming momentarily inactive.
3. **Migratory Cues from Celestial Patterns**
   - Like modern migratory animals that navigate by the stars, dinosaurs may have instinctively used the positions of celestial bodies to orient their long migrations. Herding species such as *Hadrosaurus* could have relied on natural patterns in the sky to find fertile feeding grounds or water sources.

Cosmic Mysteries and the Dinosaur Connection

The skies of the Mesozoic offer a fascinating window into how celestial and terrestrial forces intertwined. By imagining these ancient skies, we uncover deeper insights into both the physical universe and the spiritual resonance of dinosaurs as part of Earth's cosmic story.

1. **Dinosaurs as Cosmic Beings**
   - Dinosaurs lived under the same Sun, Moon, and stars that we see today, reminding us of the shared cosmic heritage of all life. Their presence on Earth is a testament to the universe's creative power.
2. **Celestial Inspiration for Modern Science**
   - The Chicxulub impact, which ended the reign of non-avian dinosaurs, serves as a stark reminder of Earth's vulnerability to cosmic events. Studying the prehistoric skies can inspire efforts to understand and mitigate similar threats in the future.
3. **Spiritual Connections to the Ancient Sky**
   - Imagining the ancient skies allows us to connect with the deep time of Earth's history, fostering a sense of awe and reverence for the universe and our place within it.

Lessons from Prehistoric Star Gazing

The interplay between dinosaurs and the ancient skies offers timeless lessons about adaptability, resilience, and our connection to the cosmos.

1. **Embrace the Cycles of Nature**
   - Just as celestial cycles shaped the lives of dinosaurs, we too can align with natural rhythms to navigate change and uncertainty.
2. **Reflect on Interconnectedness**
   - The same forces that influenced the prehistoric skies continue to shape our world today. Recognizing this continuity can deepen our appreciation for both Earth's past and its future.
3. **Find Wonder in the Universe**
   - Dinosaurs thrived under skies that were both familiar and alien to us. Their story reminds us to marvel at the universe's capacity for beauty, mystery, and transformation.

Imagining the Prehistoric Skies: A Call to Wonder

By envisioning the ancient skies of the Mesozoic, we can transcend the boundaries of time and space, connecting with the awe-inspiring history of Earth and the cosmos. The stars that once shone over the dinosaurs now shine on us, linking past and present in a timeless dance of light and shadow.

In the Dinosaur Zodiac, prehistoric star gazing symbolizes the enduring relationship between Earth's ancient life and the vast universe. By exploring the impact of celestial phenomena on dinosaurs and imagining their interactions with the ancient skies, we can deepen our connection to the cosmos and the shared story of life on our planet. Let the prehistoric skies inspire you to look upward, dream deeply, and embrace the mysteries of the stars.

Part 7: **Practical Astrology for Today**

Chapter 41: How to Find Your Dinosaur Zodiac Sign

Birth Charts and Prehistoric Wisdom

The Dinosaur Zodiac: Bridging Celestial and Prehistoric Wisdom

The Dinosaur Zodiac connects the ancient wisdom of the stars with the enduring legacy of dinosaurs. Much like the traditional zodiac, which assigns celestial archetypes based on the positions of stars and planets at the time of birth, the Dinosaur Zodiac uses prehistoric traits, dinosaur species, and celestial influences to reveal insights about personality, destiny, and growth. By creating your Dinosaur Zodiac birth chart, you can explore how the traits of these magnificent creatures resonate with your unique journey.

This chapter provides a step-by-step guide to discovering your Dinosaur Zodiac sign, interpreting its meaning, and applying prehistoric wisdom to your life. You'll also learn how to integrate the positions of celestial bodies, lunar phases, and other astrological elements into your Dinosaur Zodiac chart for a deeper understanding of yourself and your connection to Earth's ancient past.

Step 1: Identify Your Primary Dinosaur Zodiac Sign

In the Dinosaur Zodiac, each of the 12 primary signs corresponds to a dinosaur species and its unique traits, aligned with the traditional astrological zodiac.

The 12 Dinosaur Zodiac Signs

1. **Aries - Allosaurus: Bold, competitive, and pioneering.**
   ◦ **Dates: March 21 - April 19**
2. **Taurus - Triceratops: Loyal, grounded, and protective.**
   ◦ **Dates: April 20 - May 20**
3. **Gemini - Velociraptor: Intelligent, adaptable, and quick-witted.**
   ◦ **Dates: May 21 - June 20**
4. **Cancer - Camarasaurus: Nurturing, intuitive, and family-oriented.**
   ◦ **Dates: June 21 - July 22**
5. **Leo - Tyrannosaurus Rex: Charismatic, dominant, and confident.**
   ◦ **Dates: July 23 - August 22**
6. **Virgo - Ankylosaurus: Practical, detail-oriented, and resilient.**
   ◦ **Dates: August 23 - September 22**
7. **Libra - Stegosaurus: Balanced, harmonious, and diplomatic.**
   ◦ **Dates: September 23 - October 22**
8. **Scorpio - Spinosaurus: Intense, transformative, and mysterious.**
   ◦ **Dates: October 23 - November 21**
9. **Sagittarius - Brachiosaurus: Visionary, adventurous, and expansive.**
   ◦ **Dates: November 22 - December 21**
10. **Capricorn - Iguanodon: Ambitious, disciplined, and resourceful.**

- **Dates: December 22 - January 19**

11. Aquarius - Parasaurolophus: Innovative, independent, and creative.

   • Dates: January 20 - February 18

12. Pisces - Plesiosaurus: Compassionate, imaginative, and intuitive.

   • Dates: February 19 - March 20

Step 2: Map Your Dinosaur Zodiac Birth Chart

Just as traditional astrology uses a birth chart to map the positions of celestial bodies, the Dinosaur Zodiac incorporates key prehistoric and celestial elements to provide a comprehensive reading. Your Dinosaur Zodiac birth chart includes:

1. **Your Sun Sign (Primary Sign)**
   - The sign that corresponds to your date of birth, representing your core identity and life purpose.
   - Example: A person born on April 5 would have the Sun sign of Aries (Allosaurus).
2. **Your Moon Sign (Emotional Nature)**
   - Determined by the phase of the Moon at your birth, reflecting your emotional instincts and inner self.
   - Example: A Waning Gibbous Moon could align with the introspection and resilience of Spinosaurus (Scorpio energy).
3. **Your Rising Sign (Outer Personality)**
   - Calculated based on the time and place of your birth, representing how others perceive you.
   - Example: A Capricorn (Iguanodon) Rising might indicate a practical and determined outer persona.
4. **Planetary Influences (Prehistoric Alignments)**
   - Each planet corresponds to a specific prehistoric archetype, influencing different aspects of your life:
     - Mercury: Communication and intellect (Velociraptor energy).
     - Venus: Love and relationships (Triceratops energy).
     - Mars: Drive and ambition (Tyrannosaurus Rex energy).
     - Jupiter: Growth and expansion (Brachiosaurus energy).
     - Saturn: Discipline and lessons (Ankylosaurus energy).
     - Uranus: Innovation and change (Parasaurolophus energy).
     - Neptune: Imagination and spirituality (Plesiosaurus energy).
     - Pluto: Transformation and power (Spinosaurus energy).

Step 3: Determine Your Dinosaur Lunar Phase

The Moon's phase at your birth holds significant meaning in the Dinosaur Zodiac, reflecting your emotional instincts and adaptive strategies. Identify your Moon phase using a lunar calendar or an online calculator.

Moon Phases and Their Prehistoric Meanings

1. **New Moon: Beginnings and instinctual growth.**
   - **Symbol: The pioneering Allosaurus.**
2. **Waxing Crescent: Progress and determination.**
   - **Symbol: The resilient Ankylosaurus.**
3. **First Quarter: Challenge and action.**
   - **Symbol: The ambitious Tyrannosaurus Rex.**
4. **Waxing Gibbous: Refinement and preparation.**
   - **Symbol: The harmonious Stegosaurus.**
5. **Full Moon: Abundance and peak energy.**
   - **Symbol: The visionary Brachiosaurus.**
6. **Waning Gibbous: Reflection and gratitude.**
   - **Symbol: The nurturing Camarasaurus.**
7. **Last Quarter: Release and transformation.**
   - **Symbol: The intense Spinosaurus.**
8. **Waning Crescent: Rest and healing.**
   - **Symbol: The intuitive Plesiosaurus.**

Step 4: Interpret Your Dinosaur Zodiac Chart

Once you've identified your Dinosaur Zodiac placements, integrate them to form a holistic understanding of your prehistoric personality and life path.

1. **Core Identity (Sun Sign)**
   - **Represents your foundational traits and purpose.**
   - **Example: A Sagittarius (Brachiosaurus) Sun indicates a visionary personality with a love for exploration and growth.**
2. **Emotional World (Moon Sign)**
   - **Reflects your inner self and emotional responses.**
   - **Example: A Taurus (Triceratops) Moon suggests emotional stability and a nurturing disposition.**
3. **Outer Persona (Rising Sign)**
   - **Describes how others perceive you and your approach to the world.**
   - **Example: An Aquarius (Parasaurolophus) Rising indicates a creative, forward-thinking impression.**
4. **Planetary Influences**
   - **Each planet's placement adds depth to your chart.**
   - **Example: Venus in Scorpio (Spinosaurus energy) suggests intense, transformative relationships.**
5. **Lunar Influence**
   - **The Moon phase reveals your instinctual patterns.**
   - **Example: A Full Moon phase aligns with peak energy and a desire for abundance.**

Step 5: Apply Prehistoric Wisdom

The Dinosaur Zodiac offers guidance for understanding yourself and aligning with the lessons of the past. Use this wisdom to navigate challenges, embrace your strengths, and honor your connection to Earth's history.

1. **Celebrate Your Unique Traits**
   - **Embrace the qualities of your Dinosaur Sun Sign as a source of strength and inspiration.**
2. **Balance Your Emotions**
   - **Use your Moon Sign and phase to understand your emotional needs and adapt to life's cycles.**
3. **Harness Celestial Energies**
   - **Align your planetary placements with their prehistoric archetypes to enhance your relationships, career, and personal growth.**

4. **Connect with Nature**
   - **Let the Dinosaur Zodiac remind you of your connection to Earth's history and the cycles of life and the cosmos.**

In the Dinosaur Zodiac, discovering your sign and birth chart reveals a profound connection between celestial wisdom and prehistoric life. By exploring your placements and integrating their meanings, you can uncover insights into your personality, destiny, and role in the grand story of life on Earth. Let the Dinosaur Zodiac inspire you to honor the past, embrace the present, and align with the timeless rhythms of the universe.

Chapter 42: Cosmic Lessons from Dinosaurs
Learning Resilience and Strength from the Ancient World
The Timeless Wisdom of Dinosaurs

Dinosaurs, Earth's most majestic and enduring creatures, ruled the planet for over 160 million years. Their rise, dominance, and eventual extinction offer profound lessons about resilience, adaptability, and the cyclical nature of life. By examining their traits and experiences through a cosmic lens, we uncover timeless truths that transcend their prehistoric origins. These lessons not only highlight the strength and adaptability of dinosaurs but also illuminate universal principles for navigating change, overcoming adversity, and embracing growth.

This chapter explores the cosmic lessons dinosaurs impart through their evolutionary journey, linking their resilience to celestial wisdom and providing practical guidance for modern life.

1. Resilience in the Face of Change

Dinosaurs thrived in dynamic and often challenging environments. Their ability to adapt to shifting climates, changing ecosystems, and evolving predatory-prey relationships demonstrates the power of resilience.

The Lesson

Change is inevitable, and resilience is the key to thriving through uncertainty. Dinosaurs teach us that survival is not about avoiding change but about adapting to it.

Examples from the Dinosaur World

1. Adaptation to Climate Shifts
    ◦ As Earth transitioned through periods of warming and cooling, dinosaurs evolved traits to suit their environments. Feathered theropods like *Velociraptor* adapted to colder climates, while sauropods like *Brachiosaurus* thrived in lush, tropical forests.
2. Surviving Ecosystem Changes
    ◦ The breakup of Pangaea created new ecosystems, forcing dinosaurs to migrate and adapt. Herbivores diversified their diets to feed on different types of vegetation, while predators developed new hunting strategies.

Cosmic Perspective

The stars remind us that change is a constant force in the universe. Just as planets orbit and stars evolve, we must embrace the cycles of growth, decline, and renewal.

2. The Power of Collaboration and Community

Dinosaurs were not solitary creatures; many species relied on social behaviors and collective strength to survive. From herding herbivores to cooperative hunting carnivores, community was key to their success.

The Lesson

Strength comes from collaboration and community. Working together, we can achieve more than we can alone.

Examples from the Dinosaur World

1. Herding for Protection
   - Dinosaurs like *Triceratops* and *Iguanodon* formed herds to protect themselves from predators. Their collective vigilance ensured greater safety for the group.
2. Cooperative Hunting
   - Predatory dinosaurs like *Deinonychus* hunted in packs, using teamwork to take down larger prey. This behavior allowed them to thrive in challenging environments.

Cosmic Perspective

The constellations, formed by groups of stars, symbolize the power of connection. Just as stars come together to create patterns, we are stronger when we collaborate and support one another.

3. Embracing Transformation and Evolution

Dinosaurs' evolutionary journey is one of constant transformation. From the development of feathers in theropods to the eventual rise of birds, dinosaurs demonstrate the beauty of embracing change as an opportunity for growth.

The Lesson

Transformation is a natural and necessary part of life. Embracing evolution allows us to reach our fullest potential.

Examples from the Dinosaur World

1. **The Rise of Feathered Dinosaurs**
   - Feathered dinosaurs like *Archaeopteryx* marked a transition from terrestrial reptiles to the ancestors of modern birds. This evolution shows the power of adaptation in the face of new challenges.
2. **Extinction as Transformation**
   - While most dinosaurs went extinct after the asteroid impact, their evolutionary legacy lives on in birds, demonstrating that endings can lead to new beginnings.

Cosmic Perspective

Stars undergo cycles of birth, life, and death, transforming into supernovas, black holes, or new star systems. Similarly, our own transformations lead to greater growth and purpose.

4. Balancing Strength and Vulnerability

Dinosaurs displayed a balance of strength and vulnerability. While predators like *Tyrannosaurus rex* dominated their ecosystems, even they were not invincible. Herbivores like *Stegosaurus* balanced physical defenses with peaceful grazing habits, showing that strength can coexist with vulnerability.

The Lesson

True strength lies in acknowledging and balancing our vulnerabilities. Understanding our limits helps us grow.

Examples from the Dinosaur World

1. **Physical Strength vs. Ecosystem Dependence**
    - Apex predators relied on the health of ecosystems to support prey populations. Their strength was tied to the balance of their environment.
2. **Adaptations for Defense**
    - Herbivores like *Ankylosaurus* developed armored bodies, but they also relied on herds for additional protection.

Cosmic Perspective

The Moon, with its phases of light and shadow, symbolizes the balance of strength and vulnerability. Just as the Moon cycles through visibility, we too must honor all aspects of ourselves.

5. Perseverance Through Adversity

Dinosaurs endured for millions of years, surviving volcanic eruptions, shifting continents, and environmental upheavals. Their perseverance is a testament to the endurance of life.

The Lesson

Perseverance in the face of adversity leads to survival and success. Challenges are opportunities to grow stronger.

Examples from the Dinosaur World

1. **Surviving Early Extinction Events**
    - Before the asteroid impact, dinosaurs survived smaller extinction events by adapting to new environments and food sources.
2. **Post-Impact Resilience**
    - While the asteroid led to the extinction of most dinosaurs, some species' traits, like feathers and small size, allowed their descendants to thrive as birds.

Cosmic Perspective

The stars endure for billions of years, shining through cosmic turbulence. Their perseverance reminds us that even in the darkest times, light persists.

6. Interconnectedness of Life

Dinosaurs were integral to the ecosystems of the Mesozoic Era, shaping and being shaped by their environments. Their lives demonstrate the interconnectedness of all living things.

The Lesson

We are all part of a greater whole. Recognizing our interconnectedness fosters harmony and mutual growth.

Examples from the Dinosaur World

1. Ecosystem Engineers
    - Sauropods like *Diplodocus* shaped their environments by clearing vegetation and dispersing seeds, fostering biodiversity.
2. Predator-Prey Balance
    - The dynamic relationship between carnivores and herbivores maintained ecosystem stability.

Cosmic Perspective

The constellations are a metaphor for interconnectedness, with stars forming patterns that guide and inspire. Like the stars, we are connected to each other and the universe.

Applying Dinosaur Wisdom to Modern Life

1. **Resilience in Daily Challenges**
    ◦ Embrace change as an opportunity to grow. Like dinosaurs, adapt to shifting circumstances with strength and flexibility.
2. **Build Strong Communities**
    ◦ Cultivate relationships and work collaboratively. Draw on the power of collective strength to overcome challenges.
3. **Honor Transformation**
    ◦ View personal growth as a natural evolution. Celebrate the transitions that lead to a better version of yourself.
4. **Balance Strength with Vulnerability**
    ◦ Acknowledge your limits while building your strengths. Use your vulnerabilities as stepping stones for deeper connections.
5. **Persevere Through Adversity**
    ◦ In difficult times, remember the resilience of dinosaurs. Keep moving forward, knowing that challenges are temporary.
6. **Recognize Interconnectedness**
    ◦ Appreciate your role in the greater whole. Nurture your environment and relationships, fostering harmony and growth.

Conclusion: Cosmic Lessons from Dinosaurs
Dinosaurs, though long extinct, continue to inspire us with their resilience, adaptability, and strength. By viewing their journey through a cosmic lens, we uncover universal truths about life, transformation, and interconnectedness. Their story reminds us that we are part of a larger narrative, one that spans from the ancient Earth to the stars above.

Let the lessons of dinosaurs guide you as you navigate your own challenges, adapt to change, and embrace the cycles of life. In their enduring legacy, we find strength, wisdom, and a deeper connection to the cosmos.

Chapter 43: Aligning Modern Astrology with Prehistoric Cycles
Practical Tools for Deeper Connection
Bridging Ancient Earth and Celestial Wisdom
Modern astrology offers insights into the rhythms of the cosmos and their influence on our lives. Prehistoric cycles, as embodied by the reign of dinosaurs and the Earth's ancient rhythms, add a grounding element to this celestial understanding. By aligning modern astrological practices with prehistoric cycles, we deepen our connection to Earth's past and enrich our spiritual and practical lives.

This chapter explores how to integrate modern astrology with the wisdom of prehistoric cycles, offering practical tools and exercises to harmonize celestial insights with the ancient rhythms of the planet.

1. Understanding Prehistoric Cycles
Before aligning prehistoric cycles with astrology, it's essential to understand these cycles and their significance. The Mesozoic Era (Triassic, Jurassic, and Cretaceous periods) provides a framework for exploring Earth's ancient rhythms.

Key Prehistoric Cycles

1. **Seasonal Changes**
   - The Earth's tilt and orbit created seasonal cycles that influenced dinosaur migration, reproduction, and survival. These patterns mirror modern astrological themes tied to solstices and equinoxes.
2. **Lunar Rhythms**
   - The Moon's influence on tides and nocturnal activity likely shaped the behaviors of prehistoric life. Lunar phases align with astrological insights about emotional cycles and inner growth.
3. **Mass Extinction and Renewal Cycles**
   - Earth's prehistoric history includes extinction events that reset ecosystems and allowed new life to emerge. These cycles parallel astrological themes of endings and new beginnings, particularly in Pluto's transformative energy.
4. **Geological Shifts**
   - Plate tectonics, volcanic activity, and the breakup of Pangaea during the Mesozoic Era demonstrate Earth's dynamic evolution. These shifts reflect astrological themes of adaptation and resilience.

2. Integrating Prehistoric Cycles into Astrology

Modern astrology focuses on celestial movements and their influence on human life. By integrating prehistoric cycles, we create a holistic approach that connects cosmic and terrestrial wisdom.

Astrological Themes with Prehistoric Parallels

1. **Solar Events (Solstices and Equinoxes)**
   - Align the astrological meanings of solstices and equinoxes with the prehistoric significance of seasonal changes. For example:
     - **Summer Solstice**: Abundance and peak energy, mirroring the lush ecosystems of the Jurassic period.
     - **Winter Solstice**: Rest and endurance, reflecting the resilience of dinosaurs during colder months.
2. **Lunar Phases**
   - Use the Moon's phases to connect with the behaviors of prehistoric creatures. For example:
     - **Full Moon**: Align with abundance and activity, reflecting times when dinosaurs thrived in fertile environments.
     - **New Moon**: Focus on beginnings and instinctual growth, echoing the birth of new species after mass extinctions.
3. **Planetary Cycles and Prehistoric Themes**
   - Integrate planetary movements with prehistoric traits:
     - **Mars**: Action and survival instincts, connecting to predatory dinosaurs like *Tyrannosaurus rex*.
     - **Venus**: Harmony and nurturing, aligned with herding behaviors of species like *Triceratops*.
     - **Pluto**: Transformation and rebirth, paralleling extinction events and evolutionary leaps.

3. Practical Tools for Alignment

To align modern astrology with prehistoric cycles, use these practical tools and exercises to deepen your connection.

Creating a Prehistoric Birth Chart

1. **Determine Your Dinosaur Zodiac Sign**
   - Identify your primary dinosaur sign based on your astrological Sun sign (refer to the Dinosaur Zodiac in earlier chapters).
2. **Incorporate Lunar Influence**
   - Add the Moon phase and its prehistoric meaning to your chart for emotional and intuitive insights.
3. **Map Planetary Influences**

- Associate planetary placements with prehistoric traits, creating a chart that integrates celestial and terrestrial wisdom.

Meditation on Prehistoric and Celestial Rhythms

1. **Visualize Ancient Earth**
   - Close your eyes and imagine the Earth during the Mesozoic Era. Visualize lush landscapes, towering dinosaurs, and unpolluted skies filled with stars.
2. **Sync with Celestial Cycles**
   - Imagine the stars and planets influencing these prehistoric creatures, just as they influence us today. Reflect on the continuity of cosmic rhythms.
3. **Connect to Your Personal Rhythms**
   - Align your breath and thoughts with the cycles of the Moon, planets, and seasons, drawing inspiration from prehistoric resilience.

Journaling with Prehistoric Astrology

1. **Daily Reflections**
   - Record your daily experiences and emotions in relation to both modern astrological events and prehistoric cycles.
     - Example: "Under today's Waxing Gibbous Moon, I felt motivated to refine my goals, much like the adaptability of Velociraptors during dynamic ecosystems."
2. **Seasonal Insights**
   - Reflect on how seasonal transitions affect your energy and behavior, linking them to both astrological solstices/equinoxes and prehistoric survival strategies.

Rituals to Honor Prehistoric Wisdom

1. **Solstice and Equinox Ceremonies**
   - Create rituals that combine celestial and prehistoric themes. For example:
     - **Summer Solstice Ritual**: Honor abundance by placing symbolic items like ferns or fossils on an altar, representing lush prehistoric landscapes.
     - **Winter Solstice Ritual**: Light candles to symbolize resilience and survival, reflecting the endurance of dinosaurs during colder periods.
2. **Lunar Phase Activities**
   - Plan activities that align with lunar phases and their prehistoric meanings:
     - **New Moon**: Begin a new project or intention, symbolizing the birth of new species.
     - **Full Moon**: Celebrate achievements and abundance, mirroring peak energy in prehistoric ecosystems.

4. Lessons from Prehistoric Cycles for Modern Life

Prehistoric cycles offer profound lessons that complement astrological wisdom, guiding us in navigating life's challenges and opportunities.

Embrace Resilience

- Dinosaurs survived for millions of years through adaptability and strength. Use this as inspiration to remain resilient during astrological challenges, such as Mercury retrogrades or Saturn returns.

Adapt to Cycles of Change

- The Earth's dynamic history reflects the inevitability of change. Align with astrological cycles to navigate transitions with grace, much like dinosaurs adapted to shifting environments.

Balance Abundance and Rest

- Just as dinosaurs thrived during periods of abundance and endured times of scarcity, honor the balance between growth (Full Moon) and rest (New Moon).

Connect with Community

- Herding behaviors of dinosaurs like *Stegosaurus* remind us of the importance of collective strength. Use astrological insights to strengthen your relationships and communities.

5. Aligning Personal Goals with Prehistoric and Celestial Wisdom
Astrology helps us set intentions and align our actions with cosmic rhythms. By integrating prehistoric cycles, we add a grounded, Earth-centered perspective.
Setting Intentions

- Use your Dinosaur Zodiac sign and planetary placements to guide your personal goals.
  - Example: If you have a Sagittarius (Brachiosaurus) Sun and Venus in Scorpio (Spinosaurus), focus on adventurous growth while embracing transformative relationships.

Tracking Progress with Lunar Phases

- Align milestones with lunar phases:
  - **New Moon**: Set intentions.
  - **First Quarter**: Take action.
  - **Full Moon**: Celebrate progress.
  - **Last Quarter**: Reflect and release.

Honoring Evolutionary Growth

- Recognize your personal growth as part of a larger cycle, much like the evolution of dinosaurs. Celebrate your achievements while staying open to transformation.

Conclusion: Harmonizing the Stars and Earth
Aligning modern astrology with prehistoric cycles creates a holistic approach to understanding ourselves and the universe. By integrating the wisdom of celestial rhythms with the enduring lessons of ancient Earth, we connect more deeply with both the cosmos and our roots on this planet.

Let the stars guide your vision and prehistoric cycles ground your journey, blending celestial insight with the timeless resilience of dinosaurs. This harmony empowers us to navigate life's challenges with strength, adaptability, and a profound sense of connection to the universe.

Chapter 44: Dinosaur Totems and Spirit Guides
Finding Your Cosmic Dinosaur Ally
The Concept of Dinosaur Totems and Spirit Guides

Totems and spirit guides have long been a part of human spirituality, symbolizing personal connections to specific animals, plants, or celestial forces. These guides are believed to offer wisdom, protection, and insights into our journeys. Dinosaur totems and spirit guides extend this concept into the prehistoric realm, aligning individuals with the ancient wisdom and unique energies of Earth's most magnificent creatures.

A dinosaur totem serves as a cosmic ally, embodying traits that resonate with your personality, challenges, and life path. Whether you're drawn to the strength of a *Tyrannosaurus rex*, the adaptability of a *Velociraptor*, or the nurturing energy of a *Camarasaurus*, your dinosaur spirit guide reflects qualities that can inspire growth and transformation.

This chapter provides an in-depth exploration of dinosaur totems, how to find your cosmic dinosaur ally, and practical ways to integrate their wisdom into your life.

1. What Are Dinosaur Totems and Spirit Guides?

Dinosaur totems and spirit guides are symbolic representations of ancient wisdom. These totems are not just a connection to prehistoric life but also a bridge between Earth's past and our present spiritual journey.

The Role of Dinosaur Totems

1. **Embodiments of Strengths**
   - Each dinosaur totem embodies specific traits and qualities, such as courage, resilience, or adaptability.
   - For example, *Ankylosaurus* represents steadfast protection, while *Brachiosaurus* symbolizes expansive vision and growth.
2. **Guidance Through Challenges**
   - Dinosaur spirit guides help navigate life's challenges, offering lessons from their survival and dominance over millions of years.
   - A *Spinosaurus* guide, for instance, may teach you to embrace transformation and thrive in diverse environments.
3. **Connection to Earth's History**
   - Totems link us to the prehistoric cycles of Earth, reminding us of our place in the larger story of life.

2. How to Discover Your Dinosaur Totem

Finding your dinosaur totem involves introspection, intuition, and alignment with prehistoric and astrological archetypes.

Signs Your Dinosaur Totem Is Calling You

1. **Intuitive Attraction**
   - You may feel an unexplainable pull toward a particular dinosaur, whether through dreams, interests, or repeated imagery.
   - Example: Seeing *Triceratops* imagery frequently may suggest its nurturing and protective energy is calling you.
2. **Reflection on Personal Traits**
   - Consider your dominant personality traits and challenges. Certain dinosaurs align with specific energies:
     - *Tyrannosaurus rex*: Leadership and courage.
     - *Velociraptor*: Intelligence and adaptability.
     - *Stegosaurus*: Balance and harmony.
3. **Astrological Alignment**
   - Your Dinosaur Zodiac sign (Chapter 41) may indicate your totem, but your totem could also be a complementary species that supports your life path.
4. **Dreams and Meditations**
   - Pay attention to dinosaurs appearing in dreams or during meditative states. These are often signs of your totem reaching out.

A Guided Exercise to Discover Your Totem

1. **Set the Scene**
   - Find a quiet space and create an atmosphere conducive to reflection. Light candles or place images of dinosaurs around you.
2. **Meditative Visualization**
   - Close your eyes and imagine yourself in a lush prehistoric landscape. Visualize towering trees, distant mountains, and vibrant ecosystems.
   - Ask, "Which dinosaur spirit guide is here to help me?"
3. **Wait for Connection**
   - Observe which dinosaur appears. Pay attention to its size, movement, and demeanor. Is it protective, curious, or commanding?
4. **Record Your Experience**
   - After the meditation, write down your impressions and reflect on the qualities of the dinosaur that appeared.

3. Interpreting Common Dinosaur Totems

Here is a guide to the symbolic meanings of some of the most iconic dinosaur spirit guides:

1. Tyrannosaurus Rex (The Leader)

- **Traits**: Strength, courage, and dominance.
- **Guidance**: T. rex reminds you to embrace leadership and assert your power. It teaches confidence and overcoming fear.

2. Velociraptor (The Strategist)

- **Traits**: Intelligence, agility, and adaptability.
- **Guidance**: This guide encourages quick thinking and resourcefulness, helping you navigate challenges with precision.

3. Triceratops (The Protector)

- **Traits**: Loyalty, grounding, and protection.
- **Guidance**: Triceratops provides emotional security and encourages standing firm in your beliefs.

4. Brachiosaurus (The Visionary)

- **Traits**: Expansion, perspective, and growth.
- **Guidance**: This guide helps you see the bigger picture, inspiring personal and spiritual development.

5. Spinosaurus (The Transformer)

- **Traits**: Adaptability, mystery, and transformation.
- **Guidance**: Spinosaurus teaches resilience in changing environments and the power of embracing the unknown.

6. Ankylosaurus (The Defender)

- **Traits**: Protection, resilience, and stability.
- **Guidance**: Ankylosaurus offers strength during difficult times, reminding you to defend yourself and your boundaries.

7. Plesiosaurus (The Dreamer)

- **Traits**: Intuition, creativity, and fluidity.
- **Guidance**: Plesiosaurus helps you connect with your emotions and navigate life's currents with grace.

4. Working with Your Dinosaur Totem

Once you've identified your dinosaur totem, incorporate its energy into your life through rituals, meditation, and mindful practices.

Daily Practices

1. **Totem Journaling**
   - Write daily or weekly reflections on how your totem's traits align with your experiences.
   - Example: "Today, I channeled the resilience of Ankylosaurus to set boundaries at work."
2. **Visualization Exercises**
   - Imagine your totem walking beside you during challenges, offering strength and guidance.
3. **Symbolic Reminders**
   - Keep a fossil, image, or figurine of your totem in your space as a visual reminder of its energy.

Rituals to Connect with Your Totem

1. **Totem Altar Creation**
   - Build a small altar dedicated to your dinosaur guide, including items like crystals, plants, or fossils that resonate with its energy.
2. **Prehistoric Meditation**
   - During meditation, visualize your totem in its natural environment, interacting with you and offering wisdom.
3. **Lunar Phase Alignment**
   - Perform rituals aligned with lunar phases to amplify your connection. For example:
     - **Full Moon**: Celebrate your totem's guidance and express gratitude.
     - **New Moon**: Set intentions for growth with your totem's support.

5. The Spiritual Lessons of Dinosaur Totems

Dinosaur totems offer timeless lessons rooted in their survival and adaptation.

Lesson 1: Resilience

- Dinosaurs teach us to persist through adversity, adapting to life's changes with strength and grace.

Lesson 2: Balance

- The balance between predator and prey in prehistoric ecosystems reminds us to find harmony in our own lives.

Lesson 3: Transformation

- The evolution of dinosaurs, from feathered theropods to modern birds, symbolizes the power of embracing change and transformation.

Lesson 4: Interconnectedness

- Dinosaurs thrived in interconnected ecosystems, teaching us to value our relationships and environment.

Conclusion: Embrace Your Dinosaur Totem

Dinosaur totems and spirit guides are profound allies, offering wisdom from the ancient world and bridging the gap between Earth's past and your spiritual path. By identifying and working with your totem, you can access its strength, resilience, and adaptability, aligning with the lessons of the prehistoric realm.

Let your dinosaur guide remind you of the enduring power within you and the timeless connection between all living beings across the eons. Through your totem, discover the courage, balance, and transformation needed to thrive in your journey.

Chapter 45: Building a Dinosaur Astrological Practice
Tools, Rituals, and Journaling for Integration
Introduction to Dinosaur Astrological Practice

Dinosaur astrology fuses ancient celestial wisdom with the awe-inspiring legacy of Earth's prehistoric past. Building a dedicated practice allows you to integrate the lessons, energies, and archetypes of the Dinosaur Zodiac into your daily life. By combining tools, rituals, and reflective journaling, you can deepen your connection to these cosmic and prehistoric forces, enhancing personal growth and spiritual alignment.

This chapter offers a step-by-step guide to creating a Dinosaur Astrological Practice, providing practical tools, meaningful rituals, and journaling techniques to help you integrate dinosaur archetypes and celestial influences into your spiritual routine.

1. Essential Tools for Dinosaur Astrology

To build a meaningful practice, gather tools that support your exploration of both the celestial and prehistoric realms.

Key Tools for Your Practice

1. **Dinosaur Zodiac Chart**
   ◦ Create or obtain a personalized Dinosaur Zodiac chart that includes your Sun, Moon, and Rising signs, as well as planetary placements and lunar phases.
2. **Prehistoric Symbolism**
   ◦ Use items that represent your Dinosaur Zodiac sign or totem, such as:
     ▪ Dinosaur figurines or fossils (e.g., ammonites, trilobites).
     ▪ Crystals aligned with specific energies, such as smoky quartz for resilience or aquamarine for emotional balance.
3. **Astrological Calendar**
   ◦ Track celestial events, such as lunar phases, planetary retrogrades, and solstices, to align your rituals and reflections with cosmic rhythms.
4. **Journaling Supplies**
   ◦ Keep a dedicated journal for your Dinosaur Astrological Practice, including space for birth chart insights, daily reflections, and ritual notes.
5. **Meditation Aids**
   ◦ Incorporate tools like candles, incense, or sound bowls to create a calming environment for meditations and rituals.

2. Rituals for Integration

Rituals provide a structured way to connect with the energies of the Dinosaur Zodiac and celestial influences. Tailor these rituals to your personal needs and spiritual goals.

Daily Rituals

1. **Morning Alignment**
   - Begin each day by acknowledging your Dinosaur Sun Sign and its archetypal energy.
   - Example: If your Sun Sign is Sagittarius (Brachiosaurus), recite an affirmation like, "I embrace growth and expansion with courage and curiosity."
2. **Lunar Phase Check-In**
   - Reflect on the current Moon phase and how its energy aligns with your Dinosaur Zodiac sign.
   - Example: During a Waxing Gibbous Moon, consider how your dinosaur archetype would prepare for growth and abundance.

Monthly Rituals

1. **New Moon Intention Setting**
   - Use the New Moon to set goals inspired by your Dinosaur Zodiac chart. Incorporate symbolic actions, such as writing intentions on paper and placing them under a fossil or crystal.
2. **Full Moon Gratitude and Release**
   - Under the Full Moon, reflect on achievements and release old patterns. Engage in activities that honor your dinosaur spirit guide, such as meditating on its traits or journaling about its lessons.

Seasonal Rituals

1. **Solstice and Equinox Ceremonies**
   - Celebrate seasonal transitions with rituals that honor both celestial events and prehistoric cycles:
     - **Summer Solstice**: Light candles to symbolize the peak energy of the Sun, and place greenery or plants around your altar to evoke the lush environments of the Mesozoic Era.
     - **Winter Solstice**: Reflect on resilience and endurance by holding fossils or stones that symbolize strength.

3. Journaling for Reflection and Growth

Journaling is a cornerstone of Dinosaur Astrology, allowing you to track celestial patterns, deepen your understanding of dinosaur archetypes, and reflect on personal growth.

Journaling Techniques

1. **Daily Reflections**
   - Write about how the energies of your Sun, Moon, and Rising signs influenced your day.
   - Example: "As a Libra (Stegosaurus) Sun, I felt the need to mediate a conflict today, bringing balance and harmony to my environment."
2. **Lunar Phase Entries**
   - Document your emotions and experiences during each lunar phase, connecting them to your Dinosaur Moon Sign.
   - Example: "During this Waning Crescent Moon, I felt introspective, much like Plesiosaurus navigating the depths of its emotional world."
3. **Celestial Events Tracker**
   - Record how planetary retrogrades, alignments, and eclipses impact your mood, decisions, and energy. Use this as a guide for future planning.
4. **Prehistoric Wisdom Pages**
   - Dedicate sections to the lessons of your dinosaur spirit guide, exploring how its traits inspire action and growth in your life.

Prompts for Deeper Exploration

1. "How does my Dinosaur Zodiac sign reflect my core strengths and challenges?"
2. "What can my dinosaur spirit guide teach me about navigating change?"
3. "Which lunar phases feel most aligned with my energy, and why?"
4. "How do the lessons of prehistoric cycles apply to my current life path?"

4. Meditation and Visualization Practices

Meditation and visualization help you connect with the energies of the Dinosaur Zodiac, fostering spiritual alignment and personal clarity.

Guided Visualization for Connection

1. **Prehistoric Landscape Journey**
   - Imagine yourself walking through a lush Mesozoic environment. Visualize the plants, sounds, and movements around you. Allow your dinosaur spirit guide to appear and offer insights.
2. **Cosmic Alignment Meditation**
   - Visualize the stars, Moon, and planets aligning with Earth's prehistoric rhythms. Picture their energies flowing into you, blending cosmic wisdom with the grounded strength of the dinosaur archetypes.

5. Practical Integration into Daily Life

Dinosaur Astrology can be integrated into your daily life in subtle, meaningful ways.

Aligning Goals with Archetypes

1. **Career and Leadership**
   - If your sign is Leo (Tyrannosaurus Rex), focus on embracing leadership roles and inspiring confidence in others.
2. **Personal Relationships**
   - For Cancer (Camarasaurus), nurture emotional connections and create safe spaces for others.

Enhancing Decision-Making

- Use your Dinosaur Zodiac chart as a guide when facing decisions:
  - What would your dinosaur archetype do in this situation?

Symbolic Actions

- Carry a small fossil or crystal that resonates with your Dinosaur Zodiac sign to stay connected to its energy throughout the day.

6. Building a Community Practice

Sharing your Dinosaur Astrological Practice with others can deepen your connection and foster mutual growth.

Ideas for Community Engagement

1. **Astrology Circles**
   - Host gatherings to share insights, perform group rituals, or explore dinosaur archetypes together.
2. **Collaborative Journaling**
   - Exchange journaling prompts and reflections with friends to gain fresh perspectives.
3. **Seasonal Celebrations**
   - Organize group ceremonies for solstices, equinoxes, and lunar phases.

Conclusion: Your Dinosaur Astrological Path

Building a Dinosaur Astrological Practice is a deeply rewarding journey that aligns the celestial wisdom of astrology with the enduring strength of Earth's prehistoric past. By using tools, engaging in meaningful rituals, and journaling with intention, you can connect with your Dinosaur Zodiac sign and spirit guide, unlocking insights that inspire personal growth and spiritual alignment.

Let your practice evolve as you explore the cosmic and prehistoric energies at play in your life. Through these ancient lessons, you can cultivate resilience, harmony, and a profound connection to the universe.

Appendices
Appendix A: Dinosaur Zodiac Dates
Aligning Modern Zodiacs with Dinosaur Archetypes
This detailed table aligns the 12 modern zodiac signs with their corresponding dinosaur archetypes, providing specific dates, traits, and symbolic meanings for each Dinosaur Zodiac sign. These archetypes blend prehistoric wisdom with astrological traits, offering a unique way to understand your personal connection to both the cosmos and Earth's ancient past.

Modern Zodiac	Dinosaur Zodiac	Dates	Traits	Symbolism
Aries	**Allosaurus**	March 21 - April 19	Bold, pioneering, energetic, competitive, adventurous	Represents strength, leadership, and the ability to take charge, much like Allosaurus dominated its environment.
Taurus	**Triceratops**	April 20 - May 20	Loyal, patient, grounded, protective, practical	Embodies stability and security, with a focus on nurturing and protecting loved ones.
Gemini	**Velociraptor**	May 21 - June 20	Intelligent, communicative, curious, adaptable, quick-witted	Reflects intelligence and adaptability, symbolizing resourcefulness in navigating challenges.

Modern Zodiac	Dinosaur Zodiac	Dates	Traits	Symbolism
Cancer	Camarasaurus	June 21 - July 22	Nurturing, intuitive, emotional, protective, family-oriented	Represents emotional depth and care, much like the herding behaviors of Camarasaurus.
Leo	Tyrannosaurus Rex	July 23 - August 22	Charismatic, bold, confident, ambitious, leader-like	Embodies leadership and dominance, with a natural ability to inspire others.
Virgo	Ankylosaurus	August 23 - September 22	Practical, detail-oriented, resilient, analytical, perfectionist	Symbolizes resilience and practicality, with a focus on preparation and protection.
Libra	Stegosaurus	September 23 - October 22	Balanced, diplomatic, harmonious, fair, peaceful	Reflects balance and harmony, embodying the peaceful and cooperative energy of Stegosaurus.
Scorpio	Spinosaurus	October 23 - November 21	Intense, transformative, mysterious, powerful, determined	Represents transformation and adaptability, thriving in diverse environments like Spinosaurus.
Sagittarius	Brachiosaurus	November 22 - December 21	Visionary, adventurous, optimistic, expansive, free-spirited	Embodies exploration and growth, representing a far-reaching perspective and expansive vision.

Modern Zodiac	Dinosaur Zodiac	Dates	Traits	Symbolism
Capricorn	**Iguanodon**	December 22 - January 19	Ambitious, disciplined, determined, practical, hardworking	Symbolizes perseverance and resourcefulness, with a focus on achieving long-term goals.
Aquarius	**Parasaurolophus**	January 20 - February 18	Innovative, independent, creative, intellectual, progressive	Represents originality and forward-thinking, with a focus on innovation and collaboration.
Pisces	**Plesiosaurus**	February 19 - March 20	Compassionate, intuitive, imaginative, spiritual, sensitive	Embodies emotional depth and creativity, symbolizing a connection to intuition and the subconscious.

Details on Each Dinosaur Zodiac Sign
1. Aries - Allosaurus

- **Dates**: March 21 - April 19
- **Symbolism**: Represents boldness and courage, encouraging individuals to take initiative and lead with confidence.
- **Dinosaur Insight**: Like Allosaurus, known for its hunting prowess and assertiveness, Aries individuals thrive on action and adventure.

2. Taurus - Triceratops

- **Dates**: April 20 - May 20
- **Symbolism**: Embodies stability and loyalty, offering a grounding presence in relationships and challenges.
- **Dinosaur Insight**: Triceratops' protective horns and herd behaviors reflect Taurus's nurturing and steadfast energy.

3. Gemini - Velociraptor

- **Dates**: May 21 - June 20
- **Symbolism**: Represents quick thinking, adaptability, and intellectual curiosity.
- **Dinosaur Insight**: Velociraptor's agility and social intelligence mirror Gemini's versatile and communicative nature.

4. Cancer - Camarasaurus

- **Dates**: June 21 - July 22
- **Symbolism**: Reflects emotional depth, family-oriented values, and protective instincts.
- **Dinosaur Insight**: Like Camarasaurus, which thrived in herds and cared for its young, Cancer individuals value connection and security.

5. Leo - Tyrannosaurus Rex

- **Dates**: July 23 - August 22
- **Symbolism**: Embodies leadership, confidence, and charisma, commanding attention and respect.
- **Dinosaur Insight**: T. rex's dominance as an apex predator reflects Leo's natural authority and ambition.

6. Virgo - Ankylosaurus

- **Dates**: August 23 - September 22
- **Symbolism**: Represents practicality, resilience, and attention to detail, focusing on preparation and precision.
- **Dinosaur Insight**: Ankylosaurus' armored defenses and methodical survival strategies align with Virgo's meticulous approach to challenges.

7. Libra - Stegosaurus

- **Dates**: September 23 - October 22
- **Symbolism**: Reflects balance, harmony, and fairness, valuing relationships and cooperation.
- **Dinosaur Insight**: Stegosaurus, with its peaceful demeanor and iconic plates, symbolizes Libra's quest for equilibrium and beauty.

8. Scorpio - Spinosaurus

- **Dates**: October 23 - November 21
- **Symbolism**: Represents intensity, transformation, and adaptability, thriving in complexity and mystery.
- **Dinosaur Insight**: Spinosaurus' unique ability to navigate water and land mirrors Scorpio's depth and transformative energy.

9. Sagittarius - Brachiosaurus

- **Dates**: November 22 - December 21
- **Symbolism**: Embodies exploration, optimism, and visionary thinking, reaching for new heights and perspectives.
- **Dinosaur Insight**: Brachiosaurus, with its towering stature and expansive reach, reflects Sagittarius's adventurous and expansive spirit.

10. Capricorn - Iguanodon

- **Dates**: December 22 - January 19
- **Symbolism**: Reflects ambition, discipline, and practicality, focusing on achieving goals and overcoming challenges.
- **Dinosaur Insight**: Iguanodon's adaptability and perseverance embody Capricorn's determination and resourcefulness.

11. Aquarius - Parasaurolophus

- **Dates**: January 20 - February 18
- **Symbolism**: Represents innovation, creativity, and progressive thinking, valuing individuality and collaboration.
- **Dinosaur Insight**: Parasaurolophus' unique crest and vocalizations symbolize Aquarius's originality and intellectual energy.

12. Pisces - Plesiosaurus

- **Dates**: February 19 - March 20
- **Symbolism**: Embodies emotional depth, creativity, and spiritual connection, navigating intuition and imagination.
- **Dinosaur Insight**: Plesiosaurus' grace in aquatic environments reflects Pisces' fluidity and connection to the subconscious.

This alignment of modern zodiacs with dinosaur archetypes creates a bridge between celestial energies and Earth's prehistoric wisdom, empowering individuals to draw inspiration from both realms. Use this table to deepen your connection to your Dinosaur Zodiac sign and its unique lessons.

Appendix B: Celestial Events Calendar

This appendix provides a comprehensive calendar of significant celestial events for the year 2025, including solar and lunar eclipses, as well as major meteor showers. These events offer unique opportunities for observation and spiritual reflection, allowing individuals to connect with the cosmos and integrate these experiences into their astrological practices.

Note: All dates and times are provided in Coordinated Universal Time (UTC).

Solar and Lunar Eclipses in 2025

Eclipses are profound astronomical events that have been observed and interpreted across various cultures for millennia. In 2025, there will be four notable eclipses: two total lunar eclipses and two partial solar eclipses.

Date	Type of Eclipse	Visibility Regions	Description
March 13-14	Total Lunar Eclipse	Europe, much of Asia, much of Australia, much of Africa, North America, South America, Pacific, Atlantic, Arctic, Antarctica	A total lunar eclipse, where the Earth completely covers the Moon with its umbral shadow, causing the Moon to appear reddish.
March 29	Partial Solar Eclipse	Europe, northern Asia, northwestern Africa, much of North America, northern South America, Atlantic, Arctic	A partial solar eclipse, where the Moon covers a portion of the Sun, visible from the specified regions.
September 7-8	Total Lunar Eclipse	Europe, Asia, Australia, Africa, western North America, eastern South America, Pacific, Atlantic, Indian Ocean, Arctic, Antarctica	Another total lunar eclipse, offering a second opportunity in the year to witness the Moon's reddish hue.

Date	Type of Eclipse	Visibility Regions	Description
September 21	Partial Solar Eclipse	Southern Pacific Ocean, parts of Antarctica	A partial solar eclipse, primarily visible over the southern Pacific Ocean and parts of Antarctica.

Source: timeanddate.com

Meteor Showers in 2025

Meteor showers occur when Earth passes through streams of debris left by comets and asteroids, resulting in streaks of light as meteoroids burn up in the atmosphere. Below is a list of major meteor showers in 2025, including their active periods and peak dates.

Meteor Shower	Active Period	Peak Dates	ZHR*	Associated Comet/Asteroid	Description
Quadrantids	Dec 26 – Jan 12	Jan 4	120	2003 EH1	A strong shower with bright meteors, best viewed from the Northern Hemisphere.
Lyrids	Apr 16 – Apr 25	Apr 22-23	20	C/1861 G1 Thatcher	Known for producing bright dust trails; the thin crescent moon will not pose much of a problem this year.
Eta Aquarids	Apr 19 – May 28	May 6-7	60	1P/Halley	Best viewed from the Southern Hemisphere; in the Northern Hemisphere, rates can reach about 30 meteors per hour.

Meteor Shower	Active Period	Peak Dates	ZHR*	Associated Comet/Asteroid	Description
Perseids	Jul 17 – Aug 24	Aug 12	100	109P/Swift-Tuttle	One of the most popular showers, known for producing a large number of bright meteors.
Orionids	Oct 2 – Nov 7	Oct 22	20	1P/Halley	Produces fast meteors; viewing conditions are favorable this year.
Leonids	Nov 6 – Nov 30	Nov 17	15	55P/Tempel-Tuttle	Known for producing meteor storms every 33 years; this year, a modest shower is expected.
Geminids	Dec 4 – Dec 17	Dec 14	120	3200 Phaethon	Considered one of the best showers, producing colorful meteors; viewing conditions are favorable this year.
Ursids	Dec 17 – Dec 26	Dec 22	10	8P/Tuttle	A minor shower producing about 5-10 meteors per hour; best viewed from the Northern Hemisphere.

ZHR: Zenithal Hourly Rate, the number of meteors an observer would see under perfect conditions with the radiant at the zenith.

Source: Sea and Sky

This calendar serves as a guide to the celestial events of 2025, providing opportunities for observation and integration into your astrological practices. Remember to check local visibility and timing for each event, as they can vary based on your geographic location.

Appendix C: Dinosaur Astrology Glossary
Definitions of Key Terms and Concepts

This glossary provides detailed explanations of terms and concepts used throughout the exploration of Dinosaur Astrology. By understanding these definitions, you'll be better equipped to integrate the wisdom of the Dinosaur Zodiac into your astrological and spiritual practice.

A

Adaptability

- The ability to adjust to changing environments or circumstances, a key trait reflected in many dinosaur species like *Velociraptor* and *Spinosaurus*. In Dinosaur Astrology, adaptability is associated with overcoming challenges and thriving through transitions.

Allosaurus

- Representing Aries in the Dinosaur Zodiac, Allosaurus symbolizes leadership, courage, and the pioneering spirit. Known for its dominance as a predator, it embodies the energy of taking charge and embracing bold actions.

Ankylosaurus

- Representing Virgo in the Dinosaur Zodiac, Ankylosaurus symbolizes protection, practicality, and resilience. Its armored body reflects its role as a guardian and survivor.

Archetype

- A symbolic representation of universal traits or energies. In Dinosaur Astrology, archetypes are drawn from the characteristics of specific dinosaur species and their alignment with astrological signs.

B
Balance

- A state of harmony and equilibrium, often associated with Libra (Stegosaurus) in the Dinosaur Zodiac. Balance reflects the ability to navigate life's dualities and maintain fairness in relationships and decisions.

Brachiosaurus

- Representing Sagittarius in the Dinosaur Zodiac, Brachiosaurus symbolizes vision, exploration, and expansive thinking. Its towering stature represents reaching for greater heights in life.

Birth Chart

- A map of the celestial bodies' positions at the moment of birth, used in astrology to determine personality traits and life paths. In Dinosaur Astrology, the chart integrates prehistoric wisdom and celestial influences.

C
Camarasaurus

- Representing Cancer in the Dinosaur Zodiac, Camarasaurus embodies nurturing, intuition, and familial bonds. Its herd-oriented behavior reflects its protective and emotional nature.

Celestial Events

- Significant occurrences in the sky, such as eclipses, meteor showers, and planetary alignments. These events are key in Dinosaur Astrology for timing rituals and reflecting on cosmic influences.

Constellations

- Groupings of stars forming recognizable patterns in the sky. In Dinosaur Astrology, constellations like Draco (the Dragon) are connected to prehistoric myths and symbolism.

D
Dinosaur Totem

- A prehistoric spirit guide that embodies traits and wisdom aligned with an individual's personality or life journey. Dinosaur totems serve as cosmic allies in personal growth and spiritual connection.

Dinosaur Zodiac

- A system that aligns modern zodiac signs with dinosaur archetypes, blending prehistoric traits with astrological insights. Each sign corresponds to a dinosaur species and its symbolic energy.

E
Equinox

- A celestial event when day and night are of nearly equal length, marking the start of spring or fall. In Dinosaur Astrology, equinoxes are symbolic of balance and transitions, influencing rituals and personal reflection.

Extinction Cycles

- Natural cycles of mass extinction and renewal on Earth, such as the end of the dinosaurs. These cycles symbolize transformation and rebirth, a theme often associated with Pluto in astrology.

F
Fossil Zodiac

- A symbolic alignment of fossilized dinosaurs with astrological archetypes, connecting ancient Earth's history with cosmic energies.

Full Moon

- A phase of the Moon when it appears fully illuminated, symbolizing abundance, clarity, and peak energy. In Dinosaur Astrology, the Full Moon aligns with traits of prosperity and communal power.

H
Harmony

- The state of balance and peaceful coexistence, often associated with dinosaur species like *Stegosaurus*. In Dinosaur Astrology, harmony reflects interpersonal balance and alignment with natural cycles.

Herd Dynamics

- The social behavior of dinosaurs like *Triceratops* and *Camarasaurus*, symbolizing cooperation, protection, and collective strength. Herd dynamics inspire themes of community in Dinosaur Astrology.

L
Lunar Cycles

- The phases of the Moon, including New Moon, First Quarter, Full Moon, and Last Quarter. These cycles play a crucial role in Dinosaur Astrology, reflecting growth, challenges, and reflection.

Lunar Eclipse

- A celestial event where the Earth's shadow obscures the Moon. Lunar eclipses symbolize emotional revelations, endings, and transformation.

M
Meteor Showers

- Streams of meteors visible when Earth passes through the debris left by comets or asteroids. In Dinosaur Astrology, meteor showers symbolize fleeting inspiration and cosmic connections.

Moon Sign

- The zodiac sign where the Moon was located at the time of birth, representing emotions, instincts, and inner self. In Dinosaur Astrology, the Moon Sign reflects prehistoric cycles of growth and adaptation.

P
Parasaurolophus

- Representing Aquarius in the Dinosaur Zodiac, Parasaurolophus symbolizes creativity, innovation, and collaboration. Its unique crest reflects individuality and originality.

Plesiosaurus

- Representing Pisces in the Dinosaur Zodiac, Plesiosaurus embodies emotional depth, intuition, and spiritual connection. Its aquatic nature symbolizes navigating the subconscious.

Prehistoric Cycles

- The rhythms of Earth's ancient past, including migration patterns, seasonal changes, and evolutionary shifts. These cycles are mirrored in the themes of Dinosaur Astrology.

R
Resilience

- The ability to recover from adversity and thrive in challenging environments. Many dinosaur species, such as *Ankylosaurus* and *Iguanodon*, symbolize resilience in Dinosaur Astrology.

Retrograde

- An apparent backward motion of a planet in the sky, symbolizing reflection, reassessment, and challenges. Retrogrades in Dinosaur Astrology align with themes of adaptation and introspection.

S
Seasonal Transitions

- Changes in Earth's environment caused by the tilt and orbit of the planet. These transitions align with solstices and equinoxes, symbolizing growth and renewal in Dinosaur Astrology.

Solstice

- A celestial event marking the longest or shortest day of the year. In Dinosaur Astrology, solstices represent extremes of light and darkness, mirroring prehistoric cycles of abundance and scarcity.

Spinosaurus

- Representing Scorpio in the Dinosaur Zodiac, Spinosaurus embodies transformation, adaptability, and intensity. Its semi-aquatic nature symbolizes thriving in diverse environments.

T
Triceratops

- Representing Taurus in the Dinosaur Zodiac, Triceratops symbolizes loyalty, grounding, and protection. Its horns and frills represent strength and defense of the community.

Tyrannosaurus Rex

- Representing Leo in the Dinosaur Zodiac, Tyrannosaurus Rex embodies leadership, dominance, and charisma. Its apex status mirrors the energy of confidence and ambition.

Z
Zodiac Archetype

- A symbolic representation of a zodiac sign's traits, aligned with specific dinosaur characteristics in Dinosaur Astrology.

Zenithal Hourly Rate (ZHR)

- A measure of the number of meteors visible per hour during optimal viewing conditions. Used to assess the activity of meteor showers.

Conclusion

This glossary serves as a comprehensive resource for understanding the foundational concepts of Dinosaur Astrology. Use it to deepen your knowledge and integrate prehistoric wisdom with celestial insights in your personal astrological practice.

<u>Message from the Author:</u>

I hope you enjoyed this book, I love astrology and knew there was not a book such as this out on the shelf. I love metaphysical items as well. Please check out my other books:

-Life of Government Benefits

-My life of Hell

-My life with Hydrocephalus

-Red Sky

-World Domination:Woman's rule

-World Domination:Woman's Rule 2: The War

-Life and Banishment of Apophis: book 1

-The Kidney Friendly Diet

-The Ultimate Hemp Cookbook

-Creating a Dispensary(legally)

-Cleanliness throughout life: the importance of showering from childhood to adulthood.

-Strong Roots: The Risks of Overcoddling children

-Hemp Horoscopes: Cosmic Insights and Earthly Healing

- Celestial Hemp Navigating the Zodiac: Through the Green Cosmos

-Astrological Hemp: Aligning The Stars with Earth's Ancient Herb

-The Astrological Guide to Hemp: Stars, Signs, and Sacred Leaves

-Green Growth: Innovative Marketing Strategies for your Hemp Products and Dispensary

-Cosmic Cannabis

-Astrological Munchies

-Henry The Hemp

-Zodiacal Roots: The Astrological Soul Of Hemp

- **Green Constellations: Intersection of Hemp and Zodiac**

-Hemp in The Houses: An astrological Adventure Through The Cannabis Galaxy

-Galactic Ganja Guide

Heavenly Hemp

Zodiac Leaves

Doctor Who Astrology

Cannastrology

Stellar Satvias and Cosmic Indicas

Celestial Cannabis: A Zodiac Journey
AstroHerbology: The Sky and The Soil: Volume 1
AstroHerbology:Celestial Cannabis:Volume 2
Cosmic Cannabis Cultivation
The Starry Guide to Herbal Harmony: Volume 1
The Starry Guide to Herbal Harmony: Cannabis Universe: Volume 2
Yugioh Astrology: Astrological Guide to Deck, Duels and more
Nightmare Mansion: Echoes of The Abyss
Nightmare Mansion 2: Legacy of Shadows
Nightmare Mansion 3: Shadows of the Forgotten
Nightmare Mansion 4: Echoes of the Damned
The Life and Banishment of Apophis: Book 2
Nightmare Mansion: Halls of Despair
Healing with Herb: Cannabis and Hydrocephalus
Planetary Pot: Aligning with Astrological Herbs: Volume 1
Fast Track to Freedom: 30 Days to Financial Independence Using AI, Assets, and Agile Hustles
Cosmic Hemp Pathways
How to Become Financially Free in 30 Days: 10,000 Paths to Prosperity
Zodiacal Herbage: Astrological Insights: Volume 1
Nightmare Mansion: Whispers in the Walls
The Daleks Invade Atlantis
Henry the hemp and Hydrocephalus

10X The Kidney Friendly Diet
Cannabis Universe: Adult coloring book
Hemp Astrology: The Healing Power of the Stars
Zodiacal Herbage: Astrological Insights: Cannabis Universe: Volume 2
Planetary Pot: Aligning with Astrological Herbs: Cannabis Universes: Volume 2
Doctor Who Meets the Replicators and SG-1: The Ultimate Battle for Survival
Nightmare Mansion: Curse of the Blood Moon
The Celestial Stoner: A Guide to the Zodiac
Cosmic Pleasures: Sex Toy Astrology for Every Sign
Hydrocephalus Astrology: Navigating the Stars and Healing Waters
Lapis and the Mischievous Chocolate Bar

Celestial Positions: Sexual Astrology for Every Sign
Apophis's Shadow Work Journal: : A Journey of Self-Discovery and Healing
Kinky Cosmos: Sexual Kink Astrology for Every Sign
Digital Cosmos: The Astrological Digimon Compendium
Stellar Seeds: The Cosmic Guide to Growing with Astrology

Apophis's Daily Gratitude Journal

Cat Astrology: Feline Mysteries of the Cosmos
The Cosmic Kama Sutra: An Astrological Guide to Sexual Positions
Unleash Your Potential: A Guided Journal Powered by AI Insights
Whispers of the Enchanted Grove

Cosmic Pleasures: An Astrological Guide to Sexual Kinks
369, 12 Manifestation Journal
Whisper of the nocturne journal(blank journal for writing or drawing)
The Boogey Book
Locked In Reflection: A Chastity Journey Through Locktober
Generating Wealth Quickly:
How to Generate $100,000 in 24 Hours
Star Magic: Harness the Power of the Universe
The Flatulence Chronicles: A Fart Journal for Self-Discovery
The Doctor and The Death Moth
Seize the Day: A Personal Seizure Tracking Journal
The Ultimate Boogeyman Safari: A Journey into the Boogie World and Beyond
Whispers of Samhain: 1,000 Spells of Love, Luck, and Lunar Magic: Samhain Spell Book
Apophis's guides:
Witch's Spellbook Crafting Guide for Halloween
<u>Frost & Flame: The Enchanted Yule Grimoire of 1000 Winter Spells</u>
<u>The Ultimate Boogey Goo Guide & Spooky Activities for Halloween Fun</u>
Harmony of the Scales: A Libra's Spellcraft for Balance and Beauty
The Enchanted Advent: 36 Days of Christmas Wonders

Nightmare Mansion: The Labyrinth of Screams
Harvest of Enchantment: 1,000 Spells of Gratitude, Love, and Fortune for Thanksgiving
The Boogey Chronicles: A Journal of Nightly Encounters and Shadowy Secrets
The 12 Days of Financial Freedom: A Step-by-Step Christmas Countdown to Transform Your Finances
Sigil of the Eternal Spiral Blank Journal
A Christmas Feast: Timeless Recipes for Every Meal
Holiday Stress-Free Solutions: A Survival Guide to Thriving During the Festive Season
Yu-Gi-Oh! Holiday Gifting Mastery: The Ultimate Guide for Fans and Newcomers Alike
Holiday Harmony: A Hydrocephalus Survival Guide for the Festive Season
Celestial Craft: The Witch's Almanac for 2025 – A Cosmic Guide to Manifestations, Moons, and Mystical Events
Doctor Who: The Toymaker's Winter Wonderland
Tulsa King Unveiled: A Thrilling Guide to Stallone's Mafia Masterpiece

Pendulum Craft: A Complete Guide to Crafting and Using Personalized Divination Tools
Nightmare Mansion: Santa's Eternal Eve
Starlight Noel: A Cosmic Journey through Christmas Mysteries
The Dark Architect: Unlocking the Blueprint of Existence
Surviving the Embrace: The Ultimate Guide to Encounters with The Hugging Molly
The Enchanted Codex: Secrets of the Craft for Witches, Wiccans, and Pagans
Harvest of Gratitude: A Complete Thanksgiving Guide
Yuletide Essentials: A Complete Guide to an Authentic and Magical Christmas
Celestial Smokes: A Cosmic Guide to Cigars and Astrology
Living in Balance: A Comprehensive Survival Guide to Thriving with Diabetes Insipidus
Cosmic Symbiosis: The Venom Zodiac Chronicles
The Cursed Paw of Ambition
Cosmic Symbiosis: The Astrological Venom Journal
Celestial Wonders Unfold: A Stargazer's Guide to the Cosmos (2024-2029)
The Ultimate Black Friday Prepper's Guide: Mastering Shopping Strategies and Savings
Cosmic Sales: The Astrological Guide to Black Friday Shopping
Legends of the Corn Mother and Other Harvest Myths
Whispers of the Harvest: The Corn Mother's Journal
The Evergreen Spellbook
The Doctor Meets the Boogeyman
The White Witch of Rose Hall's SpellBook
The Gingerbread Golem's Shadow: A Study in Sweet Darkness
The Gingerbread Golem Codex: An Academic Exploration of Sweet Myths
The Gingerbread Golem Grimoire: Sweet Magicks and Spells for the Festive Witch
The Curse of the Gingerbread Golem
10-minute Christmas Crafts for kids
<u>Christmas Crisis Solutions: The Ultimate Last-Minute Survival Guide</u>
Gingerbread Golem Recipes: Holiday Treats with a Magical Twist
The Infinite Key: Unlocking Mystical Secrets of the Ages
Enchanted Yule: A Wiccan and Pagan Guide to a Magical and Memorable Season
Dinosaurs of Power: Unlocking Ancient Magick

If you want solar for your home go here: https://www.harborsolar.live/apophisenterprises/

Get Some Tarot cards: https://www.makeplayingcards.com/sell/apophis-occult-shop

Get some shirts: https://www.bonfire.com/store/apophis-shirt-emporium/

<u>Instagrams:</u>
@apophis_enterprises,
@apophisbookemporium,
@apophisscardshop
Twitter: @apophisenterpr1
Tiktok:@apophisenterprise
Youtube: @sg1fan23477, @FiresideRetreatKingdom
Hive: @sg1fan23477
CheeLee: @SG1fan23477

Podcast: Apophis Chat Zone: https://open.spotify.com/show/5zXbr-CLEV2xzCp8ybrfHsk?si=fb4d4fdbdce44dec

Newsletter: https://apophiss-newsletter-27c897.beehiiv.com/